Distorted Landscape

A Critique of Leftist Narratives in Media and Politics

Philip J. Eveland

iUniverse, Inc.
Bloomington

DISTORTED LANDSCAPE
A Critique of Leftist Narratives in Media and Politics

iUniverse books may be ordered through booksellers or by contacting:

iUniverse
1663 Liberty Drive
Bloomington, IN 47403
www.iuniverse.com
1-800-Authors (1-800-288-4677)

ISBN: 978-1-4759-8287-9 (sc)
ISBN: 978-1-4759-8289-3 (hc)
ISBN: 978-1-4759-8288-6 (e)

Library of Congress Control Number: 2013906237

Printed in the United States of America

iUniverse rev. date: 4/5/2013

TABLE OF CONTENTS

INTRODUCTION

I'm pro-life. I believe that human life begins at conception. I'm pretty zealous about the life issue. I've had numerous conversations about it with family, friends, co-workers, and classmates. Along with the Second Amendment and its protection of the right to self-defense, the right to life is my top policy issue.

However, I've discovered just in the past few years that whenever I discuss the life issue with pro-choicers/pro-abortionists, I am almost always playing defense. The reason, I realized, is because the whole issue is frequently framed in the context of a pro-choice narrative. That is, the issue has been co-opted by the political Left. They own the issue, and they've shaped the discussion.

To better explain how the political Left has shaped the life/abortion debate, and how they own the narrative, here's how a discussion I had recently with two pro-choicers transpired. I'll call them "the man" and "the woman."

"I don't judge anyone," the woman said with an air of moral superiority. She was sitting across from me, pretending to be only half-interested in the discussion. Perhaps it was a way of checking herself. Maybe she was trying to keep emotionally detached from the subject. In actuality, she was judging me while insisting that she doesn't judge anyone, as you'll see.

"I don't think I should tell a woman what she can and can't do with her body," the man said with an air of self-righteousness. His body language indicated clearly that he was emotionally committed to the subject. He was upright in his seat, and eager to demonstrate his moral superiority.

"Agreed," the woman said. "Who am I to tell anyone what they can and can't do with their body?"

"Do you understand, though, my position about abortion?" I asked. "Do you understand why I'm pro-life?"

"I do understand your position," the man said. "I just don't think I have any right to tell a woman what she can and can't do with her own body."

"What's my argument, then? Explain my argument," I said, confident that he couldn't.

"You believe it is okay to impose your morality on everyone else," the man said with satisfaction. "But I don't think I have any right to impose my beliefs on anybody." He'd been down this road before, and knew what buttons to push.

But, I didn't take the bait.

"Actually," I said, turning in my seat to face him, "my argument is based primarily on science. You say it's a woman's body, the unborn baby, but biological science says otherwise. For instance, every cell in a woman's body is composed of the very same genetic code as every other cell in her body – her hair, eyeballs, liver, and skin. They are all made of cells that are composed of the very same genetic code.

"Yet," I continued, "the unborn child's body, from the moment of conception, is made up of billions, even trillions of cells, and every one of them is composed of a distinct and unique genetic code that is different from both the mother's and the father's. Often, the unborn child has a different blood type than the mother. About half the time, the unborn child has a penis. Does that mean, then, that the mother has a penis for nine months? Of course not. Thus, science says that the unborn child is not part of the mother's body. It's a separate human being completely, from conception to birth and long after."

At that point, I was sorry I didn't have a white-board and some dry-erase markers. I think better with visual aids, and I often assume others do as well. A picture is worth a thousand words, yes?

"Where's the fetus?" the man asked rhetorically during a brief pause in my lecture. "It's in her body, thus it is part of her body. Yes?"

"By that logic," I responded, "if a man shoots a woman with a gun, and the bullet lodges in her torso, then the bullet is part of her body, and the man can stay out of jail by arguing that the bullet is merely a part of her body and not something that he put inside of her."

"What?" the man and woman barked incredulously in concert.

And back and forth it went for an hour or so. I kept pushing the biological science angle, and the man and woman kept pushing the It's-Her-Body argument. I heard the phrase "I don't think I should tell a woman…blah, blah, blah" over and over for an hour.

It was only later, though, a few hours after our friendly debate, when something suddenly occurred to me. A light went on and I understood something very clearly. That is, when pro-choice advocates begin an argument about abortion by insisting that they do not believe they should tell a woman what she can and cannot do with her body, they are implicitly suggesting that pro-life advocates like me *do* want to tell a woman what she can and cannot do with her body. When they start the debate with, "I don't think I should be able to tell a woman..." they are putting words in the pro-lifer's mouth, and even further, they're assigning a motive to our position. They are defining the opposition's argument in terms that fit with their narrative and assigning a motive that is from the start morally reprehensible.

But, is it true, as my two debate opponents insisted, that pro-life advocates are motivated merely by a desire to control what a woman can and cannot do with her body?

To answer that question, I decided to examine the various federal and state laws related to what individual citizens can and cannot do with their bodies. I looked at laws on tattooing, for instance. I looked at laws on drug use and food consumption. I looked at laws on plastic surgery. I looked at laws on grooming (hair and nails) and tanning. All of these activities involve people, both men and women, choosing to alter their bodies in some fashion – that is, doing what they want with their bodies.

If, as pro-choice advocates suggest, pro-life advocates are indeed motivated by a desire to dictate what a woman can and cannot do with her body, then there should be some laws on the books restricting the practices of tattooing, piercing, tanning, plastic surgery, etc., based solely on the sex of the individual seeking these services and procedures. In other words, there should be a law – federal, state, municipal, etc. – containing something to the affect: "...no female shall be permitted to tan her skin..." or perhaps, "...no female shall be permitted to receive plastic surgery..." or simply, "...no female shall [fill in the blank]..." And the author(s) of that law should be conservative and pro-life.

So, what did I find?

Regarding tattoos and piercings, no state has outlawed these procedures. Even the deep red, conservative states allow it. The only laws on the books that I could find online are related to age. Most states – even the deep blue states where folks voted for Barack Obama – prohibit tattooing and piercing of minors (that is, individuals under 18 years). But most states allow the procedures if the minor's parent or guardian is present, even the deep red states where most people voted for Romney. Thus, there are no laws that prohibit adults from tattooing or piercing or getting tattooed or pierced. In other words, conservative pro-life advocates have not passed any laws to prohibit women from getting a tattoo or having their body parts pierced. Yes, even the folks who go to church every Sunday and listen to Rush Limbaugh the rest of the week, allow adults to jack up their flesh any way they please.

Regarding plastic surgery, no federal, state, or municipal law has been passed that prohibits women from undergoing body modification procedures. Also, no law exists that prohibits women from obtaining a microdermabrasion, a facial, a chemical peel, laser wrinkle removal, hair or tattoo removal, liposuction, Botox, haircut, nail trimming, or other type of spa-like procedure. In all fifty states, adult females can enjoy these procedures, as can their male counterparts. Yes, even in those states where folks carry guns, drive pickup trucks, and listen to Dennis Prager, Hugh Hewitt, and Michael Medved.

If pro-life conservatives really are motivated by the desire to control what a woman can and cannot do with her body, then there would be at least some law somewhere prohibiting the practices of tattooing and piercing, or receiving plastic surgery, or getting fat sucked out of their bodies. But, alas, there are none, even in the deepest of red states. The fact is that most conservatives – while they may find it distasteful for a woman *or a man* to scar or blemish their body – do not want to outlaw tattooing or piercing or any of the other procedures noted above, because they believe that people should be allowed to mark up and alter their bodies any way they want.

Therefore, the whole narrative of my two pro-choice debate opponents is false. Yet, it works. It immediately puts the pro-lifer on the defensive by suggesting that anyone who opposes abortion is a fascist who wants to control people. Thus, every abortion debate essentially begins with the pro-lifer on the defensive, arguing that they're not motivated by a desire to control what a woman does with her body. That's why the pro-choicer begins with a dismissive statement that, unlike the pro-lifer, they don't want to tell a woman what she can and cannot do with her body. That's why "the woman" I debated, as I noted above, was judging me while insisting that she doesn't judge anyone – and no one saw the irony.

It's like the old adage about spousal abuse: "So, Senator, when did you stop beating your wife?" Except, it goes: "So, you're a pro-lifer, huh? When did you first discover your fascistic tendencies?" That's how the Left crafts a false narrative, and that's how they own most of the political arguments from the very beginning of the debate.

Curiously, the Leftist mayor of New York City, Michael Bloomberg, lobbied for and signed into law a restriction on the size of soda that can be sold in the city. In 2007, the city outlawed trans-fats in restaurants. The city council is debating a ban on salt, as well. Thus, one of the nation's most liberal cities – of its 51 city council members, only 4 are Republicans, and centrist Republicans at that – has placed legal restrictions on how its citizens can eat a meal. A New York City resident cannot buy a large soda and the city government is trying to prohibit them from salting their fries.

But, according to Leftists, it's the evil conservatives who want to control people's bodies. That's the narrative that is presented by Leftist politicians and their cronies in media. And no one, not even Republicans, have been able to challenge that narrative.

The Tools of the Trade

I've been an analyst for fifteen years. When I was in the navy, I was a submarine sonar technician. My job was to operate, maintain, and repair the sonar equipment designed to analyze the sounds of the ocean. Those tools included a variety of sophisticated equipment, such as spectrum analyzers, hydrophones, transducers, phased arrays, analog processors, state-of-the-art digital processors, and both analog and digital recording devices. However, even in this, the second decade of the twenty-first century, a submarine sonarman's most effective listening device remains his ears, and his most effective analysis tool is still his brain. Thus, by using my ears, my reasoning skills, as well as the boat's multi-million-dollar sonar systems, my job as an analyst was to decipher and interpret the various sounds of the ocean to determine not only what the source of those sounds were, but also to determine what threat, if any, they posed to our submarine.

Among the cacophony of noises echoing through the depths of the sea are thousands of varieties of what sonarmen call "biologicals" (i.e., fish, whales, dolphins, etc.). I remember looking forward to the winter months in Hawaii when the humpback whales paid their yearly visit to the warm tropical waters. Their distinctive songs were a welcome addition to the otherwise tedious soundtrack of the sea. I've listened to pods of hundreds of dolphins off the west coast of Canada as they gathered to feast on massive schools of fish. I've heard the infamous "boing fish" in the waters of the Hawaiian Islands. (The "boing fish" sounds remarkably like a person humming and whistling at the same time. Of note, the mysterious source of the "boing fish" sound was recently discovered to be the Minke whale. For decades, sonarmen's imaginations concocted wild tales about what the source of the sound could have been. I've heard it said that early sonarmen imagined it was the call of beautiful mermaids.)

I've also heard my share of geological noises, such as earthquakes and volcanoes. I've listened to thousands of hours of environmental sounds, as well, such as the wind, waves, and rain. The blend of all these natural sounds is called "white noise" or "static." No matter where a submarine goes in the sea, a blanket of "white noise" surrounds it. All those sounds are basically "background noise," and it's the responsibility of the sonar operator to listen "beyond" that background noise in order to hear the sounds that are of most concern to the safety of both the boat and her crew – that is, other ships and submarines; or, as we used to call them, "the unforgiving steel objects in the sea that our boat can bump into."

The two submarines I served on were both home-ported in Pearl Harbor, Hawaii. I've traveled all over the Pacific Ocean deep under the waves. I've spent hours listening to noisy Japanese trawlers, sleek and modern trans-oceanic cargo ships, old and rusty trans-oceanic cargo ships, Asian and South American naval ships, and many other vessels that I'm not at liberty to discuss. It was my job to use our sophisticated sonar systems, as well as my ears and brain, to detect and isolate from the background noise the various unique acoustic fingerprints, or "signatures," of hundreds, sometimes thousands, of ships. The bangs, rumbles, squeals, whirs, and whines of machinery such as diesel engines, gas turbines, hydraulic pumps, propellers, winches, bilge pumps, and other rotating and electrical gear and equipment on merchant ships and fishing boats, must be classified and differentiated from each other in order for the submarine to navigate safely and avoid colliding with other ocean-going vessels. It was my job to sift through the thousands of sounds and isolate the ones that posed a threat.

The greatest threat to a submarine is another submarine. That's because it operates in the very same environment as its prey – below the surface of the ocean. However, when hunting for another submarine, the job of the sonar operator is made even more difficult by virtue of the fact that submarines are designed, built, and operated in such a way as to make as little noise as possible. Staying quiet is a matter of life and death on a submarine.

Because of the unique quality of submarine operations, years of training and experience are required for a sonar operator to become proficient at detecting and classifying the thousands of sounds in the ocean and picking out the one tiny sound that may, perhaps, be from another submarine. Detecting and classifying a submarine from among the dissonance of ocean noises is akin to finding a needle in a haystack – some would even say it's like finding a needle in a needle stack! Remember, there are no windows on submarines, thus the sonar operator is the eyes and ears (literally) of the boat. The safety of the entire crew rests in his hands.

A submarine also creates its own noises, which must be

filtered out in order to effectively listen for other ships and submarines. The submarine's sonar division is responsible for tracking and measuring the boat's own noises, and taking necessary measures to silence the sounds that could make the boat detectable to other ships and submarines. A robust sound-silencing program is vital to the submarine's ability to remain undetected by the enemy.

I've witnessed young sonar operators mistakenly classify self-noise emanating from our own boat as a new "contact." They'll place a tracker on it, which sends data to the fire control system where a "solution" is calculated to determine the contact's range (distance from own ship), heading, and speed. It is part of the learning experience for young sonarmen to embarrass themselves by informing their shift supervisor that a ship has suddenly appeared off the starboard bow, only to discover that he's tasked the fire control technician and other watch-standers in the control room with tracking their own submarine. The embarrassing call from the fire control technician is not soon forgotten. Trust me. I was once that embarrassed, young sonarman.

In 1996, after six years of military service, I chose to leave the navy and pursue a career in film. I wanted to be a cinematographer, and considered applying for a film/television program at a major university in southern California. However, I was directed by a very wise submarine officer of impeccable sea-storytelling skills to begin my coursework at a community college. It would be much cheaper, he said. He was correct.

I received an honorable discharged in November 1996, and returned to Maryland, land of my birth. I moved into my sister's basement, got a job as a mall security guard, and started taking courses at the local community college. By my second semester of college, I realized that a career in film was not my best option. I switched my major to physics, and enrolled in a computer programming course, a calculus course, and a course required by the general education obligations for a liberal arts degree. That third course was Western Civilization.

After my third week of calculus and C++ programming, I came to the realization that I was not going to be the next Alfred Einstein.[1] I did, however, very much enjoy the Western Civilization course I was taking down the hall. I loved reading about politics, wars and conquests, and the long history of mankind's struggles against nature and, well, mankind. Reading about Napoleon and discussing the Great Depression was far more interesting to me than calculating the area under a curve and writing preprocessor directives. Thus, for the next five years I slowly racked up credits towards a degree in history. After two years of college, my ten-year bachelor's degree program was finally on track. I had become a student of history.

My life took an unexpected turn shortly after the dawn of the new millennium, though, when al Qaeda terrorists attacked our nation on September 11, 2001. I was one year shy of obtaining the credits required to receive a bachelor's degree in history. The terrorist attack affected me tremendously, and like most Americans I was shocked and outraged. I felt out of the loop, though, walking around campus (and the mall where I worked), wishing I could do something to help the fight against the bastards who attacked us. I was anxious to get back on the front lines of our new struggle for freedom. I had enjoyed, for the most part, being part of the world's finest military force, and felt a deep desire to put the uniform back on and take a stand against the looming Islamic-fascist threat.

So, in May 2002, I enlisted in the U.S. Navy Reserves as an intelligence specialist. I took the lessons I learned as a submarine sonar technician and a student of history and applied them to my new vocation. I was soon hired by a defense contractor and began working as an all-source intelligence analyst. I studied and reported on foreign naval forces for the Pacific Command in Pearl Harbor, Hawaii.

During those first months, I discovered that, like a sonar operator, the intelligence analyst must also learn to listen "beyond" the noise in order to "hear" the relevant information. Again, there are a host of technological tools that help decipher the relevant data from the "background noise." This is especially true for particular types, or sources, of intelligence. Yet, just as is true of the sonarman, the intelligence analyst's greatest tool is still his brain and his reasoning skills.

It takes years of training and experience to properly analyze the vast amounts of intelligence related to a particular target, and to determine which pieces of intelligence are valid and which are bogus or irrelevant. Thus, like my experience as a submarine sonar technician, I learned that an all-source intelligence analyst must rely a great deal upon logic and reason – that is, his or her brain. An intelligence analyst cannot rely solely upon technological tools to do the analyzing.

The most important lesson I learned as an intelligence analyst is that if you don't have an answer to a question, just say you don't know. It's better to admit your ignorance than to be wrong. For one thing, if you're wrong, people may die. Beyond that, you're career and reputation as an analyst depends on your honesty and commitment to the truth. It's best to just admit you don't know, but that you'll find the answer as soon as possible.

Very often, though, many of us have been trained since childhood that not knowing is akin to stupidity. Perhaps we had an older sibling who harassed us when we didn't know something. Perhaps it was a parent or teacher. After all, no child wants to be singled out in class to answer a question, only to suddenly face the embarrassment of saying "I don't know." Thus, our tendency, our instinct, is to give it a guess and hope for the best. But that doesn't work in the intelligence business.

A Shameless Culture

For many years now, I've listen to the sounds of American politics. I've sifted through the political rhetoric and filtered out the interfering background noises emanating from elected officials and the media. What I've discovered is that the American public has been sold a series of false and misleading narratives related to some of the most important social issues facing the nation today. I've also discovered that the very substance of these false narratives deteriorates immediately once the truth becomes known about the core element at the heart of the issue. The false narratives that most Americans hear from their elected officials and the media very often are the product of ignorance.

Quite frequently, Americans are treated to commentators on television who are totally ignorant of the subject they're discussing. Even more disturbing, though, are the clueless politicians who are never discouraged from expressing an opinion about a subject with which they've absolutely no knowledge or experience. But, unlike the intelligence analyst who is compelled to admit his ignorance, journalists and politicians are unable or unwilling to acknowledge that they just do not know something.

Journalism school graduates who've never handled a firearm, for instance, will confidently deliver ad hoc commentaries about the evils of large-capacity magazines, barrel-shrouds, or pistol grips, without having any clue about what those things are or whether they are truly dangerous or not. Law school graduates who've used their fine communication skills to get elected into public office, who also have never handled a firearm, will repeat what their clueless comrades in media have said about guns, and then have their equally clueless staffers dust off some restrictive gun control legislation that will, in effect, do nothing to solve the problem of violence, but which makes them all feel morally superior to their conservative, pro-gun-rights colleagues. Talking heads on cable news will wax eloquently about raising taxes on "the rich" without any clue as to whether doing so would affect the economy negatively or positively. Likeminded journalists and politicians will breathlessly warn the American people that political compromise is necessary to solve a crisis that they themselves have created, or which does not actually exist (more on this in Chapter Two).

I've discovered also that the more comfortable a person is in front of a large audience, the more likely they are to not feel obliged to understand various concepts, such as economics, law, science, or history. There's an inherent arrogance that comes with many individuals who are comfortable with public speaking. This is not to say that all good public speakers are deceptive or liars. Many people who speak to large audiences are comfortable because they are experts in their fields and are comfortable discussing their area of expertise. However, studies of psychopaths indicate that many high profile people who have a command of public communications and are in positions of power and influence, such as corporate CEOs and politicians, share many traits with serial killers and other mentally-disturbed criminals.

One study of past American presidents indicated that, like psychopaths, they all shared a lack of "guilt," a trait common to psychopaths.[2] Another study based on FBI data indicates "that some of the character traits exhibited by serial killers or criminals may be observed in many" politicians:

> While not exhibiting physical violence, many political leaders display varying degrees of anger, feigned outrage and....lack what most consider a "shame" mechanism. Quite simply, most serial killers and many professional politicians must mimic what they believe are appropriate responses to situations they face such as sadness, empathy, sympathy, and other human responses to outside stimuli.[3]

Psychologist Kevin Dutton, in his book, *The Wisdom of Psychopaths,* says that particular vocations attract sociopaths and psychopaths.[4] Among the top ten professions where one would find a psychopathic individual are CEO, lawyer, television and radio, journalism, and police officer. An occupation found on the list that is perhaps surprising is clergy, though many of my secular libertarian friends would not be surprised. Curiously missing from the list are politicians, though they are featured prominently in Dutton's book as individuals who are predisposed to psychopathy.

The two most prominent former occupations cited by members of Congress are lawyers and bankers/businessman,[5] both of which are occupations featured on the psychopathy scale found in Dutton's book.[6] In the 111th Congress, for instance, which was in office from January 2009 to January 2011, 66 percent of House members and 67 percent of Senate members with law degrees were Democrats, which indicates either that law school graduates with Leftist ideological tendencies typically chose to run for public office, or that Leftists attend law school at greater numbers than conservatives. Republicans, on the other hand, often fit the category of the business owner or executive, individuals that are also featured prominently in the psychopathy scale. Thus, there's likely as many psychopathic Democrats as there are psychopathic Republicans in public office – a strong argument for a smaller, limited government if ever there was one.

Journalists are included on the list, as are media personalities. This comes as no surprise because journalists of late are prone to subscribe to the notion that they are obligated, not to simply convey to an audience what happened during a particular event, but to actually affect policy in their reporting by crafting a narrative that pushes an agenda. Journalism students are increasingly taught to use their influence and access to institutions of power to push for political action regarding "social justice" issues, such as unionization and collective bargaining, same-sex marriage, global warming and green energy, governmental regulation of businesses, redistribution of wealth from rich to poor and the middle class, the right to a living wage, and a host of other Leftist policies. They craft Leftist narratives in their journalism in order to affect policy, and they do so shamelessly and without any sense of balance to opposing views.

The key common element of the nature of elected officials, people in high profile media jobs, and their psychopathic counterparts, is shame; or to be more precise, the absence of it. A good intelligence analyst, for instance, should have some degree of shame, or at the very least humility. He should feel compelled to admit his limited knowledge about a particular topic, so as to at least allow the listener or reader to know where facts end and speculations begin. Facts are paramount for the intelligence professional. But, as will be demonstrated in this book, many politicians and news media personalities are not so inclined.

American culture has allowed people to rise to the highest levels of society in spite of their willingness to lie and deceive and behave without any sense of shame. Hollywood stars are notoriously spinning through the revolving doors of rehab centers and divorce lawyer's offices, all while preaching to the rest of America about morality and ethics; pathological liars hold high public office while attempting to regulate the activities of their fellow citizens; American students are increasingly comfortable with cheating on exams; and plagiarism is on the rise in journalism. In many cases, individuals are rewarded for their misdeeds, either by gaining notoriety or simply by having their actions justified by Leftists who argue that society is at fault. All of these trends are manifestations of an absence of shame and humility in American culture.

Psychologists Jean Twenge and Keith Campbell, in their book, *The Narcissism Epidemic*, make a strong case that American culture is experiencing a remarkable and dangerous epidemic of certifiable cases of narcissistic personality disorder (NPD). Even worse, they argue that American culture is currently transforming into one that esteems narcissistic personalities, which they note is primarily due to the "self-admiration" movement that began in the 1960s.[7] The consequence of living in a culture that esteems narcissistic individuals, they say, is that more and more individuals that are not necessarily narcissistic are quite comfortable behaving more narcissistically.

Few observers would challenge the argument that American culture is undergoing a transformation that normalizes narcissism. Twenge and Campbell note a number of societal trends that they say represent a "rise in cultural narcissism," including "the fivefold increase in plastic surgery and cosmetic procedures in just ten years, the growth of celebrity gossip magazines, Americans spending more than they earn and racking up huge amounts of debt, the growing size of houses, the increasing popularity of giving children unique names, polling data on the importance of being rich and famous, and the growing number of people who cheat."[8]

One additional societal consequence of an epidemic of narcissism is an entitlement culture. Twenge and Campbell note that the "federal government has reached incredibly high levels of giving Americans something for nothing." The result is that:

> ...citizens have no interest at all in dealing with this reality or taking any responsibility for it. They want their entitlements and pork and will kick out of office anyone who stands in their way. In the short run, everyone gets to feel good – they get their free money and can rave about what a wealthy and prosperous nation America is.[9]

The citizens of Western European socialist states, most of which today are experiencing outrageous debt crises both individually and nationally, exhibit high levels of narcissism. The typical European living in Sweden or France, for instance, tends to concern themselves more with leisure than with work. Harvard professor of economics Niall Ferguson highlighted the difference between the typical European and American work ethic in a *New York Times* article:

> According to a recent study by the Organization for Economic Cooperation and Development, the average working American spends 1,976 hours a year on the job. The average German works just 1,535 – 22 percent less. The Dutch and Norwegians put in even fewer hours. Even the British do 10 percent less work than their trans-Atlantic cousins. Between 1979 and 1999, the average American working year lengthened by 50 hours, or nearly 3 percent. But the average German working year shrank by 12 percent.
>
> Yet even these figures understate the extent of European idleness, because a larger proportion of Americans work. Between 1973 and 1998 the percentage of the American population in employment rose from 41 percent to 49 percent. But in Germany and France the percentage fell, ending up at 44 and 39 percent. Unemployment rates in most Northern European countries are also markedly higher than in the United States.[10]

In his book *Civilization: The West and the Rest,* Professor Ferguson notes that Europeans are more likely than Americans to go on strike. Compared to Asians, says Ferguson, Europeans are exceptionally slothful: "the average Japanese worker still works as many hours a year as the average American, while the average South Korean works 39 percent more. People in

Hong Kong and Singapore also work roughly a third more hours a year than Americans."[11]

Yet, Americans, like their European counterparts, have grown increasingly embittered due to a greater sense of entitlement.[12] When an individual believes they are entitled to greater leisure time, paid vacations, higher wages, and the latest high-tech gadget to hit the store shelves – and that individual is unable to acquire those things – they become increasingly bitter and are prone to be influenced by political rhetoric that taps into that sense of entitlement, especially if their neighbor owns any of those precious items. A sense of entitlement also leads invariably to justifications for taking other's possessions and experiencing little or no shame about it, primarily because the individual feels they are a victim of circumstances or the deck was stacked against them. The thief always believes he is entitled to other people's wealth and property, and will always justify his thievery by claiming to be a victim of some sort.

Take, for instance, the increased cases of so-called "flash mob robberies." Teenagers are terrorizing convenience stores, large-box stores, and shopping malls.[13] These incidents are a recent outgrowth of modern technology. A "flash mob" is created when teenagers use social networking to arrange mass gatherings, or mobs. Once the crowds have gathered, they typically flood into a store and overwhelm the staff. Flash mobs usually end with thefts, violence, or both. Of note, National Public Radio (NPR) reported that the vast majority of "flash mob robberies" occur in predominately black urban areas.[14] It's no coincidence that these events are occurring mostly in areas where youths have been taught by angry civil rights leaders and elected officials that they are the victims of a racist system and will likely never achieve success because the game has been rigged against them.

The increased absence of shame and the epidemic of narcissism in our culture have also allowed politicians and their comrades in media to perpetuate false narratives without remorse or concern for the truth. As a result, the false narratives have become accepted as fact, and even as common sense. But, they are false nonetheless, and the politicians and media personalities who continue to push them as the truth are doing serious damage to our nation by altering the relationship between government officials and the citizens they are obligated to serve. Instead, the relationship has been reversed – today, it is the citizen who serves the government official rather than the other way round.

Terms Defined

This brings me, in a very roundabout way, to the subject of this book: the false narratives of Leftists. I have, for the last decade or so, as I noted above, observed a particular trend about the way political issues are discussed, mostly by Leftist politicians and their comrades in media. I've discovered that they basically own the narratives. They have framed every issue – from abortion, to gun control, to taxes, to war, and even the whole history of mankind – in such a way that it conforms to their ideological worldview, and so that it suits their political objectives. Leftists have crafted narratives about every important social-political issue that is relevant today. And those narratives have become so entrenched in the American conscience that it's almost impossible for the American public to think about, to discuss, and to make laws related to those issues beyond or outside the limitations of the false narrative's framework.

Before going any further, let me first define two terms: "Leftist" and "narrative." A Leftist subscribes to an ideology that emerged in the late 19th and early 20th centuries. Early pioneers and adherents of the ideology were H. G. Wells, Theodore Roosevelt, William Jennings Bryan, Robert La Follette Sr., Richard Ely, Woodrow Wilson, Jane Addams, Ida Tarbell, Walter Lippmann, John Dewey, Upton Sinclair, Eugene V. Debs, Alfred "Al" Smith, Huey Long, Herbert Croly, Father Charles Coughlin, and Franklin Delano Roosevelt. The mantle of Progressivism was taken up again nationally in the 1960s by Lyndon Johnson and is carried today by a host of Democratic politicians, including Secretary of State Hillary Clinton, President Barack Obama, and Senator Harry Reid as well as people in news media and the vast majority of Hollywood stars.

At its most basic level Progressivism/Leftism is founded upon the ideas articulated by 18th century philosopher Jean-Jacques Rousseau, who proposed that man is neither inherently good nor evil, but that ultimately it is society that shapes a human being's morality. Thus, because humans are essentially blank slates, the coercive force of government should be used to perfect humans into better creatures; kinder, more equitable, more generous, less selfish, and less judgmental. Noted economist Thomas Sowell, in his book *A Conflict of Visions,* attributes the foundations of the Progressive/Leftist ideology to a view of human nature that he calls "unconstrained," which was best articulated by William Godwin.[15]

The term "progressive" comes from the idea that history shows very clearly that human beings have failed repeatedly to construct a society that shapes human nature into more perfect creatures. Humans got things wrong in the past, and they are getting it wrong today. Therefore, Progressives believe that the wisdom of our ancestors should be dismissed, most especially the wisdom of the Framers of the Constitution and the ancients who wrote the Bible. Human beings, therefore, should devote themselves to progressing towards a perfected nature by consistently altering society until the right set of policies is found.

Conservative philosophy, on the other hand, is based more on the ideas of 18th century philosopher Thomas Hobbes, who advocated the idea that human nature is inflexible and cannot be perfected. The conservative looks at human history, sees a vast wasteland of violence and abuse, and recognizes it as evidence of an inherently imperfect and flawed creature. Thomas Sowell attributes the foundations of the conservative ideology to a view of human nature, the "constrained," best articulated by Adam Smith. When applied to government and policy, the conservative view tends to distrust human beings, particularly those who seek power and influence, especially in government.

Thus, the Framers of the Constitution – most of whom subscribed to the Hobbesian, or "constrained," view of human nature – placed severe restrictions on the power and scope of government, based primarily on their study of human history and the consistent and repeated instances of corruption, abuse, and tyranny by men in power. As a consequence, conservatives esteem and wish to conserve the wisdom of the Framers, as well as that of the ancients, most especially the authors of the Bible, each of whom argued that man is inherently flawed and must be prohibited from obtaining too much power and influence over his fellow man. Thus, the Framers defined only limited powers to the federal government, and separated federal powers into three branches. They further established checks and balances to restrain the accumulation of power at the federal level, and left whatever powers not articulated to the federal government in the Constitution to the states and the individual citizen. They placed severe restrictions on the reach of government into the lives of citizens by including the Bill of Rights.

The most significant distinction between Progressivism/ Leftism on the one hand, and conservatism on the other, is each philosophy's view of the most effective mechanism for moderating human nature. To illustrate this distinction, recall the increased narcissism in American culture discussed above. Americans are increasingly subscribing to the belief that they can live beyond their means, and also that they are entitled to other people's wealth because, perhaps, they believe that the political/economic system is rigged against them, either because it is racist, sexist, or discriminatory in some other way.

As a result, an increasing number of Americans are becoming fixated on their own economic status relative to other Americans. They feel like they are not getting what they deserve, their fair share of the pie. Alternatively, they believe that their wealthier neighbors – who perhaps have all the extravagances of wealth that they feel they are entitled to – are not paying their fair share into the system.

The imbalance is quite stark in the U.S., and a wealth gap highlights the differences between the "rich" and the "poor." Thus, the Leftist sees the world through the lens of materialism, and places the blame for narcissism on economic inequality. Remove the inequality – by redistributing the nation's wealth from rich to poor, typically by means of a progressive income tax wherein the rich "pay their fair share" – and you remedy the problem of narcissism. Leftists are therefore committed opponents of capitalism, and have over the past century transformed the American economic system into a quasi-socialist one, closer to that of many European nations where wealth gaps are far smaller. Ultimately, the goal of the Leftist is to create a socialist utopia on earth; a society free of economic inequality.

For the Leftist, the solution to narcissism – and the crime that stems from it – is to use the coercive power of government to transform the culture into a more just one, where material wealth is equally distributed, and the individual without needs no longer feels compelled to seek justice – that is, material equality. The citizen of the socialist utopia is free to devote his attention toward noble pursuits, such as the arts and science, as well as to leisure and pleasure. This is a materialist solution to the problem, based on the notion that exterior forces, in this case economic inequality, cause humans to behave selfishly and seek others possessions.

The conservative sees the increasing narcissism in American culture and recognizes it as the consequence of a spiritual rather than material transformation. Human beings are not destined to be angels on earth, nor are they to attempt to create a heaven on earth. Instead, the conservative believes that humanity's perfection will be manifested only in the afterlife. Our focus while on earth should be on the service of others individually, rather than on our material status. A focus on material and economic status breeds envy and a sense of entitlement, traits that were despised by both the ancient, modern, and post-modern thinkers whose wisdom is cherished by conservatives.

The coercive use of government for the purpose of seeking economic and social justice is anathema to the conservative. Beneficence and charity are expressed by individuals, not by society at large, for the rewards of the afterlife come only to the individual, not to the society. The care of individuals in need is most efficiently and effectively accomplished at the local level, typically through the church or civic organization, rather than through a distant, bloated, centralized bureaucracy where corruption and abuse are easier to hide and harder to remedy. This is a spiritual solution to the problem, based on the notion that an interior force, in this case a corrupt nature, is the root cause of selfishness.

Throughout this book, as I dissect Leftist narratives, the stark contrast between the unconstrained and constrained views of human nature and their respective policy implications will become readily apparent, particularly in Chapters Two and Four. The Leftist subscription to the unconstrained view of human nature, thus its insistence on using the power of government to improve human nature rather than just the conditions of human life, and to create a society that perhaps can finally bring about a utopia on earth, will be evident as each issue is discussed.[16]

What do I mean when I say that Progressives/Leftist have "crafted a narrative"? At the most basic level, a narrative is a way of communicating that includes a setting, characters, and time (that is, a beginning, middle, and end). For instance, when a small child relates to his parents for the first time a story about what happened at daycare, he's crafted a narrative.

But there is more to narrative than just a story. The most enlightened definition of narrative that I've encountered comes from Katherine Kohler Riessman, who wrote that a narrative is crafted when a "speaker connects events into a sequence that is consequential for later action and for the meanings that the speaker wants listeners to take away from the story. Events perceived by the speaker as important are selected, organized, connected, and evaluated as meaningful for a particular audience."[17]

Narrative is key to writing, and as a student of military history, my coursework often included readings of not just military history, but also studies on the practice of researching and writing about history. One book that stands out among the dozens of others I've read is John Lewis Gaddis' *The Landscape of History: How Historians Map the Past.*

In his remarkable examination of how historians do history, Gaddis argues that historians must resist the temptation to let the arrogance of hindsight affect their understanding of the past, because history is not reality, but only a "representation of reality." Gaddis warns us that:

> with the passage of time, our representations *become* reality in the sense that they compete with, insinuate themselves into, and eventually replace altogether the firsthand memories people have of the events through which they lived.... We make the past legible, but in doing so we lock it up in a prison from which there's neither escape nor ransom nor appeal....[therefore] Our responsibility as historians is as much to show that there were paths *not* taken as it is to explain the ones that were....[thus] when historians contest interpretations of the past among themselves, they're liberating it...from the possibility that there can be only a single valid explanation of what happened.[18]

Journalists are the first recorders of history. They document events as they happen, and often it is their records that provide future historians with the information required to make sense of the long chain of events that led to and will follow our present time. Journalists therefore owe present as well as future generations a truthful narrative about the paths *not* taken as much as the paths that *are* taken. That is, they are obligated to offer to their viewers, readers, and listeners, all sides of an argument, all points of view – all the "paths" of the story. They must, as Gaddis argues, "contest interpretations" that, while they may fit conveniently into the prevailing narrative of the newsroom, may legitimately represent the views of a variety, and perhaps a majority, of individuals. The narratives that journalists construct must include interpretations of events that they may have discarded because they appear extreme, radical, or out-of-the-mainstream. Only then will they liberate the truth from the prison of their own biases.

Gaddis' metaphor of the historian mapping the past, the landscape, as he calls it, suggests that journalists, as writers of current history, have an obligation to provide as true a representation of the landscape as possible. Like the historian who maps the past by both rising high above it, and also walking amongst and upon it, the journalist must venture outside of the comfort zone of their narrow perspective and explore the unfamiliar hills and valleys, rivers and oceans, of current events. Like the historian, journalists must provide as truthful a representation of the landscape as possible. That's Gaddis whole argument.

However, many journalists today are trapped in echo chambers of Leftist ideology, and the maps they draw of the current landscape are twisted representations of reality. Their maps are corrupted by their biases, and they contain distorted landscapes that bear no resemblance to reality. When a journalist reports that such-and-such politician's views are "extreme," in spite of the fact that their views may be in line with a majority of the public, the landscape is distorted and the map the journalist has drawn is corrupted and unreliable. When journalists adopt the political narratives of one party over another, they distort the landscape. When journalists offer readers, viewers, and listeners only one side of an argument, they distort the landscape. When journalists become advocates of one politician over another, they distort the landscape.

Many journalists refuse to admit that they are biased, that they are affected by their ideological predispositions, and that they are influenced by their limited experiences. In fact, many of them refuse to admit that they are limited in any way whatsoever. Many journalists insist that they only relate the facts, nothing more. Yet, no one relates only the facts – everyone has an angle, whether they know it or not. But many journalists insist that they are the only people on the planet who don't have an angle. Such arrogance is rooted in the fact that many journalists are trapped in an echo chamber and are thus unable to recognize just how biased they are and how much they are affected by ideology, and how limited they are in experience and knowledge. And, as is often the case, it is ignorance that is at the root of their arrogance.

As future historians look back and navigate the landscape of human affairs today, their paths will be guided by the maps that journalists and commentators today have drawn. However, because the maps are distorted and twisted and corrupted, historians' paths will inevitably wander chaotically across an unfamiliar landscape spotted with alien features. This book will examine the distorted landscape that many high-profile and influential journalists and commentators, as well as politicians, have crafted regarding major policy issues.

Hopefully, this book will expose the distortions and provide a better understanding of how to map the present landscape in a way that more accurately represents the truth.

What I've discovered, after years of listening to American politics, is that once the false narratives are stripped away, and the truth is revealed, and the core issues are exposed, and the American public realizes that they've been deceived once again by their elected officials and the media, the nation moves closer to the constitutional republic it was intended to be. This book will examine the false narratives that Leftist politicians and their comrades in media have crafted about (1) crime; (2) war; and (3) money.

CHAPTER ONE – THE ECHO CHAMBER

In a 1996 survey conducted by the American Society of Newspaper Editors (ASNE), over one thousand reporters from sixty-one newspapers were asked to describe themselves politically. Over 61 percent said they were either "liberal" or "Democratic," and 15 percent said they were "conservative" or "Republican."[1]

Early in 2005, just four months after the conclusion of a presidential election that pitted Republican President George W. Bush against Democratic challenger Sen. John F. Kerry of Massachusetts, the University of Connecticut's Department of Public Policy conducted a political survey of 300 journalists at news organizations all across the nation. The study's sample included 120 (40 percent) television news journalists and 180 (60 percent) newspaper journalists. The Media Research Center noted:

> In a report released May 16, 2005, the researchers disclosed that the journalists they surveyed selected Democratic challenger John Kerry over incumbent Republican President George W. Bush by a wide margin, 52 percent to 19 percent

> (with one percent choosing far-left independent candidate Ralph Nader). One out of five journalists (21 percent) refused to disclose their vote, while another six percent either didn't vote or said they did not know for whom they voted.[2]

Thus, while George W. Bush won the 2004 presidential election over opponent Sen. Kerry by a margin of 51-47 percent, the people we rely upon to inform us about politics and social issues voted in favor of the losing candidate by a margin of 52-19 percent. These numbers indicate that America's newsrooms are severely skewed politically towards one party, while the nation as a whole appears more equally divided. Other studies indicate that the margin of Democrat/liberal over Republican/conservative at news organizations, particularly those that cover national-level politics, may be even larger than the polls noted above indicate.

For instance, in 1996, Elaine Povich asked "139 Washington bureau chiefs and congressional correspondents" to identify which candidate in the 1992 presidential campaign they voted for. She found that 89 percent (124) said they voted for Bill Clinton versus only 7 percent (13) who said they voted for George H.W. Bush (two individuals said they voted for Ross Perot).[3] Studies of campaign contributions by journalists during the 2004 and 2008 presidential elections indicate that the people who report the news donate more to Democrats than Republicans by a margin of 95 percent to 5 percent on average.[4]

While there are only a few locations throughout the U.S. where Leftists outnumber conservatives by such large margins, their influence is extremely disproportionate. Manhattan is home to the nation's major network news outlets, as well as large public policy think tanks, and also home to a host of influential public relations and advertisement entities. Manhattan is also overwhelmingly Leftwing, by a margin of at least 5:2.[5] Also, when you turn on the television to watch entertainment programming, the vast majority of the shows that you welcome into your home were produced by Leftists, written by Leftists, and feature Leftist performers.

Studies of college faculties indicate ratios upwards of 44:1 Democrat over Republican, most notably in sociology departments. For political science departments, the ratio is nearly 7:1 Democrat over Republican. Only in the financial departments, like economics and business, do you begin to see faculties that consist of an equal number of conservatives and liberals.[6] However, among those "conservatives" on the faculty, the majority of them are likely only *fiscally* conservative (i.e., they support lower taxes, less banking regulation, etc.) versus *socially* conservative (i.e., they oppose abortion-on-demand and same-sex marriage, defend gun ownership and right-to-carry laws, etc.). Thus, the economics student still may come to believe by inference and by experience that someone who is *fiscally* conservative is normal while someone who is *socially* conservative is radical or extreme.

But, you may be asking, what difference does all this make? Journalists are professionals who know how to present the facts without favoring one argument over another. They're dispassionate observers, or so we're told, who do not let their feelings and biases get in the way of the truth. Journalists tell us that they are neither conservative nor liberal. They're professionals who are neither Left nor Right politically.

For instance, ABC News journalist Martha Raddatz was asked whether she's a Democrat or a Republican. Her response was instructive about how journalists view themselves:

> We don't talk about those things. We don't talk

> about those things at all. I'm an objective reporter. Uhh, we can't, uhh. We don't really talk about that. I wouldn't talk about that. I'd like you to find a reporter that does.... I'm not going to tell you anything about how I vote, when I vote, and who I have ever voted for. I am here as a journalist. I'm not here as a political representative of either party. It is not...I'm a journalist.[7]

Journalists like to believe that they are not influenced by their politics or their feelings. They want us to believe that they harbor some innate, extraordinary power that no one else in the world enjoys – the power to dispassionately view the world without feeling or emotion and to report only the objective truth. They want us to believe that they've heard all the evidence, listened to all of the arguments from all sides of the debate, and have reported an objective narrative free of personal biases. However, anyone with any rational brain knows that everyone is affected by their biases; everyone is limited by their experiences; everyone is limited in knowledge; everyone is prone to slant a story.

For instance, CNN's Soledad O'Brien, while filling in for Anderson Cooper, was caught on the air using the talking points from a far-Left online website, Talking Points Memo, during an interview with a female Republican. One conservative blogger described what happened:

> During her interview with Virginia House of Delegates Republican member Barbara Comstock, O'Brien became visibly flustered and was actually caught doing finger stress exercises as she attempt [sic] to insert editorial commentary while her guest...defended the House GOP budget, designed by Budget Chairman Paul Ryan.[8]

Ms. O'Brien was eventually confronted with the fact that she used talking points from a far-Left website during her discussion with a Republican guest. O'Brien doubled down, and tried to defend her journalistic credentials. She insisted that she was merely being a tough journalist intent on providing the truth to her audience.

> I don't think I show bias in my TV show. I think I am aggressive with people about trying to find the facts behind what they say. Am I a liberal or conservative? I'm neither. Like most Americans, I find politics very frustrating. Like most Americans, I'd like to hear from politicians the facts. That is what drives me....Editorially, I was not reading off the Talking Points Memo. The memo had an accurate, verbatim quote of what Sen. Wyden said, and when I was talking to Ms. Comstock, she was saying something that was patently untrue.

Who really believes O'Brien's insistence that she's not conservative or liberal? Does anyone really believe that on the issue of abortion, she doesn't hold a conservatives or a liberal view? On gun control? On same-sex marriage? Really?

Even more, Ms. O'Brien, instead of using talking points from a far-Left website, could have gone to the very source to get a response – that is, the congressman whom she was quoting. She could have contacted the congressman's office and gotten a direct quote. Are we to believe that Soledad O'Brien was unable to get someone from a congressman's office to comment on an issue of great importance to the presidential election? Or, that she was unable to find the congressman's quote at an online source that wasn't a repository of Leftist talking points? Of course not. Instead, her instincts were to check in with a far-Left website for talking points to challenge a conservative guest. The reason is clear: that's where she and her producers tap into the narrative.

Of course, her actions can be partially blamed on laziness. But the fact is that she, like everyone else in that CNN newsroom, is biased and relies upon Leftist talking points to keep the narrative alive. And she was caught red handed!

Another instance of this sort of bias is instructive. A week after a tragic mass shooting at a Connecticut elementary school in December 2012, Ms. O'Brien chaired a roundtable discussion on gun control that featured five guests, all of whom agreed with her that more gun control was needed to stop these terrible massacres. There were no dissenting opinions offered by any of her guests.[9] That's the echo chamber in action, and Ms. O'Brien is just another individual trapped inside the bubble.

Another example: Within hours after news broke about a mass shooting at an Aurora, Colorado, movie theater, ABC News' Brian Ross, a well-respected, veteran journalist with decades of experience, informed viewers that the shooter may have been a member of the Tea Party. When authorities in Colorado released the name of the shooter, James Holmes, Mr. Ross, without knowing anything about the shooter other than a name, walked to his desk, logged on to his computer, typed into Google the words "James Holmes" and "Tea Party," and got exactly what he suspected: a "James Holmes" from a Colorado-based Tea Party organization. Mr. Ross then went on the air and used his national platform to speculate that the Tea Party may have been linked to – nay, was likely responsible for – the mass shooting.

Of course, it turned out that the shooter had nothing, absolutely nothing, to do with the Tea Party or conservative politics. Brian Ross had made a serious mistake.[10] He was forced to apologize. But the veteran journalist's instincts were that his political opponents – ultra-conservative, extremist rightwing Tea Partiers, as he and others in the echo chamber would call them – were responsible for a mass murder. He felt no obligation to wait for the facts. He took the Leftwing narrative and crammed it down viewers' throats. That's what echo-chamber Leftists do.

Another example: After the tragic Connecticut school shooting, CBS News' Bill Plante's segment on December 19 featured three anti-gun advocates and only one pro-gun advocate – but even that gun rights advocate equivocated on the issue, likely feeling outnumbered and pressured by the glare of the newsroom's participants.[11] Thus, in essence, viewers never once heard a pro-Second Amendment voice during the debate. However, they did hear three anti-Second Amendment voices. That's how the Leftist media distorts the issue and warps the conversation – and it's how they continue to own the narrative.

When Soledad O'Brien uses memos from a Leftist website to cross examine her guest's arguments during an on-air discussion about Republican Congressman Paul Ryan's budget plan, she believes she has an obligation to her viewers to become an advocate for her guest's political opponents, the Democrats. There's nothing inherently wrong with that. That is, there's nothing wrong with that if, when cross examining a Democrat, Ms. O'Brien were to use conservative talking points and become an advocate for Republicans. But, O'Brien does not use conservative talking points when cross-examining her Leftist guests. She never becomes an advocate for Republicans. If she had, then she would have said as much in her own defense. But she didn't.

Also of note is the fact that Ms. O'Brien admitted that

she's not, as her profession demands, a dispassionate observer of events; she admitted that she's not objective about the subject matter she's discussing. She admitted that she's just like "most Americans" in that she too finds "politics very frustrating." But, isn't Soledad O'Brien one of those super-human, dispassionate journalist that Ms. Raddatz says they all are? Aren't they all well-trained professional who are dispassionate about the issues they cover? Curiously, while both women insist that they are not regular people – they're journalists – and that they're not influenced by politics like the rest of us, all evidence indicates that they are indeed swayed toward one side of the political spectrum, and thus are swayed towards one side of the issues and arguments they cover and report on – that is, the Left side.

These episodes show clearly that there is a palpable arrogance about journalists. Journalists think they are the only people on the planet with the ability to process information, not like a human being, but like a computer – a machine far superior to mere flesh and blood. It is that arrogance that emboldens them to resist revealing their political ideology while demanding it of everyone else.

But, while they insist they are not like us – and then insist, as Ms. O'Brien did, that they are just like us – we must remember that even the most obscure second-year writer at the *Washington Post* or *New York Times* enjoys access to the most powerful and influential people in the world. A lowly staff writer working a desk on the sixth floor of the *New York Times* building in Manhattan can pick up the phone, call Senator so-and-so's office, and get almost immediate access to either the senator or the senator's chief of staff – or at least get some degree of response almost immediately. Who else can boast similarly? Can the checkout girl at your local grocery store get that sort of response? Hell, can the owner of the grocery store get that sort of response? The answer is, of course not.

Yet journalists often condemn the influence of super-PACs because they're run by mega-millionaires and billionaires who they say have too much easy access to politicians. However, from the perspective of the 52-year old waitress at a roadside diner, or the 45-year old plumber on his back under a leaky sink, the young news correspondent fresh from college has much greater access to their elected officials than they do.

In light of that fact, therefore, journalists have a unique responsibility to their viewers, readers, and listeners, as well as to their profession. They should offer a full disclosure of their ideological beliefs. After all, we demand transparency from almost everyone else we welcome into our inner circle, our sphere of influence. That's exactly what we do when we turn on the television, radio, or computer, to find information about an issue – we welcome journalists into our homes and our hearts and minds. When we turn on the news, visit a website, or purchase a newspaper, we are welcoming journalists into our inner circle, our sphere of influence, and are thus allowing them to shape our understanding of the issues, to shape the landscape of current events.[12]

Above all else, journalists have a constitutionally-protected obligation to monitor the government and provide citizens with the truth about the legislation their elected officials support and the justifications their elected officials are giving for doing so; not to mention the obligation to monitor elected officials to ensure they conduct themselves legally and ethically. Of course, the First Amendment protects the right of the people to "petition the Government for a redress of grievances." But it's journalists who carry government-issued credentials to the White House, Capitol Hill, and the Supreme Court Building – credentials that grant them unmatched access to the mechanisms of power in Washington (and the fifty state capitals). Thus, the journalism profession is unlike every other profession in the level of access to the government it provides.

Therefore, at the very least full disclosure about one's political ideology should be a courtesy on the part of journalists since they're asking their viewers, the American public, to trust them as a source of information, and because of the unmatched access to the organs of government they've been granted. Shouldn't we expect mutual trust? That is, shouldn't we expect enough trust on their part to feel comfortable disclosing their political leanings? After all, if they're honest brokers – which they consistently insist they are – our only complaint would be that they're not biased toward our own ideology, and then that would be our problem, not theirs.

To press the issue a little further, consider the case of ABC News president David Westin. He spoke to graduate students at one of the nation's most prestigious journalism schools, Columbia University, just six weeks after the 9/11 terrorist attacks. There, he was asked by a journalism student: "Was the Pentagon a legitimate target [for the 9/11 attacks]?" The president of ABC News said the following:

> The Pentagon as a legitimate target? I actually don't have an opinion on that and it's important I not have an opinion on that as I sit here in my capacity right now. The way I conceive my job running a news organization, and the way I would like all the journalists at ABC News to perceive it, is there is a big difference between a normative position and a positive position. Our job is to determine

> what is, not what ought to be and when we get into the job of what ought to be I think we're not doing a service to the American people. I can say the Pentagon got hit, I can say this is what their position is, this is what our position is, but for me to take a position this was right or wrong, I mean, that's perhaps for me in my private life, perhaps it's for me dealing with my loved ones, perhaps it's for my minister at church. But as a journalist I feel strongly that's something that I should not be taking a position on. I'm supposed to figure out what is and what is not, not what ought to be.[13]

The president of ABC News could not bring himself to admit that flying a commercial airliner full of innocent passengers into a building was wrong. Noted media critic and former CBS News producer Bernard Goldberg wondered whether David Westin would have offered a similarly ambiguous response to a question about whether it was right or wrong for, say, the Klu Klux Klan to kill blacks; or for racist rednecks to beat a gay man to death; or for the Taliban to deny girls the opportunity to get an education in school. Would the president of ABC News have said, "Actually, I don't have an opinion on that"?[14]

David Westin is just another arrogant journalist who insists that he's dispassionate about every event covered by his news organization. He wanted a young, impressionable audience of aspiring journalists to believe that he was not a mere human being – he's a journalist, a true professional, an objective reporting machine, hovering high above the landscape of events, unaffected by the impact of human evil. Thousands of people were murdered in cold blood by brutal, religious zealots, on American soil, right before our eyes, and among all the people in the world, only journalists were the ones who remained unaffected by the shocking scenes? Someone alert Stan Lee; there's a new race of super-humans, and they can be found wherever the news is reported.

That's the arrogance of the echo-chamber media elitists.

Who's the Extremist?

We must acknowledge, though, that echo chamber ideology can affect everyone, from all sides of the political spectrum. When Rep. Todd Akin (R-MO) told a journalist that female rape victims often do not get pregnant because their bodies have a way of preventing conception during stressful situations, he exposed the extent to which he lives in an echo chamber; an echo chamber of pro-lifers who are willing to contrive so-called "scientific studies" to justify their stance on abortion. Rep. Akin may have just come from a meeting with like-minded individuals, and may have felt emboldened to share his views freely, without bothering to examine how his views should be presented tactfully to the general public. Instead, he became the center of attention for the wrong reason, and a distraction at a time of great importance to his political party. The congressman's gaffe became the headline for weeks, particularly due to the fact that it came just one week before the start of the Republican National Convention. However, the gaffe also served as a test case for measuring the extent to which the echo-chamber media elite skew their coverage of issues and events that they believe will reflect poorly on conservatives.

For instance, on Tuesday, Aug. 14, 2012 – just one week before Rep. Akin's "rape" comment – Vice President Joe Biden spoke to a crowd in Danville, Virginia, and said that if Republicans Mitt Romney and Paul Ryan were elected in November, "They're going to put y'all back in chains." Considering that the audience that day was composed of a large number of African Americans (some in attendance said at least half the crowd was black), all but the most sycophantic Obama supporters understood that the VP was suggesting that Republicans want to enslave blacks. It was so obvious that a number of Leftist commentators condemned his remarks.[15]

Analysts at the Media Research Center examined the amount of time the three major networks, ABC, CBS, and NBC, devoted to Biden's remarks, and the amount of time they devoted to Akin's remarks. The analysis focused on the first three days after each politician's controversial statements. They found that the big three networks' news organizations devoted 19 minutes of airtime to Democrat Biden's remark, and 88 minutes to Republican Akin's remarks – that's over four times the coverage![16] Even Leftist newsman Mark Halperin of MSNBC admitted in a rare moment of honesty, "The media is very susceptible to doing what the Obama campaign wants, which is to focus on" whatever distractions best serve the interests of the administration.[17] By devoting an inordinate amount of resources to Republican gaffes, Leftists in the media expose themselves as advocates for Democrat candidates. But, they don't see themselves that way because they live inside the echo chamber, where everyone around them views the world the same way.

Periodically, someone calls out the echo chamber for their elitist views and narrow vision of the world. Former Speaker of the House Newt Gingrich appeared on NBC News' Meet the Press and highlighted a severe and obvious bias in the media regarding the way they treat Republicans and the way they treat Democrats, particularly regarding the issues of abortion and race-relations. Gingrich said:

> I'm frankly fed up with the one-sided bias, okay? Let me give you two examples. The vice president of the United States goes to a black audience and says, "If the Republicans win, you will be in chains." Now, where's the – how can Biden remain as vice president? Where's the outrage over overt, deliberate racism? [...] Second example: The Democratic Party plank on abortion is the most extreme plank in the United States. The president of the United States has voted three times to protect the right of doctors to kill babies who came out of an abortion still alive. That plank says tax-paid abortion at any moment – meaning partial-birth abortion – that's a 20 percent issue. The vast majority of women do not believe that tax payers should pay to abort a child in the eighth and ninth month [of pregnancy]. Now why isn't it shocking that the Democrats on the social issue of abortion have taken the most extreme position in this country, and they couldn't defend that position for a day if it was made as vivid, as vivid as all the effort is made to paint Republicans [as extreme].[18]

Thomas Friedman, noted *New York Times* columnist, was a part of the panel discussion that day, and he responded to Newt Gingrich's charge. Mr. Friedman defended the Democratic Party position on abortion.[19] He, like his Leftist colleagues in the echo chamber, believes that the American people's hard-earned money should be taken under threat of force by the federal government, and used to fund abortions for babies in the ninth month of gestation, via a procedure dubbed "partial-birth abortion." The procedure consists of the following: birth is induced and the baby is delivered feet-first to avoid full extraction, because if the baby's head were to become exposed, the law would deem her a fully-protected American citizen and thus safe from the attending abortionist's efforts to terminate her life; scissors are then jammed into the base of the baby's skull and her brains are sucked into a sink; the baby's lifeless body is then discarded in the trash with the other rubbish.

By implication, also, Mr. Friedman supports the federal government taking American's hard-earned money to fund clinics where children who survive abortions are left for dead in broom closets, as has been documented repeatedly by former abortion-on-demand defenders turned pro-lifers. State Senator Barack Obama rejected a bill that would have compelled physicians performing abortions to take all necessary measures to keep babies alive who've survived abortions. He rejected the bill three times while he was an Illinois state legislator, as Newt Gingrich noted above. But, that's not extreme?

Curiously, Mr. Friedman's Leftist colleague at the *New York Times,* Nicholas Kristof, made the same point that Newt Gingrich made. He wrote: "Polls show that about one-fifth want abortion to be legal in all situations, and another one-fifth want abortion to be illegal always. The majority fall somewhere between, and these voters are the ones who decide elections."[20] Yet, it's only the Republicans who are labeled abortion zealots. Only Republicans are extremists.

Another example of the echo-chamber media openly siding with and defending the Democratic Party: Everyone, and I mean everyone, knows about Republican vice presidential candidate Gov. Sarah Palin's gaffes during the 2008 presidential campaign. However, few people have heard about then-Sen. Barack Obama's gaffes during the same campaign. For instance, then-Sen. Obama told a cheering crowd at a campaign rally that there are 58 states in the United States – he said he'd been to 57 states and had one more to go. The *New York Times* completely ignored Obama's 2008 gaffe until 2011.[21] Also, then-Sen. Obama told a crowd in 2008 that "10,000 people" had died and "an entire town" was destroyed by a tornado – it was actually 12 people that died and only a portion of the town was destroyed.[22] Additionally, then-Sen. Obama sputtered on the stump several times, yet media outlets never replayed the uncomfortable video for their viewers or listeners.[23] But, Sarah Palin's gaffes were so noteworthy, they received hundreds of hours of network and cable news airtime during the campaign, and most major television news outlets re-aired as part of their news coverage the infamous Saturday Night Live Palin-bashing sketches, just for good measure.

Even more, while media Leftists excoriated conservative Republican Congressman Akin for being out of touch with the mainstream, Leftists in the media are seldom made to feel similarly disconnected from and out-of-touch with the mainstream population. That's why in 2008, news media outlets from across the nation sent nearly 2,000 investigative reporters to Wasilla, Alaska, Gov. Sarah Palin's hometown, to dig up dirt on the *vice presidential* candidate, while sending no one to Chicago, hometown of *presidential* candidate Barack Obama, to investigate Mr. Obama's past. In their minds, a conservative from Alaska was the equivalent to an alien from another planet. They treated Ms. Palin like a specimen to be examined under a microscope. Sen. Barack Obama, though, was just an old friend whose words rang true, and whose ideological rhetoric was like a gentle caress – a tingly thrill up the leg, so to speak.

The Fabric of The Times

Noted UCLA economics and political science professor Tim Groseclose designed a thought experiment to demonstrate the degree to which major newsrooms are unrepresentative of a typical American workplace. "Suppose you randomly chose three colleagues at your work to join you for lunch," says Groseclose. "What's the chance that all three of [your lunchmates] would be right-of-center politically?"

Now, remember – the typical journalist works in an office where there are six, seven, eight, even nine liberals for every conservative, thus a journalist spends very little time around conservatives. "The answer," Groseclose says, "if your workplace has a perfect 50-50 political balance, is one out of eight." That is, if you work at an accounting office, grocery store, bank, hospital, diner or restaurant, hardware store, shopping center, or any other typical workplace where the employees were equally as likely to have voted for Obama as they were Romney, then there's a 1-in-8 chance that your three lunchmates will all be conservatives on any particular day. Groseclose continues:

> Now suppose you're a Washington correspondent and you conduct the same experiment. Then the chance that all three of your lunchmates would be right-of-center is approximately 1 in 3,000....If you engage in this social interaction twice a week, then only once every thirty years will all three of your lunchmates be conservative.[24]

A journalist at one of the nation's leading news organizations, such as NPR, CNN, *New York Times,* or *Washington Post,* likely has never had lunch with an equal number of conservatives and liberals, let alone a majority of conservatives. Thus, to their minds, conservatives are radical and extreme; they're outside the mainstream. In short, a vast majority of journalists live and work in an echo-chamber of liberal ideology.

The most notorious example of the echo chamber's effect on Leftists is from forty years ago. Richard Nixon won the 1972 presidential election over his Democratic opponent George McGovern in a landslide. Nixon won 49 of 50 states (he lost only Massachusetts); he received 61 percent of the popular vote. He won 520 of 537 electoral votes – that's 97 percent! In fact, Nixon's win that year stands as the largest landslide victory in modern American presidential politics. However, in spite of Nixon's overwhelming victory, Manhattan resident and noted film critic Pauline Kael, upon hearing the results, said, "I can't believe it. I don't know a single person who voted for him." That is what living inside the echo chamber does.

Professor Groseclose offered another thought experiment to better understand what it's like to live and work in a place where one political party outnumbers the other by 9:1. He looked for a place in the United States where Republicans (conservatives) outnumber Democrats (liberals) by as large a margin as the opposite margin in newsrooms. He discovered, so to speak, Washington County, Utah. It covers a large chunk of the southwestern corner of Utah, and any of its citizens are faithful Mormons. Most, if not all, of its residents own at least one gun. Almost everyone either served in the military or knows someone who currently is serving or has in the past. The small town of La Verkin, situated in the center of Washington County, declared itself a "United Nations-free zone," and city officials issued an ordinance banning UN personnel from entering city limits. Washington County residents formed the Dixie Republicans because they felt the establishment Republicans, including George W. Bush, were not conservative enough.[25]

If you're a centrist voter – perhaps you voted for George W. Bush in 2004, but voted for Barack Obama in 2008 – you would likely feel pretty out of place in Washington County, Utah. Imagine every pick-up truck (and there're a lot of them in Washington County) with a rifle hanging prominently in the rear window. Imagine the abundance of NRA bumper stickers. Imagine listening to the radio in your conspicuously out-of-place Volkswagen and hearing ads for gun shops and hunting outfitters during nearly every commercial break. Imagine the empty supermarket on Sunday mornings because 90 percent of the folks in your neighborhood are at church services. That's what a conservative feels like – only the opposite – in the newsrooms of America's largest television, radio, and newspaper services. That is, if there happens to be a conservative in the newsroom.

How does such an ideologically monolithic workplace affect a person's perception about their own worldview? For a Leftist at a major newsroom, viewpoints to the right are viewed as radical and extreme, regardless of where those views fit into national polling results. When everyone within your inner circle subscribes to the very same views on policy issues as you do, then all other views are dismissed as radical and extreme. When you read a news article about a Republican who opposes tax increases, or believes that life begins at conception, or opposes new gun regulations, or thinks marriage should be defined as a union of one man and one woman, or wants to eliminate or restrict public sector union's collective bargaining, then the Republican will inevitably be labeled a "conservative." They may even be labeled as "radical" or "extreme."

Yet, articles about Democrats who subscribe to a liberal viewpoint on those issues are almost invariably described simply as a "Democrat." No political label is necessary to describe a liberal Democrat when the writer of the story believes that that individual's views are in the mainstream, at least according to the journalist who lives in the echo chamber. To the liberal journalist who perhaps some years ago may have met an "extremist" with an opposing viewpoint (maybe she sat on the plane next to such a person a long time ago), the views of the liberal Democrat appear to be right down the center. To the typical echo-chamber journalist, support for abortion on demand at all stages of fetal development is the mainstream position, while Gallup polls show only 25 percent of Americans share that position.[26] Yet, articles about abortion often feature conservative politicians who fit into the majority being labeled as "extreme" or "radical." Thus, the public is misled into believing a false narrative: that the mainstream is actually the fringe, and the extreme Leftist viewpoint is the mainstream.

The conservative-run news media watchdog organization Media Research Center, and their blog *Newsbusters*, report on liberal media bias at the nation's leading news organizations. Each week, *Newsbusters* highlights newspaper articles, radio, and television news reports that feature a Republican being labeled as "conservative," "rightwing," or some other adjective. However, in those same newspapers, radio and television programs, Democrats are almost never labeled with an ideological adjective, such as "liberal" or "leftwing." They are simply described as a "Democrat." That is, unless they've committed a crime. Democrats who've committed a crime very often have their party affiliation hidden or buried, as the Media Research Center's reporting demonstrates.

The same rule applies to think tanks. When the Heritage Foundation is cited by the *Washington Post* or the *New York Times*, it's invariably labeled "conservative," which it is. But, when the Center for American Progress or the People for the American Way, or some other liberal think tanks are cited, it's almost never identified as "liberal" or "leftwing." It's the same with every liberal organization, from Planned Parenthood to ACORN; they're almost never labeled liberal or leftwing.

The reason is simple: when you're a Leftist in an ocean of Leftists, there's no such thing as a Leftist. You and everyone else who shares the same ideological viewpoint are in the mainstream. Someone once famously stated that, if you want to know what water is, don't ask a fish.[27] Similarly, if you want to know what a Leftist is, don't ask a Leftist, particularly one who eats, sleeps, and breathes Leftist ideology seven days a week.

Another consequence of the echo chamber of Leftist ideology in the newsrooms is that, as I alluded to above, political scandals are often covered very differently depending on which political party is involved. For instance, *Newsbusters* has an entire category of reports called "Name That Party." The category includes news stories about Democrats who've been charged with a crime (typically sex-related, tax evasion, embezzlement, or some other white collar crime), but which either fail to identify the criminal politician's political affiliation, or the party affiliation is buried in paragraph twelve on page eighteen, between the horoscopes and obituaries and the advertisements for upholstery stores. On television, the party affiliation of an offending Democrat is often buried deep within the narrative, if it's even mentioned at all. Meanwhile, Republicans who are charged with crimes often have their party affiliation prominently featured in the first sentence or paragraph of the story. Thus, to the average reader, listener or viewer, the only politicians who are committing crimes are Republicans.

Every so often, one of the media elitists ventures outside the echo chamber and gets a glimpse of their colleagues' biases. When this happens, and if they are honest to themselves, they invariably have to comment on it, likely due to the abject shock they experience upon being exposed to the real world.

For instance, in August 2012, outgoing *New York Times* public editor Arthur Brisbane used his last editorial to inform readers what almost everyone knew already. Mr. Brisbane noted that the newspaper's product is "powerfully shaped by a culture of like minds," what I call in this book the "echo chamber of Leftist ideology." Mr. Brisbane admitted that the echo chamber of *New York Times* writers and journalists is "a phenomenon…that is more easily recognized from without than from within." He continued: "Across the paper's many departments…so many share a kind of political and cultural progressivism – for lack of a better term – that this worldview virtually bleeds through the fabric of *The Times*."[28]

On September 28, *Washington Post* ombudsman Patrick B. Pexton wrote: "One aspect of *The Post* that particularly irks conservatives is the columnists who appear in print and online in news positions (as opposed to those on the editorial and op-ed pages and the online Opinions section). With the exception of Dan Balz and Chris Cillizza, who cover politics in a nonpartisan way, the news columnists almost to a person write from left of center."[29] This trend of newspaper ombudsman making public admissions about Leftist or Progressive slants to their newspapers isn't a sign that the profession is experiencing an epiphany about the importance of unbiased coverage of the news. It's actually a response to recent polling that suggests a mere 40 percent of Americans trust U.S. news organizations.[30]

CHAPTER TWO – TO SERVE AND PROTECT

One is hard-pressed to find a newspaper story or television news report about a crime committed with a gun that does not feature the catch phrase "gun crime" or "gun violence," or that contains some wording that suggests the gun may have committed the crime all by itself, such as "the gun went off," "killed by guns," "guns kill," or "guns took the lives." Take this line, for instance, from the Black Youth Project: "Guns are causing the deaths of thousands and thousands of children each year."[1]

This is in stark contrast to the absence of terms like "baseball bat crime" or "knife violence" or "pointy stick" violence, or the always accurate yet never used term "human violence." You'll never read a newspaper story that says "the bat struck the victim's head," or "blunt objects took the lives of thousands of people this year," or "knives and machetes kill hundreds every year." You won't find lobbyists on Capitol Hill demanding a moratorium on knife sales or a ban on baseball bats or machetes or a blunt object, though these items are used as weapons to kill hundreds (even thousands) of people every year, more so than guns are used.

In sub-Saharan Africa, for instance, the machete is the weapon of choice in intertribal conflicts because of the low cost, of course, but also because of the sheer brutality of the act of chopping the victim to death – it both terrifies and desensitizes, and makes war there especially bloody and brutal. Some estimates place the death toll from Africa's tribal and civil wars at several hundred thousand over several decades, a large portion of which are the result of "machete violence." But no newspaper reporter or television talking head has ever suggested that "machetes kill people." Only guns do that.

Take, for instance, an article about mass shootings in *The Atlantic* monthly magazine by Jeffrey Goldberg. "Guns are responsible for roughly 30,000 deaths a year in America," he wrote. In spite of Goldberg's rare balanced article on the issue – he later ponders the idea that perhaps more guns in the hands of law-abiding citizens may reduce "gun violence" – the prevailing narrative has distorted the landscape to such an extent that the phrases "guns are responsible" and "gun violence" flow as easily as any other nuggets of common sense. The terms are as common as any other phrase used by journalists.

Guns are singled out because of a prevailing false narrative. The logic of the narrative goes like this: (1) Americans own guns, lots of them; more so than nearly every other civilized, industrialized nation; (2) the right to own guns is uniquely protected by the U.S. Constitution – a flawed document that was written by evil white men who enslaved Africans and raped their way across North America's peaceful native population; (3) because the Framers were evil, the Constitution is also evil; therefore, (4) guns are evil, as are those who seek to possess them.[2]

After the tragic shooting at an elementary school in Connecticut in December 2012, American Leftists openly expressed abject hostility towards their home country and its laws. MSNBC's Ed Schultz told his radio listeners: "Hiding behind the Second Amendment can no longer be the shield for access [to guns]. The people who wrote that document owned slaves, oppressed women, and were short on tolerance."[3] He later advocated gun confiscation, whereby the government would round up privately owned firearms.[4] Michael Moore, an ardent advocate of a total ban on guns, Tweeted: "America believes in killing....A country that officially sanctions horrific violence (invade Iraq, drones kill kids, death penalty) is surprised when a 20-yr old joins in? I hate to say it, but killing is our way. We began America w/ genocide, then built it w/ slaves. The shootings will continue - it's who we are."[5]

Leftist Georgetown law professor Louis Michael Seidman described the Constitution as "archaic" and "downright evil." Why? Again, the syllogism:

> Imagine that after careful study a government official – say, the president or one of the party leaders in Congress – reaches a considered judgment that a particular course of action is best for the country. Suddenly, someone bursts into the room with new information: a group of white propertied men who have been dead for two centuries, knew nothing of our present situation, acted illegally under existing law and thought it was fine to own slaves might have disagreed with this course of action.[6]

The syllogism is also heard when anti-gun activists argue that the citizens of the United States are ignorant, immature, backward, Neanderthals, hillbillies, and rednecks. In Jeffrey Goldberg's article he quotes the father of a victim of the infamous 1999 Columbine high school massacre. Tom Mauser's son, Daniel, was among the dozen students killed by two deranged teenagers. Mauser says Americans are like "rebellious teenagers," and the nation needs to grow up and be more like the progressive and mature nations of Europe, where strict gun-control laws are enforced. Mauser says of Americans: "we don't like it when the government tells us what to do. People don't trust government to do what's right. They are very attracted to the idea of a nation of individuals, so they don't think about what's good for the collective."[7]

Of course, recent European history demonstrates very clearly what happens when individual citizens give up their identity to an all-powerful government that is able to disarm its citizens. The German people put a government in charge in 1933 that confiscated guns from law-abiding citizens, and used the power of the government to "do what's right" and "what's good for the collective." The result was a massacre of tens of millions of people. The same was true of Mussolini's and Stalin's governments, and almost every other brutal dictatorship. But, according to gun-grabbers in America, the more enlightened pathways chosen by the people of Europe should be imitated in the United States.

The tendency for Leftists, particularly those in the echo-chamber media, to hate America has been well-documented. The tragic events of 9/11 shined a bright light on the anti-Americanism of Leftists in media:

- Steven Jukes of Reuters blamed America for 9/11.
- Richard Waddington of Reuters said in September 2002, America was abusing human rights around the world, and that was what caused 9/11.

- *Los Angeles Times* columnist Joel Stein said in January 2006: "I don't support our troops....When you volunteer for the U.S. military...you're willingly signing up to be a fighting tool of American imperialism....I'm not advocating that we spit on returning veterans like they did after the Vietnam War, but we shouldn't be celebrating people for doing something we don't think was a good idea."
- CBS News icon Andy Rooney blamed America for the 9/11 attacks.[8]

While everyone knows that violence is a bad thing, it is only the Leftist who will tell you that "violence is *never* the answer." It was a Leftist who wrote, "War! What is it good for? Absolutely nothin'." The Leftist is never moved by the fact that it was war, not flowers or smiles or hugs, which brought about the end of slavery in America. It was men with guns that freed millions of Europeans from Nazi concentration camps. The Leftist doesn't recognize that violence is sometimes necessary in order to stop or prevent more violence. The Leftist doesn't understand that violence is sometimes required to stop ruthless thugs from harming people. His naiveté and commitment to Leftist ideology – born in the echo chambers of higher education and nurtured in the echo chambers of the workplace – prevent him from considering any argument that suggests guns are merely a tool, and that, perhaps, evil is rooted in the human heart, not in the cold steel of a weapon. Guns and war are bad because they make Leftists feel bad, and that's all you or they need to know.

For example, CNN contributor John Avlon, in the aftermath of the tragic mass shooting at an elementary school in Connecticut, wrote that the American public should not "let this moment pass without acting on gun control."[9] Conservative columnist and law professor Glenn Reynolds responded that, in essence, what Leftists like Avlon are "really saying is 'our arguments are so unpersuasive that they can only succeed when people aren't thinking clearly'."[10]

Another example: Leftist columnist Donald Kaul from the *Des Moines Register*, after the Connecticut elementary tragedy, wrote that he would "repeal the Second Amendment" and "[d]eclare the NRA a terrorist organization." After that, Mr. Kaul said he "would tie Mitch McConnell and John Boehner, our esteemed Republican leaders, to the back of a Chevy pickup truck and drag them around a parking lot until they saw the light on gun control."

Also, in early January 2013, in response to the Connecticut school tragedy, the White House ordered the formation of a task force to study ways to reduce gun violence. According to the Associated Press, White House aides "worry that as the shock of the Newtown shooting fades, so, too, will the prospects that pro-gun lawmakers will work with the White House to tighten restrictions." White House Press Secretary Jay Carney said: "I believe most Americans would disagree with the idea that in the wake of what happened in Newtown, Conn., that we should put off any action on the issue of gun violence."[11]

The actions of Leftists in the aftermath of the tragic shooting highlight the fact that Leftism is not necessarily about thinking, rationality, or logic. It's primarily about feelings, and in the case of mass shootings, it's all about shock-value and taking advantage of the public's temporary outrage in order to push a political agenda. In these moments, facts are dismissed and opinions are highlighted, particularly in the media. In the weeks after the deadly Connecticut school shooting, Leftist politicians and their comrades in media exposed their abject ignorance about guns and their willingness to never let ignorance stand in the way of passing new legislation, just as they had done previously on many occasions.

Take, for instance, Rep. Caroline Maloney (D-NY). Rep. Maloney was elected to office on an anti-gun platform after a tragic shooting on a New York City subway during which her husband was killed. In 2007, Rep. Maloney was one of the authors of an "assault weapons ban" bill. She appeared on television to make the case for her bill, which included several provisions for banning particular elements of an assault rifle. During an interview on MSNBC, she was asked about her gun control legislation, specifically, why did it prohibit citizens from purchasing guns that feature "a barrel shroud"?

She at first tried to duck the question, indicating that she was ignorant about her own piece of legislation, but the interviewer repeated the question: "What's a barrel shroud and why should we regulate it?" Again, she ducked the question. The interviewer asked a third time, "Do you know what a barrel shroud is?" The Congresswoman, who wrote the legislation that would have regulated barrel shrouds said: "I actually don't know what a barrel shroud is. I think it's the shoulder thing that goes up."[12]

Unfortunately, it is not. Rep. Maloney was clueless about guns, but was willing to prohibit law-abiding citizens from owning a gun with a harmless, decorative feature called a "barrel shroud" because some Leftist told her it was dangerous. That's Progressivism/Leftist in action; feelings-based ignorance.

Of course, ignorance has never prevented politicians from authoring legislation that would affect the lives of every

American. For Rep. Maloney, simply harboring a "feeling" that barrel shrouds are something bad was enough to inspire her and hundreds of other elected officials to want to ban them – never mind the fact that she and they have no idea what they are or whether they are indeed dangerous or not. Episodes like this – and there are plenty of them – give the impression that the folks on Capitol Hill really don't know what the hell they're talking about. Yet, they shamelessly push for change, without first defining where that change will take the nation.

Rapes and Murders

In 2005, Maria Besedin, a 21-year old petite brunette, boarded a Queens-bound G-train in Carroll Gardens, Brooklyn, to visit her boyfriend. She sat by herself on the subway car, updating her journal and listening to music on a pair of headphones. Her attention was drawn suddenly to a man who had moved next to her. He reached down and touched her feet. When she moved to another seat, the man, "wearing a camouflage hat pulled low over his eyes," followed and sat closer. She was so distraught by the man's behavior that she missed her stop. When the train reached 21st Street, she darted onto the platform and headed up the stairs. "The guy was running behind me and started pulling me down the stairs," she said.

As the man began to molest her, Besedin made eye contact with a Metro employee in a nearby booth:

> "I saw him and I thought, 'Oh gosh, he's gonna see me, it's gonna be okay' and – nothing....I held his gaze for at least five seconds, yelling, screaming, 'Help! Help!'"

> Said Besedin, "I always hear announcements over the intercom towards lower levels of the trains, 'This and this train isn't running' or 'Service has been stopped to here and here. Come back upstairs' or – even if someone jumps the turnstiles – 'Hey, where are you going?' – but unfortunately, he couldn't even do that."

The Metro employee did not call 911. He did only what was required of him by his administrators and by law. He pushed a button to alert the Metro command center. Meanwhile, the attack continued.

The man threatened to throw Besedin onto the train tracks, and even held her off the edge of the platform. "He held me, literally by the scruff of my neck, over the train tracks at 45 degrees…I was just shaking and thinking that I was dead, I was as good as dead."

She was assaulted sexually "several times" on the subway platform. When a subway train pulled into the station, the operator merely honked the horn and called the train command center – which is all he was required to do by the metro's policy. The assault lasted about fifteen minutes. The rapist left the scene before police arrived and has not been caught. Besedin fears using the subway, which is the cheapest way of getting around town for most New Yorkers, and suffers today from the aftereffects of the attack. Unable to travel to school and work, Besedin dropped out of Fordham University's graduate psychology program. She "struggles with depression and posttraumatic-stress syndrome, braving nightmares" and severe anxiety.[13]

Besedin got a lawyer and sued the city for negligence. A judge threw out the lawsuit. He ruled that a citizen cannot expect city employees to provide protection against criminal activity. In short, the court ruled that city employees are not responsible for the personal protection of individual citizens.

Coincidentally, the very same year that Ms. Besedin was raped in a New York City subway, the U.S. Supreme Court ruled on a case that completely altered the landscape of American law. In *Castle Rock v. Gonzalez* (2005), the United States Supreme Court ruled that the police cannot be held responsible for the personal protection of individual citizens. Here are the facts of the *Castle Rock* case:

> In 1999, Gonzales obtained a restraining order against her estranged husband Simon, which limited his access to their children. On June 22, 1999, Simon abducted their three daughters.
>
> Though the Castle Rock police department disputes some of the details of what happened next, the two sides are in basic agreement: After her daughters' abduction, Gonzales repeatedly phoned the police for assistance.
>
> Officers visited the home. Believing Simon to be non-violent and, arguably, in compliance with the limited access granted by the restraining order, the police did nothing.
>
> The next morning, Simon committed "suicide by cop." He shot a gun repeatedly through a police station window and was killed by returned fire. The murdered bodies of Leslie, 7, Katheryn, 9, and Rebecca, 10, were found in Simon's pickup truck.[14]

The *New York Times* summed up the U.S. Supreme Court ruling and what it means for every American citizen:

> The Supreme Court ruled on Monday that the police did not have a constitutional duty to protect a person from harm, even a woman who had obtained a court-issued protective order against a violent husband making an arrest mandatory for a violation.[15]

Just in case you missed that, it is well worth repeating: "the police did not have a constitutional duty to protect a person from harm." Just in case there's still some ambiguity, let's sum up the law very clearly. The federal government – the United States Supreme Court, the highest court in the land – has ruled that American citizens are solely responsible for their own protection and self-defense. You cannot sue taxpayer-funded employees, including even the police, for failure to provide personal protection if you're the victim of a crime.

The World Upside Down

Few people will recall these two disturbing stories, in spite of their impact on the nation's laws. Neither story was a prominently featured item on ABC News, CBS News, NBC News, or most other television news channels. They also weren't featured prominently in most major newspapers – they were buried deep inside the pages, if they were reported at all. They were not featured stories in *Time*, *Newsweek*, *People*, *Vogue*, or even Oprah Winfrey's magazine. They were largely ignored by the vast majority of news organizations because they do not fit the prevailing narrative. In fact, these stories completely and utterly undermine the prevailing, Leftist narrative about guns.

You see, the government – federal, state, and municipal – has declared, and the courts have ruled, that it cannot be held responsible for the protection of individual citizens. Therefore, as Mr. Spock of Star Trek would say, logic dictates that citizens are solely responsible for defending themselves and their loved ones from criminal thugs. Logic further dictates that, if we as individuals are solely responsible for protecting ourselves and our loved ones from criminal thugs, we must be able to use whatever tools we deem necessary to ensure we can protect ourselves and our loved ones from harm.

Yet, the laws in most major American cities (and in several states) ensure that criminals remain the only people walking the streets with guns – that is, they're the only ones with guns on the streets of most major metropolitan areas who are not law enforcement officers. Criminal thugs in most major U.S. cities do not fear law abiding citizens. That's a simple fact. Law abiding citizens in New York City, Boston, Philadelphia, Detroit, Baltimore, Atlanta, St. Louis, Chicago, Washington, D.C., and most other large and small metropolitan areas, are prohibited from carrying an effective (some would argue, the most effective) means of personal protection – i.e., a handgun. This in spite of the FBI's very own statistics on crime, which show very clearly that when conceal and carry laws (or, carrying a concealed weapon, or CCW for short) are passed by state legislatures, violent crime rates decline significantly.[16]

Gun-control advocates really have nothing to say to Ms. Besedin or any other victim of a violent criminal. The sad fact is that gun control laws disarm women and make them all potential victims of sexual or other violent crimes. Gun control laws ensure that criminal thugs prowling the streets are served up a buffet of helpless victims. Leftist politicians who write and institute these laws have turned the world upside-down. They've created entire communities where law-abiding citizens fear criminals, rather than the other way round.

A recent increase in rapes and sexual assaults in New York City was met with the usual dismissive wave of the hand from Leftist gun-control advocates. Women in the city walk the streets in fear of being another victim. Women are forced to gather in groups. Communities have formed bicycle escorts to keep women safe on the streets. Beat cops are telling women to avoid wearing short skirts or high heels in public because it invites rapists to attack them. A *Wall Street Journal* reporter witnessed police officers patrolling a Brooklyn neighborhood and advising women that their skirts were "too short" or "too revealing."

Thus, rather than empowering women with the ability to carry a handgun for their own personal protection – which would establish in the minds of potential rapists a lingering and haunting possibility that their next "victim" just may be their worst freaking nightmare – the New York City municipal government is reduced to telling women on the streets that they should adopt the dress code of Middle Eastern Muslim women in order to stay safe and avoid being the next victim of a violent sexual assault.[17]

Law professor Joyce Lee Malcolm of the Cato Institute, a libertarian think tank headquartered in Washington, D.C., notes that in England – where gun possession has been strictly regulated since 1953 – government-funded news organization BBC News offered legal guidelines for British citizens in how they should defend themselves on the street if they are victims of an assault:

> You are permitted to protect yourself with a briefcase, a handbag, or keys. You should shout "Call the Police" rather than "Help." Bystanders are not to help. They have been taught to leave such matters to the professionals. If you manage to knock your attacker down, you must not hit him again or you risk being charged with assault.[18]

The editors at the British-based weekly *The Economist,* during the week after the horrible mass school shooting at an elementary school in Connecticut in December 2012, called for restrictive gun laws like those in England. They suggested that "If you want to be safe, change the constitution." They were unambiguously advocating a constitutional amendment to overturn the Second Amendment.[19]

Of course, the editors of *The Economist* failed to mention that since a mass shooting in the United Kingdom in 1996, which instigated the passage of hyper-restrictive gun laws – including the confiscation of handguns – violent acts committed with handguns have doubled in number, according to British crime statistics. The island nation of Australia, which enacted similarly restrictive gun bans and gun confiscations after a mass shooting in the 1990s, witnessed a 40 percent increase in assaults and a 20 percent increase in sexual assaults in the decade following their hyper-restrictive gun laws.[20]

Additionally, the editors at *The Economist* cited the strict gun laws in Chicago as a case study on how the federal government should prohibit private gun ownership in order to decrease violence. Again, the editors failed to note that

Chicago has some of the highest gun-related crime rates in the United States. In fact, as most Americans were celebrating Christmas in 2012, Chicago marked the staggering milestone of its 500th homicide, 87 percent of which were committed with guns.[21]

Curiously, the very same people who defend restrictive gun control laws often enjoy the safety and comfort of armed personal escorts. Most notoriously, the raging anti-gun Leftists on ABC's *The View*, particularly Rosie O'Donnell, have suggested that the Second Amendment should be eliminated and replaced with a new amendment that prohibits anyone from owning a gun (handgun, long gun, shot gun, any gun), with the exception of the police and the military. Curiously, while O'Donnell sat there each day, sipping coffee with her fellow Leftist gun-haters, preaching to the American people about the evils of guns and gun owners, Ms. O'Donnell's bodyguard was applying for a conceal-and-carry permit (CCW) in order to provide the Hollywood celebrity and her family with the best protection money can buy. At that very moment, when Ms. O'Donnell's body guard applied for a gun carry permit, the abject hypocrisy of the so-called peace-loving gun-haters was exposed for all to see.

Elitists like Rosie O'Donnell and her fellow Leftist gun-haters – including the politicians who pass restrictive gun control laws – live in gated communities protected by armed security guards. They work in buildings protected by armed police who serve at their beckon call. They are chauffeured around the city, removed from the stench of the underclass, safe in their cocoons. Leftist elitists are insulated from crime, and do not feel the urgency to carry a handgun because they have guaranteed themselves a cozy, 24-hours-a-day environment where criminal thugs are something they only see on the news, read about in the paper, or watch on TV. They look down condescendingly from their high perches and sneer at the great unwashed (and unarmed) masses roaming the filthy streets below. From such lofty heights, it's easy to wax moral about guns and violence.

Interestingly, gun-control advocates in federal, state, and local government enjoy even better personal protection than the likes of Rosie O'Donnell. They also do not care that they are denying the very same comfort and safety to the people they are supposedly serving. Ironically and most infuriatingly, is the fact that it's the unarmed citizens – citizens who walk the streets at the mercy of criminal thugs – who pay for the personal protection of the very politicians who deny law-abiding, tax-paying citizens the right to defend themselves.

Jeffrey Goldberg posed a question to Washington, D.C., Mayor Vincent Gray. The Leftist politician, as Goldberg notes, "travels the city with armed police bodyguards, a service not afforded the typical Washington resident." Goldberg asked Gray whether he believes armed law-abiding citizens could prevent or stop a crime. Gray noted that the District has "3,800 police officers to protect people." He continued: "They may not be at someone's side at every moment, but they're around."[22] That's little comfort to the thousands of unarmed victims of violent crimes each year in the District. Beyond that, it's legally insane and morally reprehensible to suggest that citizens should rely upon the police for their personal protection when the U.S. Supreme Court has ruled that the police cannot be held responsible for any private individual's personal protection.

Media elitists who preach gun-confiscation also enjoy the very same protections that other elitists enjoy. From their cozy editorial boardrooms and high-rise apartments, Leftists in the media view the world from the safety and comfort of gas-guzzling SUVs that ferry them to and from their gated communities and their glass-and-steel office buildings. Their insulated lives and detachment from reality afford them the luxury of condemning guns and gun owners while living safely behind the protection of well-trained and well-compensated armed guards. That luxury also affords them a sense of moral superiority – a higher state of being from which the violence of the streets is merely the result of too many guns in the hands of too many unenlightened, uneducated dolts, and the solution to the violence is simply to get rid of all guns.

Consider this: on any given day, the U.S. Capitol Building is guarded by hundreds of police officers with guns. The heavily armed police patrol the exterior and interior of the compound; they screen every individual who enters the building with metal detectors and x-ray machines. In short, our elected officials (who call themselves "public servants") work in a highly-guarded fortress in the middle of one of the nation's most violent cities, and are protected by armed body guards who whisk them to and from work, all at taxpayer's expense. Yet, these so-called "public servants" are willing to shamelessly disarm the very taxpayers who pay their salary and who pay for their armed guards. Their laws ensure that taxpayers are far more vulnerable to violence then they ever will be.

Just ask the parents of the 20 little first graders who were massacred in an elementary school in Connecticut in December 2012, whether their children would still be alive today if their school had been protected by hundreds of armed police officers and x-ray machines and metal detectors, just as members of Congress are every day. Even more, most of our so-called "public servants" send their little angels to elite charter schools that feature a defensive barrier manned by well-compensated and highly-trained armed security guards. But, our elected officials have the audacity to call themselves "public servants." Based on this paradigm, they're more like lords and we like defenseless serfs.

Because conservatives are by far the largest segment of the population that owns and carries guns, Leftist elitists view conservatives as the source of the epidemic of "gun violence." Conservatives are the ones buying guns. Conservatives are the ones selling guns. Conservatives are the ones carrying guns. Thus, whenever a gun is used to kill or injure, somewhere along the line, Leftists believe that it a conservative is to blame for the crime. Thus, for Leftist elitists, conservatives are the problem. It's a narrative that Leftists have crafted, sold, and reinforced whenever a gun is used to kill or injure.

Stories that feature law-abiding citizens using weapons to defend themselves and others from criminal thugs are systematically ignored by the establishment media, because these stories do not fit into the prevailing narrative.[23] Because not every instance of a citizen using a gun to prevent a crime is reported to the police, the numbers of crimes that are thwarted cannot be determined exactly. Very often this is due to the fact that the gun is rarely discharged, thus no police report is required. The victim pulls the weapon, and the criminal(s) flee. End of story. Estimates are that somewhere upwards of 3 million crimes are prevented each year by law-abiding citizens with guns. But, the news seldom reports these stories.

However, when a violent crime committed with a gun cannot be ignored – either due to its magnitude (i.e., mass shootings) or the social status of the victim or perpetrator (i.e., famous people or politicians) – the media are forced to cover the story, and thus to present the story within the confines of the prevailing narrative. When they do cover the story, they either distort or ignore certain facts that do not fit the narrative. Sometimes they just make up facts out of thin air without any evidence to support them, all in order to protect the prevailing narrative.

Most people are unaware of the fact that the nation's highest court has ruled that the government cannot be held responsible if you are the victim of a crime. Your local police department cannot be expected to protect you if you're alone on a subway train at night, or your ex-husband decides that an official restraining order is irrelevant. You and you alone are expected to be able to defend yourself from criminal thugs. It's the law.

In July 2012, a Detroit-based television reporter, Charlie LeDuff, decided he was going to investigate the response time of his local police department. Detroit's economy has been in decline for decades, and the municipal government has seen harsh budget cuts, including to the police department. LeDuff's police scanner picked up a dispatch call regarding a home invasion, and he raced to the location. There he found a black female, "Mary," a single woman in her late thirties, waiting on the sidewalk in front of her east-side community home. She was afraid to enter her own house – and who can blame her?

LeDuff arrived an hour after the dispatch call and waited with the young woman for the police to arrive. They waited – for four hours!

"While we work all day," Mary said, "they [the thugs in her neighborhood] stay at home and figure out whose house they can break in, and take [the] stuff that they didn't work for."[24]

Mary and the rest of the law-abiding citizens of her

neighborhood cannot count on the police for personal protection. However, if she or one of her neighbors wanted to buy and carry a gun for protection, the government there has determined that she cannot be trusted to own and carry a gun. They have guaranteed that she remains an unarmed victim.

One is hard-pressed to find a journalist in a major news market who is willing to cover a story that highlights the need for individual citizens to be permitted to provide for their own protection. In fact, the story above wasn't intended to highlight that need. It was intended to highlight the need for more police officers. When journalists report on crime, it is usually couched in the narrative that more money should be spent on hiring more police officers. Thus, the newsroom echo chamber repeats the mantra sold by Leftists that taxes are too low, particularly taxes on the richest Americans. Raise their taxes, we're told, and the city can hire more police officers, and you'll be safe.

However, most police officers in major metropolitan areas already enjoy salaries and pensions that are far superior to their private sector colleagues. California, for instance, is going bankrupt, in part because of city worker salaries. An investigation of government employees in California found that parking meter maids in one Los Angeles suburb are paid over $90,000 a year, and receive a lucrative pension to boot. In fact, when a city employee retires (at age 62!), the cost to the city for their retirement is estimated at over $1.3 million a year.[25] Remember the small LA suburb where city officials were paying themselves salaries of $500,000 even $700,000 a year?[26] Those guys viewed the tax revenue from their citizens as a cash cow.

In Detroit, like other decaying metropolitan areas,

corruption among city officials is rampant. The lead paragraph of a city newspaper article summed it up brilliantly:

> Last week the federal government announced that it would stop sending a $50 million annual grant to the Detroit Human Services Department due to nepotism, reckless spending and corruption. In another case, the U.S. Justice Department records allege that contractor and [Detroit Mayor] Kwame Kilpatrick pal Bobby Ferguson obtained $58.5 million through extortion and other illegal means as part of the alleged "Kilpatrick Enterprise." Meanwhile, the Federal Bureau of Investigation has recently formed a special multi-agency task force in its Detroit office, declaring a war on public corruption.[27]

Yet, we're told that Detroit's taxes should be higher because the police are slow responding to emergencies?

To the Leftist in the echo chamber, the solution to rampant crime is never private gun ownership. The answer is always more police and higher taxes. In California, where the police who ticket your illegally-parked car receive a salary twice that of the average American citizen, law-abiding citizens are rarely granted a conceal-and-carry permit. California, along with five other states, has a "may issue" law, which means that the local sheriff or another law enforcement authority determines which citizens should be permitted to conceal-carry. The requestor is forced to convince her elected officials that their need for conceal-and-carry is urgent – a matter of life and death. Most states, however, are "shall issue," which means that the burden is on the state official to come up with a reason to deny the permit – you know, innocent until proven guilty. In California, as well as the other "may issue" states, the burden is on the citizen to justify conceal-carry – guilty until proven innocent.

Californians, however, are allowed to open carry. They can walk the streets with a handgun on their hip, unconcealed. Because of the exceptionally low "may issue" approval rate (0.1 percent of applicants for conceal-carry permits are granted a permit), some California residence have decided to open carry for personal protection. The gun cannot be loaded and the ammunition must be kept separate; for instance, on the hip opposite the gun. Additionally, citizens who exercise the right to open carry must agree to sacrifice their Fourth Amendment rights, and be subject to random searches by the police, to ensure their weapons are indeed unloaded in accordance with the law – guilty until proven innocent.

California Assemblyman Anthony Portantino – a Democrat (of course) who represents north Los Angeles – does not like the idea of law-abiding citizens carrying guns in public, in spite of absolutely no instances of open carriers committing crimes. Let me repeat that: there have been no cases in California of an open-carrying individual committing a crime with their weapon. None. Assemblyman Portantino, however, believes that people – not all people, just law abiding people – walking the streets with guns on their hips just may make other people uncomfortable. "Just because one person is comfortable with their weapon," Assemblyman Portantino said during an interview with a libertarian media organization, "doesn't mean that that gives that person the right to infringe on the rights of other people who aren't comfortable."[28]

The right to be comfortable? The interviewer didn't ask the assemblyman to cite the source of the so-called "right to be comfortable." One would imagine that it's somewhere in a neo-Marxist tract tucked snugly between the latest copies of *The Nation* and *The New Republic*. Besides, "comfortable" is such an ambiguous definition, and were it to appear as a right in public policy, a fascist state would be necessary in order for it to enforced. Imagine if a law were passed that guaranteed that no one would ever be made to feel uncomfortable by anyone else. Imagine a "comfortable police" patrolling the streets and checking on the comfort level of the citizenry.

I suppose, then, that the assemblyman believes that this new right to be "comfortable" overrides the First Amendment, which would thus empower the government to prohibit all speech that may make some people uncomfortable. Replace his use of "gun" with "word," for instance, and imagine an elected official making this argument: "Just because one person is comfortable with their *words* doesn't mean that that gives that person the right to infringe on the rights of other people who aren't comfortable." Perhaps it is this same mindset that is behind the movement to ban films that "insult" the "prophet of Islam," as President Obama has suggested.

"You don't need a handgun to order a cheeseburger," the assemblyman said during a session of the assembly. "You don't need a handgun to get a cup of coffee," he added. (Of note, the use of the *non sequitur* is common among Leftists, because reason and logic are irrelevant.) Assemblyman Portantino said these things while defending his bill to prohibit law-abiding citizens from open carrying handguns. While he's at it, Assemblyman Portantino could tell Mr. Besedin – the New York City subway rape victim – that she didn't need a handgun to ride the subway the night she was attacked and brutalized by a thug rapist. But, the Leftist position on gun control is never challenged, least of all by anyone in the echo-chamber media.

Portantino is just the latest politician who has tried to change California's open carry law. Assemblyman Lori Saldana, Democrat (surprise!) from San Diego, tried to ban open carry in 2010, but her efforts failed. Assemblyman Portantino was emboldened to retry after the tragic Tucson shooting in January 2011 (more on this below). Leftist politicians often exploit tragedies to obtain more power and control over the law-abiding citizen. That's their *modus operandi*.

Assemblyman Portantino said the following during the interview with Reason:

> **Portantino**: The Second Amendment of the Constitution allows people to defend their private property.
>
> **Reason**: And that includes your person, right?
>
> **Portantino**: That includes your person, but when you're out in 'Mainstreet' California, we also have sworn officers who are there to serve and protect the public.

Tell that to the woman in Detroit who waited four hours for the police to arrive! Tell that to the victim of a violent crime who was merely walking home from work, minding their own business. Tell that to the tens of thousands of victims who thought they didn't need a gun to get a cup of coffee, or ride the subway, or get cash from an ATM, or get some exercise and some fresh air. Hell, tell that to the U.S. Supreme Court! After all, they've ruled that the police are not responsible for the protection of individual citizens. Imagine if they were. Imagine all the lawsuits every time someone was the victim of a robbery or burglary or some violent crime. The litigation would bankrupt municipalities.

The fact is that the police are responsible for deterring and investigating crimes. They are "law enforcement," not personal protectors. It's common sense, really. A police department large enough to provide for the personal protection of every individual citizen at all hours of the day would be enormous and outrageously expensive – far more expensive than a handgun. But, Leftist politicians never shy away from a tax increase, and they never hesitate to concoct a false narrative that the police are somehow responsible for individual citizens' personal protection. And, by subscribing to this narrative, politicians ensure that police unions contribute to their reelection campaigns, and the police guarantee themselves exorbitant pensions. It's a win-win for everyone but the unarmed, law-abiding, taxpaying victim of thug criminals on the streets.

Unlike the single black female in Detroit who waited four hours for the police to arrive at her burglarized home, Assemblyman Portantino or D.C. mayor Vincent Gray probably never waited very long for law enforcement to come to their rescue. Safe and comfortable in their big leather chairs in offices protected by well-armed, taxpayer-funded police officers, these politicians can say with smug indifference that the citizens should rely upon the police for personal protection. But what will these politicians say to the victim of a crime who comes to them complaining that the police failed to protect them? Tens of thousands of citizens are victims of criminal violence every year, but they cannot sue the police for failure to protection them. Therefore, all these elitist politicians can say to the victim is: Too bad, so sad, pass the potato salad. Oh, and "vote for me!"

But, what happens when a municipality goes broke and cannot afford to keep a robust police force on the streets? In San Bernardino, California, city officials have run the government into the ground. The city is flat broke. They've been forced to lay off police officers. Thus, the city's attorney, Jim Penman, held a press conference and advised residents that they should lock themselves indoors and load their guns.[29] Law-abiding citizens in California have been made wards of the state. They, like the citizens of every major metropolitan area governed by Leftist Democrats, cannot walk the streets without fear, because the law forbids them from carrying their own means of self-protection – in California, they can open carry but, as was noted above, the ammunition must be kept separate. The logical conclusion of Leftist ideology is that criminals can walk the streets without fear of law-abiding citizens, rather than the other way round. That's what happens when feelings, rather than logic and reason, drive policy.

After the tragic shooting at a Sikh temple in Wisconsin in August 2012, Philadelphia Mayor Michael Nutter called (again) for stricter gun control laws. Echoing an almost identical statement he made after the mass shooting at an Aurora, Colorado movie theater just a month before, Mr. Nutter told his fellow mayors assembled at the U.S. Conference of Mayors – an organization of mayors from almost 1,300 cities and town across the nation – that guns need to be taken off the streets and out of the hands of criminals. But, who doesn't want guns out of the hands of criminals? It's the *non sequitur*, again. Leftists argue that, in order for criminals to be unarmed, all law-abiding citizens must also be unarmed. This argument often comes shortly after a moment of heightened sensitivity due to a violent, highly publicized event, when the nation is in shock. Leftist never let a tragedy go to waste; it's always seen as an opportunity to press for radical legislation.

The reality is that Leftists in government and media are committed to disarming all law-abiding citizens, regardless of the facts, the law, or the consequences. Their only interest is in obtaining and keeping the power and prestige that comes from high office, and they have crafted a series of false narratives in order to keep American citizens ignorant, envious, and fearful. In the case of the assemblyman from California and the mayors from Philadelphia and Washington, D.C., the false narrative is that the police should be our only means of personal protection when we leave our homes. The insanity of this ideology is demonstrated every time another law-abiding citizen is victimized by a criminal thug.

Leftist politicians and their media comrades use tragedies like mass shootings to exploit the American people. They incite fear about guns, rather than fear about the evil that resides in the hearts of their fellow citizens. They do so in order to expand the power of the state and to increase their control over the individual. Expanding the power and scope of the government has been and remains the goal of Leftists and the false narratives they have crafted about guns and violence have been and remain their most effective tools to achieve that goal.

For instance, just one week after the school massacre in Connecticut, President Obama cited the tragedy during a press conference in order to pressure Republicans to agree to his budget proposal. The president said: "And when you think about what we've gone through over the last couple of months, a devastating hurricane and now one of the worse tragedies in our memory, the country deserves folks to be willing to compromise on behalf of the greater good, and not tangle themselves up in a whole bunch of ideological positions that don't make much sense."[30]

As almost two dozen families grieved the deaths of their first grade children in Newtown, Connecticut, the president used their tragic loss to browbeat his political opponents into agreeing on a budget plan. The president's egregious and shameless exploitation of a highly emotional moment in the nation's history for political purposes exposed the fact that politicians are concerned more about obtaining and maintaining political power than actually solving problems. Of course, according to President Obama, it's always the Republicans in Congress who are tangled up ideologically, not him and his Democrat allies in Congress. And of course, according to the president, it's the Republicans who "don't make much sense."

Also, after the tragic mass shooting at the elementary school in Connecticut, talking heads and newsreaders on TV, who are supposed to report the news, consistently injected their anti-gun views into every discussion about the tragedy, revealing the fact that they are advocates for Leftist policies rather than news reporters. CNN anchor Don Lemon, for instance, said during a segment: "We need to get guns and bullets and automatic weapons off the streets." It was a curious comment, since the killer of the 26 school children – twenty of which were first graders – didn't use an automatic weapon, because automatic firearms have been banned from public use since 1934. But, Leftist talking heads on TV will never let facts stand in the way of a good old fashioned false narrative.

Lemon also said that firearms "should only be available to police officers and to hunt al-Qaeda and the Taliban and not hunt elementary school children." He was on a roll when he said: "Who needs an armor-piercing bullet to go hunting? Who needs an assault rifle to go hunting?"[31] Apparently, to the Leftist/Progressive, the Bill of Rights is actually the Bill of Needs, and it is they who will tell us what we need – and guns certainly won't be on the list.[32]

In the shadow of the Connecticut school massacre, ABC News' Good Morning America did a segment on gun control, and pushed the narrative that there are too many guns "on the street," a turn of phrase intended to inspire images of gangs of armed citizens wandering the streets looking for trouble. They hyped and sensationalized the tragic shooting at the elementary school and beat the anti-gun drum for days. They even suggested that one "solution" to the mass shooting problem would be to prohibit the production of new weapons. One journalist breathlessly delivered this piece of information: "Here's some facts that might surprise you. There are more registered gun dealers and stores than major supermarkets. More gun sellers than McDonald's restaurants....if we stopped gun production in this country today, we would still be years and years away from a solution on that path....the country is going to have to figure out how to deal with the mental health issues and the guns that are already on the street."[33]

CNN's Soledad O'Brien argued, yes, argued, with a guest about gun control laws on the air in the days after the Connecticut school massacre. She interrupted him and berated him repeatedly, and said his views are irrational. She began the conversation with the question: "How does that possibly make sense to you?" and concluded the segment: "it just boggles the mind, honestly, and if you were to come here and talk to the people in this town, they'd be stunned by you."[34] The guest, economics professor John Lott, had the audacity to cite facts about guns and crime that contradicted the prevailing false narratives that the folks at CNN were trying to sell to the American public. And Soledad O'Brien just could not hide her hostility to an opposing viewpoint. That's the state of journalism today.

CNN's Piers Morgan became emotionally unhinged during an interview with a pro-gun advocate on the air less than a week after the Connecticut school shooting. Morgan called his guest a liar, an "idiot," and an "unbelievably stupid man." He ended the interview this way: "You know what? You wouldn't understand the meaning of the phrase high-level argument. You are a dangerous man espousing dangerous nonsense and you shame your country."[35] Here was a major figure on one of the nation's largest and most respected cable news network calling his guest childish names on the air, interrupting him numerous times, speaking over him like a small child does his parents, and berating him for five minutes.

Does anyone really think that Piers Morgan is emotionally capable of dispassionately weighing the costs and benefits of new gun control legislation? Is this the state of American intellectual discourse today?

Virginia Tech and Tucson

On April 16, 2007, Seung-Hui Cho killed 32 people at the Virginia Polytechnic Institute in Blacksburg, Virginia. He wounded only 17 people. Police reports state that the deceased had all been shot at least three times.

The carnage began very early in the morning. Cho shot and killed two student residents in his dormitory, and then returned to his dorm room. He removed the hard drive from his computer, left the dorm, disposed of the hard drive at some unknown location, went to the post office and mailed a package, and headed for the engineering building across campus.

Two hours after the first shooting, Cho entered a classroom on the second floor of Norris Hall where he shot and killed a professor and nine students. Cho found more unarmed victims across the hall where he shot and killed a professor and six students. He proceeded to the adjacent classroom, which was almost empty. Most of the students had jumped to safety from the windows. They were given a few precious minutes to escape when their engineering professor, Holocaust survivor Liviu Librescu, barricaded the door and briefly prevented the shooter from entering the classroom. Cho shot and killed the professor and one student.

For twenty minutes, Cho moved fearlessly from room to room, without concern of return fire. Cho was confident that his victims were, unlike him, law abiding citizens who left their guns off campus. Cho knew where he lived. He was in the United States of America – a civilized society. And, as everyone knows, civilized societies must have laws, and citizens of civilized societies must be willing to abide by the law. If they didn't, then chaos would ensue. Thus, Cho, knowing full-well that he lived in a civilized society, knew also that the law had served him up an entire campus of unarmed, law-abiding victims.

Cho killed five professors and 27 students and wounded 17 others. He did not use an "assault rifle." He did not use an AK-47. He did not use an RPG or an Apache attack helicopter. He used a 9mm semi-automatic handgun, a very small weapon made large by the fact that Cho encountered no resistance whatsoever. The law had made Cho an army-of-one against a campus of unarmed, law-abiding, civilized victims.

In the aftermath of the tragedy, troubling stories of Cho's emotional instability began to emerge. It was also reported that, because of privacy laws, no one was legally bound to advise Virginia Tech administrators about Cho's mental disorder and potential for violent behavior. Thus, when he was charged with stalking two female students, the university was unaware of Cho's past, and was unable to make an informed judgment about his true mental state. To those who knew him, though, Cho was a ticking time bomb. Nonetheless, legislators in the Commonwealth of Virginia created a situation where a lunatic was loosened upon a civilized society of law-abiding, unarmed citizens without knowledge of Cho's mental history, and without access to a means of defending themselves.

On the morning of January 8, 2011, a mentally disturbed young man, Jared Lee Loughner, purchased ammunition for a handgun at a Wal-Mart outside Tucson, Arizona. He ran a red light on his way to the store, but the police who stopped him found no outstanding warrants for his arrest, thus he was allowed to continue on his way. Loughner eventually left his car somewhere and took a taxi to a Safeway supermarket where Rep. Giffords (D-AZ) was holding a "Congress on Your Corner" town hall meeting.

At approximately 10:10 a.m., Loughner walked through the small crowd that had assembled in the parking lot and approached Rep. Giffords, who was seated at a table with several other people. Loughner pulled a pistol and started shooting. He killed six people, including a 9-year old girl and a federal judge, and injured 13 more, including Rep. Gabrielle Giffords (D-AZ).

All evidence indicates that Loughner was a paranoid schizophrenic. His former classmates at Pima Community College said they feared for their lives when Loughner was around. One young woman said she sat near the classroom door because she was certain that Loughner would do "something bad," and another classmate said he believed Loughner may bring a gun to school and kill everyone. The school received numerous emails from students who expressed fear that Loughner would eventually commit a mass school shooting.[36] Campus police responded five times to calls about Loughner's disturbing behavior.[37] His math professor said he feared Loughner would bring a gun to school, and he warned campus officials about Loughner's deranged behavior. Loughner ultimately was expelled from the class, and eventually from school the year before the shooting.[38]

During the last 30 years, mentally ill people who would have once been institutionalized by the state, have been allowed to walk the streets without supervision and without medication. Mentally disturbed people make up the bulk of the homeless population and are responsible for a disproportionately large percentage of violent crimes. Some research indicates that mentally disturbed individuals, specifically paranoid schizophrenics like Loughner, are responsible for the vast majority of rampage murders. All evidence points to the fact that the Tucson shooting is at heart a mental health issue. How a mentally disturbed young man – one who was clearly suffering from paranoid schizophrenia and was clearly exhibiting violent tendencies – was allowed to walk the streets among civilized society, and how he was able to obtain a gun, should have been the preeminent subjects of discussion in the aftermath of the shooting.[39]

However, the mental health issue was not the main focus of discussion in the weeks and months following either of these shootings. Both shooters had been recognized by the people around them as mentally disturbed and dangerous. But officials in both cases were hesitant to take any action because the laws about compulsory institutionalization are confusing, and the costly threat of lawsuits always looms large. The tendency of those in position to prevent these tragedies is to pass the buck and let someone else deal with the troubled mind of a potentially violent individual.

After the Tucson shooting, for instance, instead of discussing our current mental health laws and the need to institutionalize potentially violent paranoid schizophrenics like Loughner and Cho, the echo-chamber media seized on the tragedy in Arizona as an opportunity to accomplish two goals: (1) politicize the gun control debate and (2) silence conservative voices.

Within hours of the Tucson tragedy, Pima County Sheriff Clarence Dupnik, an outspoken liberal Democrat who had previously called Tea Party members racists, held a press conference to brief reporters on the tragic events of the day. During his short time behind the microphones, just hours after the tragic shooting, as reporters scrambled for details about the victims and the shooter, Dupnik urged Americans to stop the "vitriolic rhetoric" heard on the radio and TV "day in and day out." The sheriff informed the American public that politics, specifically conservative talk radio and Fox News, had inspired Jared Loughner to assassinate Rep. Giffords.

Dupnik's gut instincts as a career law enforcement officer, it seemed, had led him to believe that Loughner was a political operative, and was perhaps linked to several previous incidents involving Rep. Giffords, most notably her election campaign headquarters had been vandalized the year before the shooting. Sheriff Dupnik seemed to be making the case that Loughner was part of a larger problem in Arizona. The Democrat sheriff was connecting dots, and they all seemed to suggest that Democratic Rep. Giffords was assassinated as part of a larger plot designed to change the political landscape in Arizona – a landscape that had taken a turn for the worse in Sheriff Dupnik's view – a turn toward conservatism!

During his brief press conference, Dupnik conveniently left out key details of the crime and the history of the disturbed man who carried it out. For instance, the sheriff neglected to inform the public that his office had been involved with Jared Loughner on numerous occasions, and had turned him over to health officials for psychiatric evaluations. None of those previous encounters with Loughner had anything to do with politics. They had nothing to do with Tea Party rallies, Republicans, or conservative talk radio. They were all related to Loughner's being a paranoid schizophrenic. Yet, the sheriff did his best to make it appear that Loughner's previous encounters with the police were somehow indicative of a politically motivated killer rather than a mentally disturbed individual.

Dupnik also did not explain why his office failed to assign a uniformed officer to a highly publicized political event in a supermarket parking lot – a highly publicized event that was hosted by a Congresswoman whose headquarters had recently been the target of violence.[40] Dupnik's press conference was a political statement, not a news briefing, and the facts apparently were irrelevant. He had a bone to pick with conservatives, and the tragic massacre was an opportunity to tell the world about the evil that had swept across his state and was changing the political landscape.

Thus, instead of explaining why he and his officers failed to provide protection for a member of the House of

Representatives; instead of providing evidence to sustain his case that Loughner was acting on behalf of a conservative cause; Sheriff Dupnik lashed out against the citizens of Arizona, a state that Dupnik believed had become the home of conservative bigots. He noted that immigration laws recently passed in the state legislature proved that bigots were running the government. He told the American people that conservatives are prone to political violence, and can be set off at the drop of a hat. He attacked conservative talk radio – specifically Rush Limbaugh – and Fox News for creating a climate of hatred that drove Loughner to assassinate, or at least try to assassinate, a Democratic politician. The sheriff was in full attack mode and the target was his political opponents.

Immediately after Dupnik's press conference, within minutes in fact, the echo-chamber media jumped on the "political rhetoric" bandwagon. Leftists at every major news outlet across the nation accepted the sheriff's explanation for what motivated Jared Loughner – in spite of the fact that Dupnik presented no evidence to sustain his case. Every mainstream establishment media organization across the country (and overseas) made "political rhetoric" the main theme of their coverage of the tragedy. Every discussion was framed in the context of the "hostile," "dangerous" and "toxic" political rhetoric. Images of high profile conservatives flashed on television screens as psychiatrists and other mental health professionals discussed political violence. Noted Leftist commentators reminded viewers that Rush Limbaugh and other talk radio personalities were the manifestation of pure evil.

Throughout the weekend, no evidence was provided to substantiate Dupnik's claims that Loughner was inspired by political rhetoric. By Monday morning, news reports noted that Loughner's favorite books, as listed on his Facebook page, included the radical writings of big-government Leftists, including *The Communist Manifesto* and *Mein Kampf*. Yet, no one in the media ever suggested that Loughner was a fascistic Leftist like Hitler or a Communist like Mao or Stalin (or a socialist like President Obama). Loughner's own political influences were all standard Leftist propaganda, yet the media continued pushing the narrative that he was a conservative hate-monger like Rush Limbaugh.

A big break for the establishment media's narrative came when, by Saturday evening, just hours after the shooting, all the major news outlets had focused their attention towards a map on a website operated by Sarah Palin's political action committee (PAC). A map of the United States was posted on the PAC's site, and it was dotted with crosshairs, each one indicating Congressional districts that Republicans were encouraged to target with political advertising and campaign contributions. They were districts that the Republican Party (aka the Grand Old Party, or the GOP) and Palin's PAC believed had vulnerable Democrat incumbents. Those damning crosshairs were all the evidence the establishment media needed to indict and convict Sarah Palin. The echo-chamber Leftists in media had found evidence that linked Sarah Palin to the shooting of a beloved female Democrat. Remember, Sarah Palin was the woman who never missed an opportunity to highlight her hunting experiences in Alaska. Remember the infamous image of her and her father posing with a murdered animal? Remember her support for legislation that allowed wolf hunting from helicopters? Sarah Palin: killer!

Media personalities and public officials jumped on the

Palin map like the Baltimore Ravens' defense on a fumbled football. The narrative took a turn – no longer was it just Rush Limbaugh and talk radio. Now it was Sarah Palin – the women who once accused Barack Obama of "palling around with terrorists"; the woman who sparked a conservative movement that lifted Sen. John McCain's poll numbers and almost won the election; the woman who spoke with the folksy twang of middle-America; the woman who loved to hunt and kill furry, little, innocent creatures; the woman who said you could see Russia from Alaska. It was Sarah Palin's map and Sarah Palin's hatred that were responsible for the assassination attempt. That was the narrative, and the echo-chamber media ran with it.

Again, no evidence was cited to substantiate the narrative. It was accepted as fact that Loughner – whose favorite political writings were all the works of noted Leftists (the very same works that are sitting on the bookshelves of every one of Barack Obama's closest advisors) – was a secret Sarah Palin devotee who took direction from the former Alaska governor and tried to kill Democrat Rep. Giffords. The narrative was set in stone and sold to the American public as fact.

By the end of the weekend, the smear campaign was in full swing on every TV and radio news program and in every major newspaper. Matt Lauer on NBC's Today Show reported: "Sarah Palin has been coming under some criticism. While there is no evidence her Web site featuring a target on Giffords' district had anything to do with this attack, some are asking if today's political rhetoric is inspiring the lunatic fringe?" Meredith Viera added: "This shooting came with the state of our politics seemingly nastier than ever."[41] The "political rhetoric" narrative was being crafted. Every major news outlet pointed fingers at Sarah Palin, her "violent rhetoric," and her evil map of potential victims. There was blood in the water, and the sharks were in a frenzy:

- Chris Matthews said Palin and Fox News were responsible for the shooting.[42]
- NBC's Andrea Mitchell blamed Sarah Palin for the shooting.[43]
- NBC's Lee Cowan blamed Palin's map for the shooting.[44]
- CNN's Wolf Blitzer and Jessica Yellin blamed conservative talk radio and Sarah Palin for "creating the environment that allowed this kind of instance to happen."[45]
- Tom Brokaw blamed conservative rhetoric for the shooting.[46]
- The Associated Press blamed Sarah Palin for the shooting.[47]
- CBS's Nancy Cordes blamed Sarah Palin for the shooting.[48]
- The *Washington Post*'s Eugene Robinson blamed conservatives for the shooting.[49]
- CNN's Jessica Yellin cited Sarah Palin's map as motive for shooting.[50]
- NBC's Kelly O'Donnell blamed the Tea Party's rhetoric for the shooting.[51]
- The *Chicago Sun-Times* editorial staff blamed conservatives for the shooting.[52]
- ABC's David Wright blamed Sarah Palin's map for the shooting.[53]
- Politico's Roger Simon blamed Sarah Palin for the shooting.[54]
- *New York Times* columnist and Nobel Laureate Paul Krugman blamed Fox News for the shooting.[55]

- CBS's Bob Schieffer blamed Sarah Palin's map for the shooting.[56]
- MSNBC's Keith Olbermann blamed the Tea Party and Fox News for the shooting.[57]
- Rep. Robert Brady (D-PA) blamed the shooting on Sarah Palin.[58]
- CNN's Martin Savidge interviewed a Leftist Arizona columnist who blamed conservatives for the shooting.[59]

Before Saturday's news cycle had ended, and as the victims' families hurried to the hospital for news about their loved ones, the "political rhetoric" theme had been successfully implanted into every conversation about the tragedy. Every conversation about the tragedy was framed in the context of political rhetoric, and Sarah Palin's face was shown on television screens alongside video clips of the bloody crime scene. The notorious map with its revealing and damning crosshairs was superimposed over the crime scene in Tucson. The message was clear: Sarah Palin was responsible for the shooting. The message from the echo-chamber media was particularly clear in this important regard also: all that deep-seeded hatred you've been harboring for Sarah Palin since November 2008 – well, guess what? It's justified now. Go ahead and hate and feel damn good about it. Sarah Palin deserved all the vitriol you can dish out, for she is evil incarnate.

The *New York Times* editorial staff further fanned the flames of hatred: "It is legitimate to hold Republicans and particularly their most virulent supporters in the media responsible for the gale of anger that has produced the vast majority of these threats, setting the nation on edge."[60] Far Leftist commentator Amy Goodman interviewed an Arizona Democrat shortly after the tragedy, and framed the whole discussion in the context of political rhetoric. Her guest, Rep.

Raul Grijalva (D-AZ), singled out Sarah Palin's rhetoric as especially irresponsible, and again the notorious map was highlighted. Grijalva and Goodman never once presented any evidence to substantiate the claim that Palin was responsible for the shooting.[61] None was necessary.

Amidst all the noise over the weekend about Sarah Palin's map, facts started to trickle out about the true nature of Loughner. Those closest to Loughner told Fox News that he was not motivated by any political rhetoric, either from Sarah Palin, Glenn Beck, or any other conservative pundit. Loughner's best friend from high school said the shooter never listened to talk radio or Fox News. He said Loughner never attended a Tea Party rally.[62] Yet, all of these facts did not alter the prevailing narrative that Sarah Palin and Fox News inspired Loughner to kill a Democrat. These facts were simply ignored by the echo-chamber media. After all, they had a narrative to sell to their viewers and readers, and certain facts did not fit that narrative were just dismissed.

The most egregious example of post-tragedy reactionary Leftism was from Nobel-prize winning economist and *New York Times* columnist Paul Krugman. Within hours of the shooting, with the sidewalk in Tucson still wet with blood, Krugman wrote: "We don't have proof yet that this was political, but the odds are that it was." He blamed the Tea Party, Palin's map, Glenn Beck, Rush Limbaugh, and conservatives in general for creating a "climate of hate."[63] By the day after the shooting, as Loughner's insanity appeared to be the most likely motive, Krugman ignored the evidence and stubbornly wrapped himself in the safety and comfort of the prevailing narrative: "It's true that the shooter in Arizona appears to have been mentally troubled. But that doesn't mean that his act can or should be treated as an isolated event, having nothing to do with the national climate."

In the hours and days after the Tucson shooting, as the survivors healed and grief-stricken family members struggled to make sense of the tragedy, the message from the echo-chamber media to the American people was that Sarah Palin and all the other evil conservatives were responsible for the shooting. The narrative was created in the first few hours after the shooting, and in spite of all evidence to the contrary, it prevails even today.

The result of the echo-chamber media's incessant attention to the Palin map took its toll on the truth. All the evidence, including from those who knew him best, contradicted the media's narrative that Palin's map and Tea Party rhetoric caused Loughner to kill people. Nonetheless, just a few weeks after the shooting, thirty-five percent of Americans said they believed the false narrative.[64] A Pew Research poll of media coverage taken shortly after the shooting indicated that the "political rhetoric" issue was discussed more than the shooter or the tragedy he perpetrated on innocent victims.[65]

If their goal was to convince Americans that conservatives were responsible for the Arizona mass killing, then the echo-chamber media were successful. They managed to dupe over one third of Americans into believing a false narrative. The consequences of the false narrative are far reaching, beyond just affecting public opinion about Republicans and conservatives. Prosecutors in the Loughner case said in the months after the shooting that Sheriff Dupnik's comments could hamper their efforts to seek justice. The Pima County attorney general's office ordered Sheriff Dupnik to stop talking for fear that it would negatively affect their case.[66] Even more, the Sheriff's behavior begs some serious questions about his competence as a public safety officer. Noted historian Victor Davis Hanson highlighted something curious and condemning about the Arizona sheriff:

> More disturbing still, if Dupnik were right that a pre-existing climate of conservative-engendered hate was not only pervasive in Tucson, but might also prompt an unstable person to kill, why had he not dispatched at least one of his 500 officers to patrol the open-air public event sponsored by Democratic congresswoman Gabrielle Giffords?[67]

The sad fact is that the sheriff had become a national hero to those in the echo chamber for his bravery and his willingness to call out evil Republicans for their role in the tragedy; for his no-nonsense condemnation of Arizona's bigots. Thus, his failure to protect Rep. Giffords was overlooked.

While all the post-tragedy focus was directed to a map – which, outrage of all outrages featured crosshairs in a political context – several examples of similar maps were curiously overlooked by the echo-chamber media. Why? They did not fit the prevailing narrative that Republicans are evil, and Democrats and Leftists are not.

For instance, Democrats created a map of the United States during the 2004 campaign and put bull's-eyes on it to highlight conservative politicians who they believed were vulnerable politically.[68] Bulls-eyes! Like the ones you find on a shooting target! One Democrat wasn't satisfied with targets on a map. He put his Republican opponent in rifle crosshairs in a television advertisement.[69] Yet, none of this was presented to the viewers and readers of America's leading news organizations in the days and weeks following the shooting. These things just didn't fit the narrative. That narrative is composed of two main themes: (1) conservatives are responsible for creating an environment of hate; and (2) liberals are innocent of anything similar.

However, a quick search on the internet provides plenty of ammunition – er, I mean examples – to undermine that argument. Even more, some of the evidence is pretty damning for liberals, Leftists, and Democrats in general. Remember, none of the following examples were offered to viewers and readers of the leading news organizations in the weeks and months after the Tucson shooting, for to do so would have put Palin's map in proper context and upset the prevailing narrative:

- Liberal Democrats put a bull's eye on Congresswoman Giffords' district – apparently, she was too damn moderate for their taste.[70]
- Barack Obama told a crowd of supporters at a fundraiser in June 2008: "If they [Republicans] bring a knife to the fight, we bring a gun."[71]
- A *Washington Post* columnist, who blamed conservatives for the Tucson shooting in 2010, wrote in 2009 the following about Tea Partiers: "I want to knock every racist and homophobic tooth out of their Cro-Magnon heads."[72]
- A Leftist columnist wrote that he and his fellow Democrats were "firing warning shots across the bow of ultra-safe Democrats." Again, they were apparently too moderate.[73]
- A former Democratic Congressman from New York suggested that someone should shoot his political opponent.[74]

- An MSNBC producer wanted Obama to put a gun to people's heads.[75]
- MSNBC's Chris Matthews, a staunch Leftist and ardent Obama supporter, said he wanted Sarah Palin "erased."[76]
- The *New York Times* columnist Paul Krugman urged his fellow Progressives to "hang Joe Lieberman in effigy."[77] Lieberman is a moderate, and is viewed by the far Left as a threat to their political power in Washington. Again, too moderate.
- Rep. Barney Frank (D-MA) joked and laughed about a failed 2007 assassination attempt of then-VP Dick Cheney.[78]
- Leftist radio talker Thom Hartman called Glenn Beck and Sarah Palin terrorists. He accused them of inciting lone wolfs to kill political opponents, just like Bin Laden had done with sleeper cells – he called their actions "stochastic terrorism."[79]
- CNN hosts and reporters used the term "crosshairs" numerous times when discussing political issues.[80]
- Leftist Bill Maher called Sarah Palin a "dumb twat" and a "cunt." He also called Michele Bachmann a "nutcase."[81] He donated $1.5 million to President Obama's 2012 reelection campaign. The president, as of the writing of these words (August 2012), has not returned the money.
- A Democrat on the House floor said on January 19, 2010, that opponents of the Healthcare reform are Nazis. Yes, Nazis.[82]
- Another Democrat said repealing the healthcare law will kill people.[83]
- Leftist MSNBC host Lawrence O'Donnell interviewed

> Rep. Bob Filner (D-CA), and discussed whether Loughner was a Jew-hater who wanted to start a revolution that would benefit Republicans.[84]

Curiously, all of these people were silent about toxic political rhetoric and hate speech during the eight years of the George W. Bush administration, when the most outrageous examples of hatred and political terrorism were on display.

From 2002 through 2008, anti-war protesters called the President Bush and Vice-President Dick Cheney Nazis, and some even called for their assassinations. Leftists did this not just once or twice, but at nearly every anti-war rally and anti-Guantanamo Bay protest – and there were over a hundred of them. At one rally, Leftists marched down the streets in full view of the public towing a cart with a guillotine on it. Under the guillotine was a basket with President Bush's head in it. They carried signs with rifle crosshairs superimposed over images of Bush and Cheney.[85]

These were not isolated incidents. They were the rule for nearly eight years. Yet, there was no outrage from the establishment media. The silence was deafening. In fact, when President Bush was portrayed as a Nazi-Satan hybrid during a rally in Boston, a CNN reporter called it "a look-a-like."[86] Filmmakers even produced a movie that featured President Bush being assassinated.[87]

But it wasn't just Leftist protesters dressed in wild costumes that were doing these outrageous things. A host of so-called academics wrote articles and delivered speeches that equated President Bush to Hitler.[88] Again, there was no outrage because the vast majority of people working in the echo-chamber media all agreed that Bush was Hitler. It wasn't controversial to them.

By far the most blatant example of hypocrisy on the

Left regarding mass shootings was demonstrated by how the media reacted to the Arizona shooting and how they reacted to the Fort Hood shooting. For days and weeks after army major Hasan shot and killed 13 and injured 30 of his fellow soldiers at Fort Hood, Texas, commentators, talking heads, and politicians took to the airwaves, newspapers, and cyberspace to urge their fellow citizens to avoid jumping to conclusions about what could possibly have motivated the Muslim psychologist – who, by the way, shouted "Allahu Akhbar" as he pulled the trigger over and over and over again, and who had been in contact via email with one of al Qaeda's leading figures.

On November 8, 2009, the *New York Times* urged its readers to "avoid drawing prejudicial conclusions from the fact that Major Hasan is an American Muslim whose parents came from the Middle East." The paper cited President Obama's similar warning about "jumping to conclusions" before all the facts were known.[89] They wanted caution and introspection rather than accusations and hyperbole.

Yet, one day after the Tucson shooting, the *New York Times* editorial staff apparently couldn't resist accusations and hyperbole with regard to the motives of Jared Lee Loughner. The *Times* warned it readers about "a widespread squall of fear, anger and intolerance that …produced violent threats against scores of politicians and infected the political mainstream with violent imagery. With easy and legal access to semiautomatic weapons like the one used in the parking lot, those already teetering on the edge of sanity can turn a threat into a nightmare." They insisted that the "rage, stirred by talk-radio hosts," had inspired Loughner to try to kill a Democratic politician. They condemned all conservatives: "Many on the right have exploited the arguments of division, reaping political power by demonizing immigrants, or welfare recipients, or bureaucrats. They seem to have persuaded many Americans that the government is not just misguided, but the enemy of the people."[90]

The same hypocrisy was on display at CNN. For days and weeks after the Fort Hood shooting, the talking heads on Ted Turner's cable-based Kremlin called for calm and urged viewers to avoid jumping to conclusions about what motivated Hasan to kill his fellow soldiers. But, they just couldn't resist the urge to blame their political opponents, those evil conservatives, when news of the Arizona shooting broke. Unfortunately for Loughner, he wasn't a brown-skinned Muslim taking aim at Americans in uniform, for if he had been, he would have enjoyed the protective diversions of media Leftists. But, alas, he was a white male, thus he was considered fair game for speculation and rumors.

As was noted above, and as the *New York Times* editorial indicates, politicians maneuvered to push for their pet agendas, and used the Arizona tragedy as an opportunity to get legislation passed. It is obvious that the shooter's real motivation and political rhetoric were of no concern to Leftists determined to gain a political advantage in the midst of a tragedy. Some political strategists let the cat out of the bag when they offered advice to Democratic leaders about seizing on the moment to get their agenda through Congress.

For instance, after the tragic Tucson shooting, former *Newsweek* editor Howard Fineman advised President Obama to use the tragedy to get his political agenda through Congress.[91] *Newsweek*'s Jonathon Alter also advised President Obama to use the shooting to get his political agenda through Congress.[92] As was noted above, Leftists in the California

Assembly resurrected their pursuit of disarming all law-abiding citizens after the tragic shooting.

Additionally, the tendency of politicians to want to "do something" in the midst of a crisis was demonstrated after the Tucson shooting as calls for more restrictions on speech (the First Amendment be damned) were issued by Leftist politicians. The irrationality of the political class stems from their addiction to the perks of public office, which exerts a compulsion to act when tragic events occur. Because their terms last only two years, House members must begin campaigning for reelection almost immediately after settling into their big, cozy, leather chairs in January. Thus, they seize upon every opportunity to offer some type of legislation that is intended to "fix" something that, more often than not, does not need fixing.

Here are some examples of the knee-jerk lunacy of Leftist Democrats in the aftermath of the Tucson shooting:

- Rep. Robert Brady (D-PA) introduced legislation to outlaw symbols that may "incite" violence.[93]
- Rep. James Clyburn (D-SC) called for restrictions on free speech and wanted to prohibit symbols and words that he deemed dangerous.[94]
- Rep. Ruben Hinojosa (D-TX) offered his support for legislation to outlaw certain speech or symbols deemed "dangerous."[95]
- Rep. Chellie Pingree (D-ME) wanted Republicans to change the name of a bill. The bill's name was "Repeal the Job Killing Health Care Law Act." Pingree believed that getting rid of the word "killing" in a piece of legislation just may prevent paranoid schizophrenics from killing people.[96]

Politicians are elected, thus they can be replaced. However, Leftist lunatics in Hollywood hardly ever go away of their own accord. Their commitment to the false narratives of Leftist ideology is unique in that their statements permeate and infect the public discourse in ways that most politicians can only wish to emulate. Angelina Jolie enjoys a massive following that the vast majority of elected officials could only dream of emulating. Ask anyone: Who is the current Chairman of the House Judiciary Committee? Who is the current Vice Chair of the Senate Select Committee on Intelligence? Who cast the deciding vote in the Senate to table legislation on gun control last year? A blank stare is what you'll get.

Ask a young voter today to tell you which Hollywood celebrity just got divorced or entered drug rehabilitation (again), and, without hesitation, you'll likely get the correct answer. Ask that same young voter to tell you what nation is currently expanding its influence into Africa and setting up new oil rigs and exploring for precious metals, and you'll likely get the hallmark blank stare of the clueless youth voter (also known as an Obama supporter). Ask young voters which nations continue to reject sanctions against Syria's tyrannical regime, and you can wager a year's pay that they'll get that one wrong as well.

CBS News reported: "Pew Research Center for the People and the Press found that 21 percent of people aged 18 to 29 cited 'The Daily Show' and 'Saturday Night Live' as a place where they regularly learned presidential campaign news." The cluelessness of so many young voters can be explained by the fact that a Hollywood comedian is their primary source of information. Imagine what America would have looked like fifty years ago if the Greatest Generation relied upon Jackie Gleason or Lucille Ball as their source for news on public policy issues. If that had been the case, Congress very well could have crafted legislation requiring every citizen to take a tablespoon-full of "Vitameatavegamin" after every meal.

Hollywood celebrities have been and remain today relatively effective proponents of Leftist ideology, and have been and remain today reliable purveyors of the false narratives of Leftist ideology. For instance, Leftist television host Bill Maher is cited as a person who many people rely upon for information about current events. However, Mr. Maher is ignorant. He's ignorant about nearly everything important. And he's hateful to boot – a very sad and disturbing combination.

Within a week after the Tucson, Arizona shooting, Mr. Maher was on the Tonight Show with Jay Leno ranting about evil Republicans. He swerved into full-lunatic mode when he suggested that conservatives want to kill people who disagree with them. Unfortunately for Maher, the audience that night just wasn't buying his argument – his trademark condescension likely didn't help his cause very much either. For instance, after the audience seemed to sour a bit on his vitriolic diatribe, and stopped applauding at his every utterance, and even hissed a few times, Mr. Maher asked the audience sarcastically, "Do you read?"[97] Clearly, Mr. Maher had grown too accustomed to an audience of sycophants who think every word that whistles passed his lips is a precious gift to humanity – a sacred wind from God to be remembered, recited, and treasured for all eternity.

During his four-minute diatribe about evil conservatives and their angry, dangerous and vitriolic hate-speech, Mr. Maher (1) suggested that all conservatives are hysterical, irrational, gun-toting lunatics who are itching to shoot anyone who disagrees with them; (2) said Newt Gingrich is the "right-wing douchbag" that he "hates" the most; (3) said gun owners are addicted to guns like alcoholics are addicted to liquor; (4) said America is populated with violent lunatics [again, the illogical syllogism rears its ugly head]; and (5) called gun owners "assholes." Did Mr. Maher not hear all the calls for civility in the days and weeks after the Tucson shooting, particularly the calls from President Obama to turn down the angry rhetoric?

Ironically, as he was characterizing his political opponents as armed lunatics ready to kill at the drop of a hat, Mr. Maher condemned Newt Gingrich for "characterizing his political opponents as the enemy," a practice that Mr. Maher suggested may inspire "borderline people" to harm their political adversaries. The hypocrisy and irony of his statements was lost only on him and his sycophantic groupies.

Mr. Maher also suggested that Leftists don't engage in the same sorts of violent rhetorical insanity as conservatives. Leftists don't treat their political opponents as the enemy like conservatives do, he said. However, a cursory search of the Internet reveals numerous examples of violent rhetoric from comedian Bill Maher:

- Bill Maher called Republicans "a deadly enemy."
- Maher's friend and guest Rob Reiner equated the Tea Party to Hitler; Maher laughed heartily.
- Bill Maher wished Glenn Beck had been killed.
- Maher joked about Sarah Palin reincarnated as a wolf and being shot.
- Bill Maher said he was sorry that the assassination attempt on Dick Cheney failed.
- Joy Behar and Bill Maher laughed about Dick Cheney's heart attack.

- Maher wondered why Rush Limbaugh didn't die from drugs instead of Heath Ledger?[98]
- Maher called Sarah Palin a "dumb twat" and a "cunt," mocked her son who has Down's Syndrome, called GOP Rep. Michele Bachmann "a boob," repeatedly targeted Palin's family for vicious attacks, and then gave $1.5 million to President Obama's reelection campaign. The money was not returned, and the echo-chamber Leftist media never gave a damn.[99]

Yet, there he was in the wake of the Tucson shooting, Bill Maher, lecturing Americans about being civil. And people still take this clown seriously?

Filmmaker and propagandist Michael Moore believes that gun owners are racists. Therefore, not only are guns themselves evil, but anyone who owns one is evil. It's a convenient narrative for the Leftist because it eliminates any need for further discussion. If you support gun ownership, you're evil – a Nazi. No further debate is required. Remember the syllogism used above to explain Leftists' opposition to private gun ownership? Michael Moore is a living testament to that illogical syllogism described above.

A few days after the Tucson shooting, Moore appeared on far-Leftist Rachel Maddow's show on MSNBC. He wondered aloud about why Americans own so many guns. "Why us?" he asked. His answer:

> The vast majority of these guns are owned by people who live in safe parts of town, or mostly in suburbs and rural areas. Places where there are very few murders....So, why do you have a gun, then? Why do you have a gun? What are you afraid of? What is that thing that we're afraid of

> that we want to have a gun in the house? [...] On this particular day, Martin Luther King Day, this needs to be said. That imaginary person who's going to break into your home and kill you, who's that person look like? You know. It's not freckle-faced Jimmy down the street. [...] We never really want to talk about the racial or the class part of this, in terms of how it's the poor or it's people of color who we imagine – that we're afraid of. Why are we afraid? And it's been a fear that's existed for a very, very, long time. [...] We also need to address the issue of why we're such a violent people, and not just personal, domestic violence, but the nation that invades other countries, that has such a huge weapons budget, that just seems so intent on violence being the answer.[100]

Michael Moore outlined, in that short diatribe, the whole "gun-haters" syllogism. Why do Americans own guns? They're racists. Why is gun ownership protected in the Constitution? Because racists wrote the Constitution. Why are they racists? Because they're white, and whites have been oppressing and enslaving the brown people of the world for, as Michael Moore said, a "very, very long time."

In addition to the narrative that Palin's map and Tea Party rhetoric inspired Loughner, the establishment media added another element of the syllogism, "guns are evil," to the narrative. In fact, the ABC News website, as of late 2012, still featured videos made during the aftermath of the Tucson shooting in which the whole false narrative describe above was crafted and disseminated as fact. Sarah Palin's map is prominently featured in the video report, and the whole narrative revolves around the demonstrably false and easily debunked notion that "easy access to guns," "political rhetoric," and "Sarah Palin's map" were the root cause of the violence witnessed that day in Tucson.[101]

PJTV's Bill Whittle, shortly after the Tucson shooting, noted that over the two years from 2010 to 2011, there were two mass shootings: Ft. Hood, TX, and Tucson, AZ. The population of the United States is 330,000,000. Two Americans in 24 months perpetrated mass murders with guns. Thus, the failure rate of American citizens is approximately 0.000000006 percent. That's six-billionth of one percent per year. Yet, politicians on the Left wait with baited breath for any opportunity to dismantle the Second Amendment and outlaw certain forms of speech that are protected by the First Amendment, but which they find inconvenient. The actions of an infinitesimally small minority of people, says the Leftist, should shape the nation's policies.

But, it's conservatives who are the extremists?

Aurora Theater Massacre

During a midnight showing of the premier of a summer blockbuster movie on July 20, 2012, a deranged lunatic entered a movie theater, Century Theaters, in Aurora, Colorado. He was armed with an AR-15 semi-automatic rifle. After tossing two gas canisters into the crowded auditorium, James Holmes opened fire on the unarmed mass of moviegoers. He killed 12 people and injured 58 others.

As expected, the narrative reared its ugly head. NBC's Today Show co-host Savannah Guthrie teased viewers about her upcoming segment. She exposed in "an undercover report...just how easy it can be for anyone, even violent criminals, to buy assault weapons, no questions asked." Her findings? "Colorado has some of the weakest gun laws in the country," she said. Colorado is letting violent criminals buy guns?

However, investigative journalist Jeff Rossen opened his segment with this curious statement: "It turns out this shooter, this alleged shooter in Colorado, had no rap sheet, so he was able to buy his guns in a store legally." Rossen, realizing that his comments pose a threat to the narrative, injected quickly: "But even if he had a violent criminal record he still could have bought them."[102]

In 2007, a man shot and killed two teenagers at a Christian camp in Colorado. He then drove to a mega-church in Colorado Springs and shot two people in the parking lot. When he entered the crowded church with the intention of killing even more people, he encountered a woman, Jeanne Assam, who had a concealed and carry permit. She pulled her weapon and shot the gunman, preventing the deaths of dozens, if not hundreds, of churchgoers that day.[103]

You probably never heard about that story. Such stories are never mentioned by echo-chamber Leftists because it does not fit the narrative. Incidents where armed, law-abiding citizens stop crimes far outnumber mass shootings, but they are almost entirely ignored by media elitists in the echo chamber.[104] Shock value may be one reason – after all, there were only two dead bodies from the Christian camp shooting. But, the evidence is pretty clear that Leftists have an anti-gun agenda. Stories of people using their legal guns to prevent or stop crimes are ignored because they do not promote the Leftist agenda to ban all firearms.

Here's one fact about concealed carry laws that no one ever hears from Leftists/Progressives. It was articulated by economist John Lott on CNN during a discussion about gun control in the days after a tragic mass shooting at an elementary school in Connecticut. CNN's Soledad O'Brien berated Professor Lott and interrupted him repeatedly throughout the short segment, but he managed to get in this curious fact:

> Take the Columbine case. Do you know that Dylan Klebold, for example, was lobbying against the concealed handgun bill when it was before the state legislature? He was writing his state legislators, he was strongly against it, he was particularly upset about the part of the law that would allow concealed handguns on school property, and do you know the day the Columbine attack occurred? It occurred on the day of final passage of the state concealed handgun law. At Columbine, how many times do you talk about that?[105]

One of the two Columbine school shooters was lobbying his state representative to vote against a law that would allow conceal and carry on school campuses, and the bill passed the state legislature on the very day he and another student went to their school and killed 13 people. But the news media never reveal that little fact because it undermines their false narrative.

One disturbing fact about the Aurora shooting is that the movie theater's owners created a false sense of security by putting up stickers to inform their customers that no guns are allowed on the premises, even concealed carry weapons – which is, by the way, permitted by state law. David Kopel explained it this way:

> [The Concealed Carry Act passed after the Columbine High School mass shooting] allows government buildings to be declared "gun-

> free zones," but Colorado law insists that when a government promises a gun-free zone, the government must keep the promise: Licensed carry may be forbidden in a government building only if all entrances to the building are controlled, and if the public entrances have metal detectors manned by armed guards. [...]
>
> The Concealed Carry Act did not disturb the property rights of business owners – if they wish to, they may prohibit concealed carry on their business premises. Fortunately, very few Colorado businesses have done so. But one that did was Century Theaters. Compounding the problem, Century Theaters did not create an actual "gun-free zone" (as some government buildings in Colorado have). Instead, Century Theaters created a *pretend* gun-free zone. Century Theaters did nothing to prevent armed criminals from entering the theater.[106]

These details are never shared with views, readers, and listeners of the echo-chamber Leftist media. They don't fit the narrative. They're inconvenient facts that must be ignored. The common sense law that the Colorado legislature passed to protect its citizens allowed for private businesses to prohibit guns on their premises. But, these business owners are not required – nor should they be required – to provide assurances that guns will not enter their premises. Citizens are free to go to the movies at a theater where they can bring their guns, or they can watch a movie at a theater with a "pretend" gun-free zone, as they did that night in Aurora. Unfortunately, the consequences of pretending to be safe were deadly.

Michael Moore was a guest on CNN's Pier Morgan on July 25, 2012. They discussed the Aurora shooting, and Moore shared with the viewing audience his understanding of the Founding Fathers and the Second Amendment:

> ...when [the Founders] said "the right to bear arms," I think, you know, an arm back then was – you could only fire one shot at a time. You had a little, a little ball bearing-like bullet, and you'd stuff it in the thing, and you had to do this [here he mimics using a ramrod to pack powder and a bullet into an imaginary musket barrel], and gun powder, and, you know, it took you about fifteen minutes before you could fire one shot. Now, if the Founding Fathers could have looked into a crystal ball and seen AK-47's, and Glock semiautomatic pistols, I got a feeling they wouldn't – they'd want to leave a little note behind and probably tell us, "you know, that's not really what we mean when we say 'bear arms'." So, I think, I think, that, um, um – I think most intelligent people would, would see that it kinda makes sense, what they were thinking. I don't think we have to go back into their minds at all. And I wish that we would just live in this century. I think they'd want us to do that.[107]

Just in case you actually attempted to follow Michael Moore's logic, let me first explain that it will be an exercise in futility, because there is absolutely no logic present in his argument – none. First, Michael Moore tells us what he thinks the Founders really meant (as if he's actually read what they wrote). Then, he tells us that we do not really need to try to understand what they wrote (because Michael Moore will tell us). Then, he tells us what they probably would want us to do today (see, I told you he'd tell us).

Michael Moore is an ignoramus – but he's a confident and shameless ignoramus because he knows that there are at least a handful of people who are just as shameless and ignorant as he is, and thus will believe that what he says is actually rational. As you watch Mr. Moore talk about the Framers of the Constitution, you can rest assured that there are a handful of people sitting at home on the couch, sniffing their fingers and nodding in agreement, who know, perhaps, even less about the Framers than he does, if that's even possible. Unfortunately, many of those finger-sniffers are journalists at America's major news organizations – like ABC News' Brian Ross who instinctively reported that the Aurora shooter was a Tea Party member, and was later forced to apologize for just making it up from whole cloth (see Chapter One).

Racial Overtones

Black Americans disproportionately feel the brunt of the consequences of restrictive gun control legislation. Criminals rule the streets in many metropolitan areas, and law-abiding black Americans are forced to lock themselves in their homes in a futile effort to feel safe. However, instead of voting for politicians who will enable citizens to protect themselves, black Americans consistently and overwhelmingly vote for Left-wing Democrats who support increasingly restrictive gun control laws.

Statistics from the U.S. Department of Justice indicate that nearly half of all victims of violent crimes are black, yet blacks represent only 12 percent of the total U.S. population. Most troubling, though, is the fact that of the approximately 8,000 black murder victims in the United States each year, 93 percent are killed by someone of the same color.[108] The vast majority of these crimes are committed in cities that either prohibit handgun possession or have very strict regulations on gun ownership. Yet, in spite of laws prohibiting handgun ownership and possession, blacks are using guns to kill each other at disturbingly high rates.

One of the prevailing narratives promoted by gun control advocates is that more restrictive gun control laws reduce crime rates. However, all evidence indicates otherwise.[109] In fact, in Washington, D.C. alone, violent crime rates skyrocketed immediately after the city banned private handgun ownership in 1975. The District has remained one of the most violent cities in the U.S. for forty years. Whole neighborhoods are held captive by gangs of violent thugs, and law-abiding citizens fear walking the streets, even in daylight.

One fact that is not part of the narrative of any of the commentaries about confiscating guns from law-abiding American citizens and overturning the Second Amendment – commentaries that often highlight the fact that so-called "gun violence" is far higher in the United States than it is in other civilized nations[110] – is the fact that the staggering number of murders committed with guns in the United States occur disproportionately in black neighborhoods. Remove the gun-related deaths of black Americans at the hands of other black Americans from the nation's overall crime statistics, and the gun murder rate in the United States becomes comparable to other industrialized nations, and thus far less of an outrage and useful talking point for the media.[111] In fact, the homicide rate for black Americans is seven times that of whites – 26.5 per 100,000 versus 3.5 per 100,000 (more on this later).

The debate about the cause of the disproportionate violence

among young black males is a very sensitive one. Poverty, unemployment, illegitimacy, drug use, and gang membership are all suspected culprits. Conservative commentators often note the abundance of children of single-parent homes in American prisons, and suggest that a spiritual crisis in the black community is the main cause of the horrific statistics. Leftists argue that systemic racism, economic inequality, and underfunded schools are the main culprits.

However, it must be noted that 90 percent of black Americans consistently vote for Leftist Democrats, and those very same politicians consistently disarm law-abiding black Americans. Almost every major metropolitan area is run by Leftist Democrats, and has been for over 30 years. Thus, the question must be asked: Will black Americans ever consider the possibility that perhaps the policies of their elected officials, all Democrats, may be, at least partially, a contributing factor to their predicament?

Dick Heller, a federal police officer from the District of Columbia, was sick and tired of living in fear of street thugs. He joined five other District residents in a lawsuit, arguing that D.C.'s total handgun ban was a violation of his Constitutional right to keep and bear arms. Of note, two of the six plaintiffs in the lawsuit were black.

Being a federal police officer, Heller was permitted to carry a handgun as part of his job, but was prohibited from owning and possessing a handgun for personal protection in his home. Heller and the other five plaintiffs in the case lived in high crime neighborhoods in the District, and each recalled personal horror stories about the violence they had either witnessed or experienced themselves. One plaintiff recounted a story about using a handgun to thwart violence he experienced while he was a resident of San Jose, CA. That plaintiff was assaulted because he was gay, and he used a handgun to defend himself. That plaintiff knew firsthand that carrying one's own personal protection was vitally important to being and feeling free and secure in America.

In 2008, the U.S. Supreme Court struck down the District' handgun ban (*District of Columbia* v. *Heller*), but left in place a variety of restrictions, including a ban on conceal-and-carry (CCW).[112] Thus, citizens of the District still walk the streets as unarmed victims, fearful of violent thugs. Today, nearly five years after the Supreme Court decision, the news media in the D.C.-Metro region feature news stories almost every night about violent crimes, occurring almost exclusively in the District and neighboring Prince Georges County, Maryland, both of which have very restrictive gun control laws and both of which are beset with high violent crime rates. Curiously, in the cities and counties of northern Virginia, where private handgun ownership, conceal and carry, and even open carry, are all legal, violent crime rates are markedly lower, and news stories about violence occurring in those cities and counties are relatively rare.

Two years after the *Heller* case, the U.S. Supreme Court struck down Chicago's restrictive ban on handgun ownership in *McDonald* v. *Chicago*.[113] After the *Heller* and *McDonald* decisions, gun-control advocates warned of skyrocketing gun violence in those two cities, as if the violent crime rates weren't high enough already. Elected officials (that is, Democrats), establishment media talking heads, newspaper columnists, opinion writers, and civil rights activists marched in protest and expressed their outrage at the Court's decisions. They warned of a return to the days of the Old West, with gun fights in the streets at high noon and body bags in the thousands. Sadly, the citizens of Chicago and the District were already experiencing some of the nation's highest violent crime rates, in spite of the fact that their laws already prohibited handgun ownership.

The idea that individual citizens should be able to carry their own means of protection is deemed by gun control advocates as archaic, outdated, and reminiscent of the barbaric Wild West days of Wyatt Earp. However, academic studies of the relationship between conceal and carry laws and crime rates are revealing and surprising only to those who live inside the Leftist echo chamber. States, counties, and municipalities that have passed conceal and carry laws experience an almost immediate drop in violent crime rates.[114] The reason is obvious: would-be criminals are less inclined to rape, mug, and rob people when there's uncertainty about which people are concealing a handgun and which ones are not. In short, when law-abiding citizens carry their own means of protection, or the laws allow them to carry a handgun, criminals begin to fear law-abiding citizens, which is the way it's supposed to be in civilized society.

The right to keep and bear arms is clearly articulated in the U.S. Constitution. The Second Amendment states: "A well regulated Militia, being necessary to the security of a free State, the right of the people to keep and bear Arms, shall not be infringed." Scholars have debated for over a century whether the right defined in the amendment was an individual right or merely a collective right reserved to the states. Conservative scholars argue that the use of the term "the people" in the Second Amendment indicates clearly that the right was intended for individuals. They note that everywhere in the Constitution where the term "the people" is used, such as it is in the First Amendment, the Framers meant the individual citizen.

The Framers were very specific when they wrote the Constitution. If they were referring to the states, they wrote "the states." If they were discussing the Congress, they wrote "the Congress." If they were referring to the president and his cabinet, they wrote the "Executive." And so on. Thus, when the Framers wrote "the people" in the Second Amendment they actually meant "the people," or individuals, not the states or some other collective group. In fact, over forty academic legal studies have been conducted to determine what the Framers of the Constitution meant when they wrote the Second Amendment. The vast majority of them concluded that the right is indeed an individual right and not a collective right.

However, not everyone is convinced that the Second Amendment is a guarantee and a protection of the rights of individual citizens from government usurpation. Some Leftist scholars have argued that the amendment was a way for the Framers of the Constitution to defend the right of states to form militias. Law professor Carl T. Bogus argues that the Second Amendment was intended as a collective right, reserved only for the states. He insists further that it was ratified to appease the fears of whites in the South who were worried about violent slave revolts.[115] Mother Jones columnist Stephanie Mencimer cited Professor Bogus' work as evidence that the Constitution is a racist document – again, as usual, the anti-American syllogism rears its ugly head.[116]

Curiously, gun-control advocates like President Obama, Professor Bogus, and the host of others who believe individual citizens should be unarmed when out in public, fail to see the obvious implications of their argument; that is, that guns were kept out of the hands of slaves in the South in order to keep them oppressed and subservient to the white majority. Strict gun bans kept guns out of the hands of newly freed slaves, just as law-abiding black Americans today are kept defenseless by laws that prohibit them from owning and carrying the most effective means of self-protection. Gun bans kept blacks oppressed in the 19th and 20th centuries, and they keep blacks oppressed today. Leftists refuse to acknowledge that fact that the solution to slavery wasn't gun control – the solution to slavery was armed citizens of the Northern States rallying and killing the armed citizens of the Southern States. It's that simple.

The racial history of gun control legislation in America was a significant part of Associate Justice Clarence Thomas' opinion in the *McDonald* case.[117] After a lengthy and thorough examination of hundreds of years of judicial precedents pertaining to the issue of individual versus collective rights, as well as the Privileges and Immunities Clause of the Fourteenth Amendment and a host of other technical legal issues, Justice Thomas revisited American history, specifically the period just before the Civil War and just after, known as Reconstruction.

Justice Thomas reminded the Court that black slaves during the antebellum period were prohibited by state laws from owning or possessing firearms. There were some exceptions for certain slaves to hunt on their master's property, using their master's firearms, but in general slaves could not own or possess a firearm of any sort. Abolitionists during the antebellum period often argued for the rights of all people, black or white, to keep and bear arms for their personal protection. They recognized that firearm possession was a great equalizer, enabling freed blacks to defend themselves from those who would seek to oppress and thus re-enslave them.

After the Civil War, noted Justice Thomas, white gangs such as "the Ku Klux Klan, the Knights of the White Camellia, the White Brotherhood, the Pale Faces, and the '76 Association," roamed the post-Civil War countryside terrorizing blacks. They raped and pillaged black towns across Reconstruction South. Justice Thomas noted that during an eighty-six year period, between "1882 and 1968, there were at least 3,446 reported lynchings of blacks in the South." Of course, whites carried out these horrors only after disarming their black victims. Many whites in the South, still stinging from a humiliating Civil War defeat, voted for state legislatures, city officials, and sheriffs who were willing to pass and enforce strict gun control laws to prohibit black citizens from owning firearms. Justice Thomas noted also that on several occasions it was elected officials who engaged in violence against freed blacks – for instance, it was local sheriffs who led the infamous Colfax Massacre, and a state militia that carried out the Hamburg Massacre.

Justice Thomas brilliantly dismantled the misguided notion that the Second Amendment and the Fourteenth Amendment protect only a collective right to keep and bear arms, rather than an individual right. That idea, he wrote, "enabled private forces, often with the assistance of local governments, to subjugate the newly freed slaves and their descendants through a wave of private violence designed to drive blacks from the voting booth and force them into peonage, an effective return to slavery."

Justice Thomas continued: "Without federal enforcement of the inalienable right to keep and bear arms, these militias and mobs were tragically successful in waging a campaign of terror against the very people the Fourteenth Amendment had just made citizens." In short, the Framers of the Constitution were clear: the right to keep and bear arms is an inalienable right that cannot be limited to state officials, for history has demonstrated repeatedly that state officials are prone to abuse unchecked power over the individual citizen.

The vociferous defense of private gun ownership that Justice Thomas penned in the *McDonald* case was both historic and historical. He offered it on behalf of Otis McDonald, the black man who is the namesake of the notorious case – a law-abiding citizen who fought for his Constitutional right to own a handgun to protect himself from the "gangbangers" who he said were keeping law-abiding citizens oppressed in Chicago.[118]

In spite of the clear historical facts regarding race and gun control, black and white Leftist politicians, as well as the editorial staffs of most echo-chamber news organizations, continue defending restrictive gun laws by insisting that gun possession should be limited to the police and the military. Even worse, these Leftists have demonstrated a willingness to lie and deceive in order to perpetuate a false narrative about guns and race.

For instance, during the heated debate about federal health insurance and the $800 billion stimulus package in early 2009, a group of citizens calling themselves the "Tea Party" emerged. It was composed primarily of conservatives, primarily Republicans, who were outraged at the growth of the federal government during an economic crisis. The members of this new grassroots organization held protests and rallies in hundreds of cities across the nation, and town halls with elected officials were scenes of anger and outrage.

In the midst of the heated political season, President Obama traveled to Arizona in August 2009, and discussed his plans for a federal healthcare program. Protesters a few miles down the road from the location of the president's speech carried placards and shouted slogans against the uncontrolled growth of the federal deficit and the outrageous public debt. Among the protesters, one man in particular got special attention. He was carrying what gun-illiterate news people called an "assault rifle" over his shoulder. As the scene rolled onscreen, MSNBC newsreader Contessa Brewer informed her viewers:

> Yesterday, as President Obama addressed the Veterans of Foreign Wars in Phoenix, a man at a pro-health care reform rally just outside wore a semiautomatic assault rifle on his shoulder and a pistol on his hip. The Associated Press reports about a dozen people in all at that event were, uh, visible, carrying firearms.....And the reason we're talking about this...[is] because people fell like, yes, there are Second Amendment rights, for sure, but also because there are questions about whether this has racial overtones. I mean, here you have a man of color in the presidency, and white people showing up with guns strapped to their waist or to their legs.[119]

What MSNBC failed to share with its viewers was the fact that the protester they were insisting was a white racist – the one with the assault rifle over his shoulder – was in fact a black man. In fact, the staff at MSNBC intentionally edited the video to deceive its viewers into believing that the man with the rifle was white. The complete video of the man was several minutes long, but MSNBC cut it down to the three seconds that showed him from the waist down, while his arms were crossed, thus his "black" hands were not visible. It was one of the most obvious examples of intentional deceit designed to keep an echo-chamber Leftist narrative alive.

But to the echo-chamber Leftists at MSNBC, the man's skin color had to be concealed from the viewers because it did not fit the false narrative – the narrative that white racists were intent on killing the first black president of the United States. They intentionally deceived their viewers because they held little regard for the truth, and even less regard for the integrity of their profession, and absolutely zero regard for their viewers, whom they treated as mere ciphers to be manipulated into outrage in order to serve the larger political needs of the Progressive, Leftwing President Barack Obama. The sheer absence of shame among these media elitists makes them unfit to run a news organization.

While the echo-chamber media continued to develop their false narrative about Tea Party racism during President Obama's first three years in office, events in Florida soon provided them with a golden opportunity to reinforce the false narrative that white men with guns are a threat to blacks in America.

Trayvon Martin and George Zimmerman

On the night of February 26, 2012, a young black child, Trayvon Martin, was shot and killed by a twenty-eight year old white male, George Zimmerman. The innocent child was returning home with candy and iced tea he had purchased at a local convenience store in Sanford, Florida. Another innocent black child murdered by a white devil.

At least that was the narrative that was crafted in the first few days after the story broke nationally. The narrative consisted of the following items: Trayvon Martin was minding his own business when an angry white man hunted him down and murdered him in cold blood; the local police, consisting of equally angry white men, let the white killer go, just as they had done numerous times during the days of Jim Crow and segregation and lynching.

The narrative that was sold to the American public was driven home with a series of misleading images and outright deceptions. Television news stories about the shooting, as well as websites, newspapers, and magazines, featured photos of Trayvon Martin that were taken when he was around 12 or 13 years old, at least five years before the shooting. One photo in particular was repeatedly shown – Trayvon's big, innocent eyes peeking out from underneath a white hooded sweatshirt. That photo became the iconic image of the story, and has been featured on countless placards at rallies across the nation, and is the go-to photo whenever the story is discussed on television. That photo, as well as the hooded sweatshirt, has become synonymous with black victims of racist white violence.

Shortly after the story went national (and viral on the internet), photos of the shooter, George Zimmerman, started appearing on television, newspapers, websites, and magazines. The photos indicated that Zimmerman was Hispanic, which did not fit the narrative of a white racist killing an innocent black boy. However, several so-called "journalists" with an apparent penchant for creative writing concocted a brand new ethnicity; one that fit better into the prevailing narrative. George Zimmerman would be called a "white Hispanic,"[120] a phrase that had been used only very rarely (in fact, almost never) before this incident.[121] But, it served its purpose because it helped move the false narrative forward. The storyline in the first weeks the story broke was that an innocent black child had been murdered by an angry "white" man, and the white man was set free by racist white cops.

Noted media critic and former CBS News producer Bernard Goldberg commented on the use of the new ethnic category. Goldberg suggested that, had George Zimmerman done something good, like win a race or prize or save someone from drowning, he would never have been identified as a "white Hispanic." He would simply have been identified as a "Hispanic." Thus, Goldberg said, the use of the new phrase betrayed a desire by the establishment media to craft a narrative that a black was murdered by a white.

The irrationality of the term "white Hispanic" was obvious to everyone, even some of the Leftists at the *Huffington Post.* However, not everyone was willing to accept the charge that the creation of a new ethnicity from whole cloth was part of a larger conspiracy to contrive a false narrative. Yet, as the evidence below will demonstrate, the echo-chamber media have a vested interest in false narratives, particularly those related to race relations and violence. During the first few weeks after the shooting, the echo chamber crafted a narrative that an innocent black child was murdered by an angry white man, and that narrative took root and grew rapidly, fed by hyperbole, deceit, and lies.

For instance, in the pages of the *New York Times,* Robert Gooding-Williams, Professor of Political Science at the University of Chicago, wrote an opinion piece in which he suggested that the Sanford police chief's willingness to accept Mr. Zimmerman's story about the incident represented the reinstitution of the Fugitive Slave Laws of the antebellum South:

> It is hard to resist the thought that race matters here, for who believes that, had an adult African

> American male killed a white teenager under similar circumstances, the police would have taken him at his word and so declined to arrest him?....
>
> In short, it appears that whites (or other non-blacks) may hunt down blacks with immunity from arrest so long as they leave behind no clue that they were not acting to defend themselves...
>
> If it seems a stretch, finally, to paint Zimmerman in the image of the slave catchers of yesteryear, recall that he himself invited the comparison when, while stalking the African-American teenager against the advice of a 911 dispatcher, he complained, using an expletive to refer to Trayvon, that they "always get away."[122]

The professor was reluctant to clearly define Zimmerman's ethnicity, of course, for it allows him to keep the prevailing narrative alive. He wrote: "there is some controversy as to whether Zimmerman should be identified as white, or Hispanic, or both, although no one seems to be claiming he is black." In fact, controversies about race classification exist only among Leftists, who are determined to label people in order to keep racial animosity alive and well in America.

The professor also referenced something Zimmerman said to the 911 dispatcher; that they "always get away." The truth is that criminals often do get away after they've burglarized a home. Zimmerman suspected that he had caught a criminal in the act of either staking out a potential home for burglary or had perhaps already burglarized a home. Zimmerman made a call to 911 dispatchers that night believing he had encountered a burglar, not a runaway slave as the professor suggested. The fact is that the neighborhood which Zimmerman was patrolling had been hit by a series of burglaries over the previous weeks, and no one had been caught. Thus, as Zimmerman suggested, they always get away.

On March 21, just three weeks after the shooting, a break in the story came by way of the audio from Zimmerman's emergency 911 phone call. The quality of the tape recording was rather poor, but the folks at CNN were able to detect a key phrase – one that proved beyond a doubt that Zimmerman was a racist. Wolf Blitzer was sitting in for Anderson Cooper that night, and he spoke with reporter Gary Tuchman and guest Rick Sierra, "one of the best audio experts in the business,"[123] According to the audio expert, George Zimmerman can be heard calling Trayvon Martin – the young, innocent, black child with candy and iced-tea who was minding his own business – a "fucking coon."[124]

The audio was played over and over again on CNN, with particular attention to the racist epithet uttered by Zimmerman. CNN dubbed the revelation "a major development" in the case.[125] The damning phrase was breathlessly presented to CNN's viewers:

> "I should warn you right now you're going to hear some strong language," Blitzer says in the segment posted Wednesday. "You might want to send your kids out of the room."[126]

News of this revelation spread like wildfire. Commentators and civil rights activists took to the airwaves and editorial pages to express their outrage. Leftists who had been saying for years that America is a racist society had been vindicated. Young, black, innocent children like Trayvon Martin were being targeted for murder by white racists, and the police in Sanford let a white murderer walk free, just like they had always done. According to the echo-chamber Leftist media, Zimmerman had "grumbled the phrase 'f**king c**ns' moments before shooting and killing Trayvon Martin."[127] One *Mediaite* writer concluded:

> Given the emotional punch of this story, [CNN reporter] Tuchman's presentation is a bit clinical, but that detachment doesn't blunt the impact of hearing that phrase over and over again. As Cooper pointed out, the Sanford Police are saying that they didn't hear the slur, not that they "missed it," as has been reported. Although reporter Tuchman maintains that the recording is not definitive, this should help clear things up a lot for the police. It's also an example of CNN putting its technological resources to excellent journalistic use.

On March 16, *New York Times* columnist Charles M. Blow wrote that the Trayvon Martin case is evidence that "the burden of black boys in America" is that they have to walk the streets in fear of being shot and killed by white racists.[128] Mr. Blow lives in Brooklyn, where every week a young black kid is shot to death by another black kid. So, while Mr. Blow says he fears his two sons will someday encounter a Zimmerman, none of the dozens of murders of young black kids in Mr. Blow's city touched his conscience and inspired a series of op-ed articles[129] as had the death of Trayvon Martin. Why? Two words: "white Hispanic."

The New Black Panther Party held a press conference and put out a $10,000 bounty on Zimmerman's head. "He should be fearful for his life....You can't keep killing black children," said Mikhail Muhammad, leader of the local NBPP branch.

Filmmaker Spike Lee posted Zimmerman's home address on Twitter in the hope that someone would avenge the slaughter of an innocent black child (unfortunately, it was the wrong address, and an elderly couple was forced to leave their home for several days in fear that they would become targets of revenge).[130]

Curiously, while President Obama commented within days after the story went national (and viral) – before all the facts were known about the case – and said that if he had a son, he would "look like Trayvon," he never commented on the inflammatory and arguably illegal actions of the New Black Panther Party, Spike Lee, and the host of other hate-mongers who used the tragedy as a tool to inflame hate and discontent.[131]

With news of Zimmerman's "f*cking coon" comment circulating, the Reverend Jesse Jackson and the Reverend Al Sharpton, accused for years by racist crackers for being nothing more than race hustlers, suddenly found themselves vindicated. All the white racism (or, in this case, "white Hispanic" racism) that they said was lurking in the hearts of white Americans had been exposed by a scratchy 911 call from Sanford, Florida. The two civil rights leaders were getting national attention again, all thanks to Zimmerman's "f*cking coon" remark. The Old Guard of the civil rights movement was relevant again – Praise the Lord!

And then, just as quickly as the good news had arrived and the systemic racism of America's judicial system and the white people who'd invented it had finally been exposed for all to see, sadness swept the news rooms across the nation. After further review, it seemed that the "f*cking coons" comment was not what everyone had hoped it was. Apparently, the "white Hispanic" shooter had merely said "f*cking cold," a reference to the unusually cold weather in Florida that winter – the same cold weather that had compelled Trayvon Martin – the young, innocent, black child with candy and iced tea who was minding his own business – to pull up the hood on his sweatshirt. Later, it was determined that Zimmerman may have said "f*cking punks." Either way, it was not a racial epithet.

CNN eventually had to inform their viewers that Zimmerman hadn't uttered a racist epithet. The disappointment was palpable. However, undeterred by that minor setback, the echo-chamber media pressed on with their false narrative. NBC News took up the cause and fabricated another falsehood. They took the 911 call, ran it through their "racism generator," and produced a highly edited 911 phone call that was guaranteed to prove that Zimmerman was a bigot. Jesse and Al and the rest of the Old Guard, don't you worry. NBC News has got your backs!

NBC's Today Show, NBC News, and its cable affiliate MSNBC, aired a new version of the 911 call. Here's what they played for their viewers, and here's what they published on their websites:

> ZIMMERMAN: This guy looks like he's up to no good ... he looks black.

Forget the "f*cking coon" thing. This was big! This was Zimmerman, in his very own voice, speaking just like the racist that everyone knew he was (because, you know, he's a "white Hispanic"). The short sound-bite from Zimmerman's 911 phone call fit the narrative perfectly. Those in the media crafting the narrative abandoned the "fucking coon" piece, and molded a new reality, one that consisted of the following storyline: Of course Zimmerman didn't say "fucking coon."

That's too old school, even for an angry white guy. George Zimmerman, only in his twenties, would not say "coon." However, he would, of course, equate the color of the victim with suspicious behavior. Zimmerman saw a black child, and that alone was suspicious. So, he shot him like a runaway slave. Just listen to him! He's clearly a racist!

However, the actual phone conversation with the dispatcher contained a little more substance than what the Today Show, NBC News, and MSNBC presented to their viewers and online readers. What they presented was a carefully edited version of the call. The actual conversation during which the comment about race was made was just a bit longer, but that little bit completely altered the narrative. Here's the portion of the conversation between Zimmerman and the 911 dispatcher that NBC News didn't want their viewers and readers to know about because it didn't fit the narrative:

> ZIMMERMAN: This guy looks like he's up to no good, or he's on drugs or something. It's raining and he's just walking around, looking about.
>
> 911 DISPATCHER: Okay, is this guy – is he white, black, or Hispanic?
>
> ZIMMERMAN: He looks black.

Online news blogger Dan Riehl of Breitbart.com broke the story about NBC News intentionally editing the call. Riehl noted that the issue of race was raised by the dispatcher, not by Zimmerman.[132] Once again, the narrative had suffered another setback. To even the untrained observer, it began to look as if a false narrative was being crafted to intentionally inflame race hatred, and NBC News was falsifying evidence in order to make a case that there remains widespread racial hatred in the United States.

NBC News and MSNBC eventually apologized for intentionally editing the phone call,[133] but remain to this day unwilling to discuss the controversy on the air. They have refused to admit the obvious: that the edit was an intentional attempt to portray Zimmerman as a racist; a "white Hispanic" racist.[134]

While it was part of the narrative that a racist "white Hispanic" man shot an innocent black child, the reality is far different. For instance, Trayvon Martin at the time of the shooting was a troubled young man of seventeen years, not the little innocent child that every news organization portrayed him as being. A 200-page autopsy report on the crime noted traces of THC in Trayvon Martin's blood, indicating that he'd smoked marijuana either hours or days before the incident. The Leftist online news and opinion cite *Huffington Post* reported: "The amount described in the autopsy report is such a low level that it would have played no role in Martin's behavior, said Larry Kobilinsky, a professor of forensic science at John Jay College of Criminal Justice in New York."

However, the question of whether or not marijuana affected Trayvon's behavior is irrelevant. The narrative that was sold to the American public was that Trayvon was a little angel – in fact, a five-year-old photograph featuring Trayvon's angelic face looking into the camera was the one almost exclusively used on television, the internet, and in newspapers, while more recent photos of Trayvon hamming it up gangsta-style were seldom, if ever, shown. The narrative that was crafted and sold to the American people was that Trayvon was just an innocent child, an angel, who did nothing wrong besides buy candy and iced tea from a convenience store and walk on a street where an angry white racist was out hunting for black boys to murder.

Drug use did not fit the narrative, thus the presence of THC in Trayvon Martin's blood was not reported on the major news networks. Also missing from most news reports from major outlets was the fact that George Zimmerman – who told the police the day after the shooting that it was Trayvon Martin who knocked him down and beat him with his fists – showed clear signs that he had been roughed up pretty good. Zimmerman had a broken nose, black eyes, cuts on his face, and large, bloody wounds on the back of his head – wounds consistent with Zimmerman's story that he was attacked by the six-foot-three-inch teenager. Again, those facts did not fit the narrative, thus they were downplayed or simply ignored.

By the time the medical condition of George Zimmerman was reported on CBS News on the night of May 16, nearly eight weeks had passed since the story first went national (and viral).[135] For two months, the American public was told that Trayvon Martin was an innocent child, a little angel, who was minding his own business, walking home with candy and iced tea, when an angry white man with a gun – an angry white man who called the innocent child a "fucking coon," and who saw Trayvon's black skin and thought "criminal" – shot and killed the young, innocent child (an innocent child of perhaps 12 or 13 years of age, based on the photograph repeatedly shown on television, in newspapers and magazines, and online). News of Zimmerman's wounds fell on deaf ears, just as the media had planned it. Public opinion had been shaped by a false narrative composed of outright lies and deceptions, and boring little details trickling out months later were never going to alter that narrative.

In the first weeks of the coverage of the shooting, civil rights leaders and other activists warned that, unless Zimmerman was arrested and charged with murder, there would be riots in the streets. The media-hounds at the New Black Panthers went to their trusted playbook on publicity stunts and posted a bounty on the head of George Zimmerman, thus the prospect of widespread violence loomed large, which is just how the Panthers like it. The narrative reached critical mass when a special prosecutor, Angela Corey, announced that the shooter, George Zimmerman, would be arrested and indicted on manslaughter charges in the death of Trayvon Martin. Jelani Cobb of *The Daily Beast* wrote:

> Amid the bounty of ugliness unearthed by the case, and the many more profane moments we're likely to witness before this is over, what people will remember is that it took nearly seven weeks for charges to be brought against a Hispanic man who shot an unarmed black teen. They will have learned that such a killing warrants only the most cursory of police examinations and that a simple arrest of the assailant requires incessant media attention, massive rallies in Miami, Sanford, New York, Atlanta, and Chicago, [and] the palpable threat of social unrest.[136]

The FBI released the findings of its independent investigation into the Trayvon Martin-George Zimmerman case, and discovered that the Sanford Police Department's lead investigator, Chris Serino, had been pressured by several of his fellow police officers – three of which are black and one Hispanic (who has a black spouse) – as well as several supervisors, to file charges against Zimmerman, in spite his belief that the shooter was justified and had "targeted Trayvon because of his attire, the circumstances and recent burglaries in the area, not the color of the teen's skin."[137]

The police officers and their supervisors were concerned that the black community would be outraged if Zimmerman remained free. The riots following the Rodney King verdict – during which hundreds of millions of dollars of private and public property were destroyed and several people were killed – was a stark reminder about what can happen when black citizens feel slighted by the justice system. Calls for riots and violence from national black civil rights leaders indicated that violence would likely ravage the nation if Zimmerman was not arrested and prosecuted.

An FBI report on the way the Sanford Police Department handled the aftermath of the tragic events revealed that political pressure was applied to the lead investigator. The decision to release Zimmerman without charges appeared to be the sticking point. Civil rights leaders, New Black Panthers, and news media were all conspiring to get Zimmerman arrested to rectify the injustice. However, there was no justification for an arrest. A justification had to be contrived in order for there to be an appearance of social justice. Zimmerman had to be charged with something, but the law stood in the way. That's where the whole episode turned into a fiasco. The FBI report found clear violations of procedure, and abject politicization of the law.

The *Tampa Bay Times* reported: "The lead Sanford police investigator who sought manslaughter charges against George Zimmerman told the FBI that a sergeant and two others officers tried to pressure him into making an arrest in the controversial case – even though he didn't think there was enough evidence." The article noted further that two of the officers who pressured the investigator were friends of Trayvon's father, Tracy Martin. Mr. Martin originally understood why charges were not pressed against Zimmerman, but was pressured by local civil rights officials into pushing the racial profiling narrative and seeking retribution against the police and Zimmerman.

> Records released Thursday show that Barnes, a 25-year veteran of the department, told the FBI that he believed the black community would be "in an uproar" if Zimmerman was not charged. "The community will be satisfied if an arrest takes place," the FBI quoted him saying. Barnes "felt the shooting was not racially motivated, but it was a man shooting an unarmed kid."

Curiously, the *Times* reporter covering the FBI investigation demonstrated a certain degree of naiveté when addressing the Sanford Police Department's actions. She wrote: "The report does not make clear why [lead investigator] Serino would feel pressure from Barnes and the other two officers he mentioned when he had the backing of the police chief." Then, in the very next sentence, she answered the question herself: "Chief Bill Lee was fired last month for his role in the widely disparaged investigation."[138]

Clearly, everyone in that police department felt the heat, and the pressure burst like a bubble. Not only was Zimmerman arrested because he was not black, and because he shot someone who was, but Chief Bill Lee was fired in order to appease black civil rights leaders (and the likes of Spike Lee and other race hustlers). Lead investigator Chris Serino, "a 15-year veteran of the department who was a major-crimes investigator, was demoted," the Times reported, "to overnight patrol." The message was clear: police should arrest all "white Hispanics" who shoot blacks, regardless of the evidence and the law. The police can no longer trust their years of experience, their gut instincts. Now, they must treat every non-black who defends themselves as a criminal. And it was all because Leftists pushed a false narrative, and lied about George Zimmerman in order to keep the false narrative alive.

Urban Crime and the War on Poverty

As we've seen above, the Leftist in both media and elected office see violence as an opportunity to exploit the American electorate. They often take advantage of the heightened sensitivities of the general public following a tragedy to push an agenda. In reality, though, their agenda is to either silence dissention, restrict Second Amendment rights, or simply to reinforce their belief that American citizens are particularly violent, racist, or both.

For instance, after the mass shooting at a Connecticut elementary school in December 2012, many talking heads on television as well as some elected officials crafted a narrative that the United States is unique among industrialized nations in the rate of violent crimes, especially crimes committed with guns. Certain catch phrases were used by the echo-chamber news media and Leftist politicians to sell the false narrative, such as when a *New York Times* news article from Jan. 5, 2013, noted that there had been an "expansion of gun violence in America."[139]

A *Chicago Sun-Times* headline on Dec. 28, 2012, read: "Gun violence reverberates through nation in a year of mass killings."[140] In January 2013, the Obama White House ordered the formation of a task force to study policies to reduce "gun violence."[141] Yet, the FBI's crime statistics show very clearly that the violent crime rate in the United States had been declining steadily for twenty years.

In 1992, the violent crime rate in the U.S. was 757.7 per 100,000, and the murder rate was 9.3 per 100,000. In 2011, the violent crime rate had dropped to 386.3 per 100,000 (a 51 percent decrease), and the murder rate had dropped to 4.7 per 100,000 (a 50.5 percent decrease). The incidences of rapes and robberies had been halved during the same period.[142] The rate of murders with guns also declined significantly.[143]

However, if you relied solely upon the news media and politicians to determine whether the nation's crime rates were going up or down, and to determine whether you're safer in 2013 then you were two decades before, you would have been compelled to believe that violence, particularly violence committed with guns, was on the rise in America. However, if you were to come to that conclusion, you'd be wrong – dead wrong.

But, why was the narrative of a crisis in "gun violence" being crafted and pushed so strongly when the evidence showed very clearly that no crisis existed?

A close examination of the crime statistics in the U.S. indicates that the violent crime rate in urban centers with populations greater than 250,000 is nearly twice that of the national average (754.5 versus 386.3 per 100,000). Also, while the percentage of the U.S. population that is black is 12.6 percent, the percentage of murders committed in the U.S. by blacks is 37.7 percent.[144] A whopping 80 to 90 percent of their murder victims are also black. If you break the numbers down further, and count only murders committed by 13-29 year olds, blacks committed 3394 murders and whites committed 2278 in 2011. Yet, blacks represent less than one-fifth of the white population.[145]

The statistics seem to suggest that young black men are far more violent than their white counterparts. While men in general commit far more violent crimes than women, and young men are far more violent statistically than older men, it appears that young black men are statistically the most violent group in the U.S. That's a remarkable assertion, though, and if the evidence does indeed suggest it is true, then perhaps that would explain why certain statistics are not discussed by Leftists committed to a particular narrative.

But, if it is true, the question must be asked, why are black men the most violent group in the U.S.?

Studies of suicides indicate that men, in general, kill themselves at much higher rates than women. Warren Farrell noted in *USA Today*: "Boys and girls at age 9 are almost equally likely to commit suicide; by age 14, boys are twice as likely; by 19, four times; by 24, more than five times. The more a boy absorbs the male role and male hormones, the more he commits suicide."[146]

The same is true for violence in general. Boys are generally more violent than girls, and men are far more violent than women. This fact has been known for thousands of years. Boys make the best young soldiers. Entire cultures have flourished by harnessing the power of testosterone-laden young men. In ancient Sparta, young men were intentionally separated from their mothers and shaped into fighting machines. In many ancient cultures, young men were trained from early age to fight as part of an army. The fact that men are the more violent of the two sexes is indisputable.

But, when even a half-decent father is present in a boy's life, and a society esteems a nuclear family unit, a boy's chances of behaving violently are far less than when a father is absent. Thousands of years of human history and tradition indicate very clearly that a father is vital to the development of an adolescent boy; to teach him how to deal with the massive surge of testosterone running through his veins. Centuries of evidence seems to indicate that the absence of fathers in young men's lives is the likely root cause of outrageous rates of violence.

But the Leftist – whose view of human nature is based on Jean-Jacques Rousseau's ideas – sees these staggering statistics and says that economic inequality and systemic racism are to blame for the violence in the black community. As I noted in the Introduction, the Leftist sees the world through the lens of materialism. All problems and all solutions are material in nature. When Leftists talk of money and evil, they say that "money is the root of all evil." When Leftists talk of crime and violence, they say that guns and economic inequality are the problem.

However, the conservative argues that, as the Bible says, is it "the love of money that is the root of all evil" (1 Timothy 6:2), not the money itself. The conservative argues that, as the Bible teaches, from the "callous heart comes iniquity" (Psalm 73:7), and sin in the heart angers God (Psalm 66:18). The conservative argues that the individual must take responsibility for his actions, and cannot place blame on inanimate objects like money and guns. The conservative argues that the solution must be found within, not without.

Therefore, the conservative view of human nature – which is based on Thomas Hobbes, Adam Smith, and the ancients who wrote the Bible – sees these troubling statistics and recognizes that the problem likely is spiritual in nature. There are deep character flaws in people who chose a life of crime and violence, regardless of the color of their skin; regardless of their economic status; regardless of the history of their family. The decaying black culture is a symptom of a deeper problem – a character problem. Thus, the solution to the problem is spiritual in nature.

The problem can only be solved by healing the wounds of the soul and rebuilding character. Receiving free handouts from faceless bureaucrats in a distant capital city is not the solution, as the Leftist would have us believe; nor is forcefully redistributing wealth from rich to poor. The establishment of a new bureaucracy, or the expansion of an existing bureaucracy, is also not the answer. The answer has been known for thousands of years. It's family.

A host of studies show a clear link between out-of-wedlock birth rates and poverty. Children born to unwed mothers are far more likely to end up in poverty than those born into two parent families. And children raised by unwed mothers are far more likely to choose a life of crime. The rate of unwed births for blacks is a whopping 72.3 percent. For whites, it's 28.6 percent.[147] The solution to the problem in the black community is a stable, two-parent family.

Black *Washington Post* columnist William Raspberry attended a gathering of Christian ministers who discussed the collapse of the American family, particularly the black American family. Raspberry noted: "The absence of fathers means…that girls lack both a pattern against which to measure the boys who pursue them and an example of sacrificial love between a man and a woman." He noted further that the problem is not external or material, as the Leftist would have us believe, but internal and spiritual:

> …black America's almost reflexive search for outside explanations for our internal problems delayed the introspective examination that might have slowed the trend. What we have now

> is a changed culture – a culture whose worst aspects are reinforced by oversexualized popular entertainment and that places a reduced value on the things that produced nearly a century of socioeconomic improvement. For the first time since slavery, it is no longer possible to say with assurance that things are getting better.[148]

Senator Daniel Patrick Moynihan conducted a study and authored a report in 1965 entitled, "The Negro Family: The Case for National Action," which suggested that the disintegration of the family would bring about chaos in black communities. Curiously, in spite of a vast array of data to support his argument, Leftists denied that the root cause of the relatively high poverty and crime rates in black neighborhoods were associated in any way with a character or spiritual problem evident in the high rates of unwed births. Instead, they argued that the root cause was systemic racism, poverty, and lack of opportunity. They criticized Moynihan for "blaming the victim," and continued pushing the narrative that racism was the root cause of the problems in America's black communities.[149]

Curiously, while Leftists today push the narrative that American was and remains a uniquely racist nation, and that a racist system is the root cause of the poverty, crime, and unwed motherhood rates in the black community, studies of the effect that Leftist policies have had on the black community are dismissed. They are dismissed because they don't fit the narrative. Yet, the evidence is rather compelling that Leftist public policies indeed have severely affected inner cities, and not for the better.

For instance, the Brookings Institute's George A. Akerlof and Janet L. Yellen note that a confluence of factors contributed to the increased rates of out-of-wedlock births for American women of all races beginning in the 1960s.[150] The first factor was easier access to abortion and contraceptives, and the concomitant decline in "shotgun weddings." The stigma of unwed pregnancy declined as access to these resources increased. Women entered the workforce in greater numbers, and men's views of women changed significantly, as they themselves were also freed from the consequences of casual sex. The "sexual revolution" altered the relationship dynamic between men and women.

The second factor was expanded public subsistence and welfare. Easier access to welfare checks displaced fathers as key figures in the lives of their children. Once men realized that their responsibilities to a pregnant woman had been taken over by the state, they felt less urgency to stick around. With unwed mothers receiving government assistance in the form of a monthly check, men felt less obligated to fill the role of provider, and women felt less obligated to keep the man around as a provider. The result, of course, was a decline in fathers and an increase in unwed mothers.

The third factor was the liberalization of sexual behavior, a direct consequence of Leftist social attitudes about marriage and sex that emerged during the "free love" movement of the 1960s. The "sexual revolution" movement actually began in the early 20th century, and especially flourished in the 1920s. However, the Great Depression interrupted the revolution temporarily. When it reemerged in the 1960s, it was reinforced by the development of oral contraceptives, as was noted above.

In each case, we see Progressive/Leftist ideals being embraced by the culture, and in each case we see those ideals negatively affecting society. The Progressive ideal of sexual promiscuity, coupled with Leftists' insistence that expanded federal anti-poverty programs are the solution to the problems plaguing poor communities, were embraced by a population that was already in the process of remedying those problems. In short, a consistently declining poverty rate was completely dismissed or overlooked, and a false narrative was crafted in which the federal government was seen as the only mechanism to solve a problem that was already being remedied by forces other than the federal government.

In 1964, when Democratic President Lyndon B. Johnson's administration and a Democratic Party in Congress passed several key pieces of legislation to fight a "War on Poverty," the poverty rate in the U.S. had been declining steadily for five years. But Leftists, as they always do, insisted that a crisis existed and a massive bureaucracy (which in essence means more bureaucracy and more federal spending) was needed to fix it. As a result of the "war on poverty," which began officially in 1965, welfare spending began to increase, slowly at first.

But by the 1970s, government bureaucrats with a vested interest in keeping their bureaucratic jobs, pointed out that the poverty rate was still rising, which it was, in spite of their already expensive poverty-fighting programs. Congress voted to expand "war on poverty" programs, and the level of welfare spending skyrocketed. Spending on means-tested welfare programs (cash, food, housing, medical care, etc.) for the poor grew from less than $75 billion in 1964, to $200 billion in 1974, to $600 billion in 1996. By 2011, the cost of the "war on poverty" had grown to nearly $1000 billion per year.[151]

What did all that spending get us?

When the Johnson administration, as well as a Democrat-controlled House and Senate, insisted that increased federal spending was required to fight a "war on poverty" in America, the poverty rate was in decline already, and had declined steadily from 22.4 percent in 1959 to approximately 16 percent in 1965, when the vast majority of War on Poverty programs went into effect. By 1970, the rate had declined to approximately 13 percent. However, by 1993, the rate had increased to 15 percent and remained consistently high through 2009.[152]

In short, before Lyndon Johnson and a Democratic-controlled Congress started their "war on poverty," the poverty rate had fallen by 28 percent in just six years. However, after spending trillions of taxpayer dollars over four decades to fight poverty and help the poor, the federal government was able to reduce poverty by a measly 10 percent. Yet, the Leftist will arrogantly insist, as they always do, that more spending on government programs will reduce crime and violence in America's most troubled communities.

Meanwhile, crime and out-of-wedlock birth rates skyrocketed as a direct result of these poverty programs, as well as the "sexual revolution." The Leftist will never admit that their policies have harmed the black community; by driving out fathers and sentencing millions of young black men to a life of poverty, crime, violence, and incarceration. They will never admit that their policies are responsible for creating a vicious cycle of perpetual decline and hopelessness.

Instead, Leftists continue to push the false narrative that systemic racism and economic inequality are the root causes of violence in America's inner cities, and that more spending on bloated, centralized bureaucracies in a distant capital, as well as greater restrictions on guns and the Second Amendment, are the solution. And, as was demonstrated above, they are willing to lie and deceive and demonize their political opponents in order to keep the false narrative alive, no matter who gets hurt in the process.

This explains why when dozens of black teens were shot by other black teens over a single weekend in July 2012, in President Obama's hometown of Chicago, he said nothing. There were no White House press releases, nor were there any task forces created to solve the epidemic of violence in black neighborhoods in America's cities. Yet, when a so-called "white Hispanic" man shot one black teenager in Florida, President Obama held a news conference to highlight it and draw national attention to it, and even suggested that if he'd had a son, he would have looked very much like the young black teenager who was shot.

In President Obama's mind, the former story doesn't fit the narrative. However, the latter story fits very nicely into the narrative that America is a nation of racists, and it's that racism that is causing the violence in America's inner cities.

When It Does Not Fit the Narrative...Just Ignore It

Just two days after the mass shooting at a Connecticut elementary school in December 2012, a man with a gun entered a Chinese restaurant in San Antonio, Texas. It was 9:30 p.m. The man, Jesus Manuel Garcia, 19, was an employee of the restaurant and was looking for his former girlfriend, who had recently broken up with him. She was not in the restaurant.

Garcia was determined to kill someone, and when the employees fled the restaurant and ran to a nearby movie theater, he followed. Garcia shot a bullet into the windshield of a police car, and entered the theater in pursuit of the fleeing employees. When Garcia fired several shots inside the theater, people fled in panic, fearing a mass slaughter.

An off-duty Bexar County Sheriff's Department officer, Sgt. Lisa Castellano, who was on scene providing security, returned fire and struck Garcia with four rounds. Garcia was taken to a hospital in stable condition. Sgt. Lisa Cuello Castellano was awarded a Medal of Valor for her actions.[153]

This incident was (nearly) completely overlooked by Leftists in the echo-chamber media, as were numerous other instances of citizens using a gun to prevent a determined killer from taking lives.[154] In fact, CBS News covered the San Antonio movie theater shooting, but only on their website where few people are likely to see it. And the story CBS News offered its readers only briefly noted the fact that a gun was used to stop a mass shooting – the narrative of the CBS News story was that a gunman shot some people and caused some panic at a movie theater.[155]

The National Rifle Association (NRA) has been collecting stories about armed citizens preventing or stopping crimes for many years, and those stories are legion.[156] However, few of them are covered by the national news media, giving the general impression that guns are never used by law-abiding citizens in self-defense, but are only used by lunatics committing mass murder.

The lack of coverage of the hundreds of thousands of cases of law-abiding citizens in America preventing or stopping crime is not necessarily intentional. The old adage "if it bleeds, it leads," is quite true. However, if there were far more journalists who felt that these incidents were important to crafting or sustaining a particular narrative, then perhaps more of them would get attention.

But, as has been demonstrated, Leftists in the echo-chamber media do not hear about these stories, and even if they did, they would not understand their significance to the overall narrative about violence in America. Thus, they ignore them because they just don't fit the narrative that guns are evil, and anyone who owns them is either a racist, Neanderthal, or cowboy lunatic.

CHAPTER THREE – THE PRAETORIAN GUARD

On Friday, October 11, 2002, five months before U.S. and coalition forces invaded Iraq, both houses of Congress approved a resolution that authorized President George W. Bush to use military force against Saddam Hussein's regime in Iraq.[1] In the House of Representatives, 215 Republicans and 81 Democrats voted in favor of the resolution. In the Senate, 48 Republicans and 29 Democrats voted in favor. It was a bipartisan resolution, and it contained 23 "whereas" clauses – that is, Congress made 23 separate arguments to justify the use of military force against Saddam Hussein's regime.

The bulk of the arguments focused on Saddam Hussein's rejection of United Nations resolutions – seventeen of them! Here's a summary of the arguments made by the U.S. Congress in its authorization of the use of force against Saddam Hussein:

- Iraq's non-compliance with the demands of the cease fire in 1991, including his repeated attempts to deceive UN weapons inspectors.
- Iraq's weapons of mass destruction (WMD) and WMD programs.

- Iraq's "brutal repression of its civilian population."
- Iraq's history of using WMD on the Iranian military and Iraqi citizens.
- Iraq's 1993 assassination attempt of former President George H. W. Bush.
- Iraq's firing on coalition aircraft enforcing the United Nations-mandated no-fly zones throughout the 1990s.
- Iraq's harboring of al-Qaeda members.
- Iraq's continued efforts "to aid and harbor other international terrorist organizations," including terrorist organizations determined to kill Americans.
- A Constitutional obligation for Congress and the President to fight terrorists and to confront nations that harbor them.
- Iraq's unprovoked wars against Iran and Kuwait created instability in the region – neighboring states Turkey, Kuwait, and Saudi Arabia feared that Saddam Hussein would target them next.
- Saddam Hussein paid families of suicide bombers $50,000 dollars, creating a financial incentive for continued martyrdom attacks around the world.
- The Iraq Liberation Act of 1998, a bipartisan Congressional resolution, made it the policy of the United States government to remove Saddam Hussein and his Ba'ath Party regime from power, and to promote a democratic replacement.[2]

Only three of the nearly two dozen arguments made by Congress in its authorization for the use of force in Iraq were related to Saddam Hussein's WMDs or WMD programs. The remaining *whereas* clauses were all related to other factors, such as his continued violation of UN resolutions, his history of using chemical weapons on both Iranians and Iraqis, and his history of invading neighboring states. Yet, it's the WMD issue that is most remembered, not the tyrant's brutal history.

As a result, a prevailing narrative persists today about the Iraq War which says that President Bush lied about Iraqi WMD. The narrative also says that Bush rushed the nation into war without consulting anyone outside the administration. Another false narrative concocted by echo-chamber Leftists says that the Bush administration tortured foreigners, via a practice called "enhanced interrogation techniques," in direct violation of international law. All of these narratives will be explored in this chapter.

Also, this chapter will examine the way the media has confronted the use of unmanned, remote-controlled drones by President Obama in his administration's "war on man-made disasters." Finally, it will examine President Obama's handling of the two wars he inherited from the previous administration, as well as the war on terrorism, and how the echo-chamber media altered its narratives about those wars following the election of a Democratic president.

Going It Alone

When President Barack Obama was confronted with the growing violence in Libya in February 2011, the echo-chamber media started to ratchet up the narrative that, unlike Bush, Obama was not going to "go it alone" and invade an Arab country unilaterally. President Obama addressed the nation on March 28, 2011, and made the case for using the U.S. military against the regime of Libyan dictator Muammar Qaddafi. The president reminded Americans that his actions in Africa would not be viewed as unilateral. He said that America was not acting alone, but had been "joined by a strong and growing coalition." He stressed that it was "a broad coalition." He noted further that "American leadership is not simply a matter of going it alone..."[3] President Obama insisted that he was not like his predecessor, the cowboy president from Texas.

While President Obama made his case, his Leftist comrades in newsrooms across the nation formed a circle around their Leftist president – a Praetorian Guard, of sorts. Reuters, for instance, reminded readers that "Obama is committed to partnering with other countries rather than going it alone as did his predecessor George W. Bush." The author made certain to highlight how President Obama was "struggling to fashion a cohesive Middle East policy that can encompass his decision to launch military action in Libya alongside his hesitant response to repression elsewhere."

The reporter deftly maneuvered his way around President Obama's silence in the face of brutal oppression by the Islamic regime in Tehran just a year before the Libya crisis. The Iranian regime had cracked down on protesters and thousands of people were killed or injured, and the brutality of the regime was broadcast around the world via social media. President Obama not only refused to act, he refused to even comment on the scenes of slaughter that were being posted on websites around the world. Crowds of protesters called for America's assistance or support, but those calls were ignored by the Obama White House. President Obama got a pass from the echo-chamber media for refusing Iranian freedom seekers any assistance, even a simple condemnatory press release. Even more, his failure to respond was cited as evidence that he was a true statesman who would chose his battles wisely rather than rushing into the darkness.

Not content to just draw a stark contrast between presidents Bush and Obama, Reuters reminded readers in 2011 of the "serious challenge" facing the Obama administration vis-à-vis the crisis in Libya, and how it's "not easy to strike a balance between pragmatism and principle."[4] Reuters had raised their shields to deflect criticism away from a Leftist administration, and a narrative was carefully crafted by a variety of echo-chamber media outlets. The Obama White House couldn't have written it any better.

The echo-chamber media pushed the prevailing narrative hard in order to make their case that Bush was a rogue warmonger while Obama was a thoughtful statesman and foreign policy expert:

- Journalist Jonathon Alter offered a defense President Obama: "...he's a reluctant warrior. So it's not as if he's converted to being a cowboy. So I think people recognize the difference between him and former Pres. Bush."[5]
- *Newsweek*'s Eleanor Clift said Bush went into Iraq "all alone."[6]
- A *New York Times* journalist wrote in 2011: "Mr. Obama made much of his commitment to a multilateral foreign policy, in contrast to President George W. Bush's unilateral invasion of Iraq.... the United States can no longer afford another big, go-it-alone military campaign."[7]
- Rep. Anthony Weiner (D-NY) said Bush went it alone in Iraq, but Obama was obligated to use the U.S. military. He asked rhetorically: "What's the value of being a great, powerful country if we're not going to

step in against tyrants that are slaughtering their point and that's the point the President made tonight."[8]

- A *New York Times* opinion writer defended Obama's actions in Libya and made the distinction between the former cowboy-in-chief and the Harvard-trained lawyer: "In his deliberative fashion, Obama ultimately saved countless lives." He added: "Republicans can't cope with a president who tries to think before he leaps."[9]
- The *Los Angeles Times* editorial staff condemned Bush's "go-it-alone cowboyism" and praised Obama for creating a "multilateralist's dream."[10]
- CBS News highlighted how "poised" the Obama administration was during the crisis, and their national security correspondent, David Martin, reminded viewers and readers that Obama "does not want to go to it alone here."[11]
- NBC News' Andrea Mitchell in March 2011 praised Obama's Ambassador to the United Nations Susan Rice for her "remarkable job at the UN," and her "adept diplomacy." Rice had managed to get a resolution passed to condemn the Libyan dictator's brutal crackdown on his own people.
- CBS News' Norah O'Donnell said in October 2011 that the removal of Qaddafi "will no doubt burnish his credentials as a world leader, as a President who can fight terrorism."
- NBC News' David Gregory said in October 2011: "This is a leadership moment for the President....This is a President who has been tested now repeatedly in that arena, and I think it's something that he'll try to use as a club against Republicans in the debate."[12]

Throughout the coverage of the events in Libya, the narrative was repeated over and over again. President Obama was a breath of fresh air; a statesman who would repair the harm done to America's image around the world by the cowboy president George W. Bush. The narrative's chief feature was that unlike Bush, Obama was not "going it alone."

A writer at the conservative think tank The Heritage Foundation dissected the argument often made by echo-chamber Leftists in media that "Bush went it alone" in Iraq. Nile Gardiner noted that when the U.S. military entered Iraq, there were "over 145,000 Coalition personnel from over 30 nations serving in Iraq…including 23,000 non-U.S. military personnel." In addition, thousands of coalition personnel were on their way to Iraq, "including 3,000 from South Korea." The coalition consisted of "21 nations from Europe, and nine from Asia and Australasia," including "12 of 25 members of the European Union, as well as 16 of the 26 NATO (North Atlantic Treaty Organization) member states."[13]

Back in 2002 and 2003, with a large coalition allied with the United States against Iraq, Gardiner recalls that, in spite of the echo-chamber Leftist narrative, "opposition of French President Jacques Chirac and German Chancellor Gerhard Schroeder to the U.S.-led liberation of Iraq" did not represent "Europe as a whole." Rather, "a majority of European governments backed the U.S. decision to liberate the Iraqi people." Leftists in the echo chamber and in Congress, though, who were opposed to a U.S.-led invasion to end Saddam Hussein's regime found themselves allied more with France and Germany than with the host of nations joining the U.S. in their effort to end a tyrannical regime. The vast majority of European nations sided with Bush, while the vast majority of echo-chamber Leftists sided with France and Germany, and with Saddam Hussein.

President George W. Bush, after going to Congress to seek authorization, went to the United Nations on September 12, 2002, and made his case for removing Saddam Hussein from power. As a result of his efforts, and as a consequence of his presentation to the world community, the United Nations Security Council, on November 8, 2002, passed United Nations Security Council Resolution (UNSCR) 1441, which stated that the Iraqi dictator was being given "a final opportunity to comply with its disarmament obligations," or face serious consequences. The resolution passed the UNSC by a vote of 15-0, including "yes" votes from noted oppositionists Russia, China, France, and even a host of Arab nations.

The differences in the way echo-chamber media elitists treated two presidents at a time of war was stark: On the one hand, you had a president of the United States, George W. Bush, going to Congress to obtain authorization for using America's military. You had a president going to the United Nations in person and making his case for using America's military to remove Saddam Hussein from power. You had nearly nine months of an administration making a robust case for war to both a foreign and domestic audience. You had a president who built a coalition of 30 nations who were willing to commit their military, their money, and their time and precious resources, to a military cause in an Arab state.

On the other hand, you had a president, Barack Obama, who felt it unnecessary to seek Congressional approval for using America's military – and received a bipartisan rebuke for failing to do so.[14] You had a president who never once bothered to go to the United Nations himself, as Bush had done, to make the case for using America's military in an Arab state. You had an administration that was able to rally, not thirty, but a mere eight other nations to commit their resources and treasure to the cause.

And the media elitists in the echo chamber still insist that Bush "went it alone."

Why Iraq?

In early 2011, former Secretary of Defense Donald Rumsfeld appeared on Comedy Central's "The Daily Show" with Jon Stewart. Rumsfeld was promoting an autobiography and the discussion turned almost immediately to the Iraq war. Stewart asked Rumsfeld why the Bush administration singled out Saddam Hussein's Iraq, rather than seeking a regime change in, say, Libya or Pakistan. Rumsfeld should have reminded Stewart and his viewers that the authorization for war came from Congress, and the vote for the authorization was bipartisan. Rumsfeld should have reminded Stewart that, in 1998, the Clinton administration made it the official policy of the U.S. government that Saddam Hussein's regime should be eliminated. In fact, the groundwork for the passage of the "Iraq Liberation Act of 1998" was laid by none other than Bill Clinton himself in a February 1998 speech:

> Iraq admitted, among other things, an offensive biological warfare capability, notably, 5,000 gallons of botulinum, which causes botulism; 2,000 gallons of anthrax; 25 biological-filled Scud warheads; and 157 aerial bombs. And I might say UNSCOM inspectors believe that Iraq has actually greatly understated its production....
>
> Over the past few months, as [the weapons

> inspectors] have come closer and closer to rooting out Iraq's remaining nuclear capacity, Saddam has undertaken yet another gambit to thwart their ambitions by imposing debilitating conditions on the inspectors and declaring key sites which have still not been inspected off limits....
>
> It is obvious that there is an attempt here, based on the whole history of this operation since 1991, to protect whatever remains of his capacity to produce weapons of mass destruction, the missiles to deliver them, and the feed stocks necessary to produce them. The UNSCOM inspectors believe that Iraq still has stockpiles of chemical and biological munitions, a small force of Scud-type missiles, and the capacity to restart quickly its production program and build many, many more weapons....
>
> Now, let's imagine the future. What if he fails to comply and we fail to act, or we take some ambiguous third route, which gives him yet more opportunities to develop this program of weapons of mass destruction and continue to press for the release of the sanctions and continue to ignore the solemn commitments that he made? Well, he will conclude that the international community has lost its will. He will then conclude that he can go right on and do more to rebuild an arsenal of devastating destruction. And some day, some way, I guarantee you he'll use the arsenal.[15]

The people nestled comfortably in the echo chamber are willingly ignorant of the fact that it was a Democratic president who made it the policy of the U.S. government to seek the end of Saddam Hussein's regime. It doesn't fit the narrative, thus it's ignored. Jon Stewart was unaware of this fact, which is why he asked his abjectly ignorant question, "why Iraq?" He was unaware of the fact that, unlike Pakistan or Libya, Saddam Hussein's Iraqi regime had been targeted for destruction by Democratic President Bill Clinton and a bipartisan Congress.

Why did the U.S. government single out Saddam Hussein and his Baath Party regime? Among all the tyrannies around the world, why did the Iraqi regime draw so much attention from Congress and the President of the United States? Here is a timeline of events related to Saddam Hussein's actions from 1990 to the time of the passage of the bipartisan "Authorization for Use of Military Force Against Iraq Resolution of 2002." Each of these events was cited by Congress in its authorization for the use of force, and each was considered by President Bush as he weighed the decision to use the American military to remove Saddam Hussein from power:

- August 2, 1990: Iraqi forces invaded Kuwait.
- August 2, 1990: UNSCR 660 condemned Iraq's actions.
- August 6, 1990: UNSCR 661 established sanctions against Saddam Hussein's regime.
- August 25, 1990: UNSCR 665 established a shipping blockade in the Persian Gulf.
- November 29, 1990: UNSCR 678 authorizes member states to "use all necessary means" to bring Iraq into compliance with previous UN resolutions.
- January 17, 1991: Coalition forces began bombing in Baghdad, Operation Desert Storm starts.
- April 3, 1991: UNSCR 687 authorized a ceasefire (the official end of Gulf War I).

- April 5, 1991: UNSCR 688 called for Hussein to immediately cease hostilities against Iraqi civilians, but did NOT authorize a no-fly zone.
- June 17, 1991: UNSCR 700 approved the Secretary-General's guidelines on an arms and dual-use embargo on Iraq.
- August 15, 1991: UNSCR 706 allowed emergency oil sale by Iraq to fund compensation claims, weapons inspection and humanitarian needs in Iraq.
- August 15, 1991: UNSCR 707 condemned Iraq's non-compliance on weapons inspections as a "material breach" of Resolution 687, and incorporates into its standard for compliance with SCR687 that Iraq provide "full, final and complete disclosure ... of all aspects of its programs to develop" prohibited weaponry. Also grants permission for UNSCOM and the IAEA to conduct flights throughout Iraq, for surveillance or logistical purposes.
- October 15, 1994: UNSCR 949 Condemns recent military deployments by Iraq "in the direction of ... Kuwait", demanded an immediate withdrawal and full co-operation with UNSCOM.
- April 14, 1995: UNSCR 986 authorized the "oil for food" program, allowing $1 billion in oil sales every 90 days for humanitarian purposes.
- June 12, 1996: UNSCR 1060 condemned Iraq's refusal to allow access to sites designated by the Special Commission.
- June 21, 1997: UNSCR 1115 condemned the repeated refusal of the Iraqi authorities to allow access to sites and demanded that Iraq cooperate fully with UNSCOM.

- October 23, 1997: UNSCR 1124 reaffirmed Iraq's obligations to cooperate with weapons inspectors after Iraqi officials announced in September 1997 that "presidential sites" are off-limits to inspectors. The resolution also threatened travel bans on obstructive Iraqi officials not "carrying out bona fide diplomatic assignments or missions" if non-cooperation continued.
- February 20, 1998: UNSCR 1153 permitted an increase in the cap on Iraqi oil sales to $5.256 billion.
- September 9, 1998: UNSCR 1194 condemned the decision by Iraq ... to suspend cooperation with [UNSCOM] and the IAEA.
- October 31, 1998: President Clinton signs the Iraq Liberation Act, which made it the official policy of the U.S. government to support the removal of Saddam Hussein from power.
- December 16-19, 1998: Operation Desert Fox. President Bill Clinton authorizes missile and aircraft strikes on suspected Iraqi WMD sites.

Thus, in response to the question, "why Iraq?" the answer is obvious. No other nation had racked up the outrageous litany of abuses of the international community's demands – 17 UN resolutions were ignored. No other nation was actively attacking U.S. military aircraft enforcing UN no-fly zones. No other nation could claim, as Hussein's Iraq could, that the will of international community meant nothing. The fact is that Saddam Hussein had exhausted the patience of the world, and America was willing and able to act, and to draw a line in the sand and exact justice on a rogue tyrant.

Polls indicate that Jon Stewart may be the single largest source of news for America's newest generation of voters –

who, by the way, voted overwhelmingly for Barack Obama over John McCain in 2008. If Mr. Stewart actually took that responsibility seriously, perhaps he or his producers would have devoted a few minutes to finding out about the facts surrounding one of the century's most significant global events – the March 2003 invasion of Iraq. They would have recognized that Saddam Hussein was a uniquely dangerous threat to peace in the Middle East and elsewhere. But, that's what living in the echo chamber does. It makes you ignorant, or at least naive. It makes you ask, "why Iraq?"

Bush Lied, People Died

In 2004, as the Iraq war effort stumbled and the death toll rose, echo-chamber Leftists in both media and elective office began to focus their attention towards the absence of Saddam Hussein's weapons of mass destruction (WMD). Curiously, the attention devoted by echo-chamber Leftists to the WMD issue far outweighed the issue's significance in the justification for war. In other words, the WMD issue was only one aspect of the justification for war – there were a host of other justifications. As we saw at the top of this chapter, the issue of Saddam Hussein possessing WMD was only part of the argument for going to war.

Of course the threat Saddam Hussein posed via those WMD was highlighted by the Bush administration, as it should have been by anyone interested in preventing another 9/11 attack. An attack on American soil with biological, chemical, or radiological weapons would have devastated the nation's economy and global interests. It would have severely affected the nation's sense of safety even further in the shadow of 9/11.

Thus, echo-chamber Leftists couldn't argue that Saddam

Hussein had not thumbed his nose at the international community by violating the demands of 17 UN resolutions. The evidence was overwhelming that he had. They couldn't argue that Saddam Hussein was a nice guy – though propagandist Michael Moore did his best in "Fahrenheit 911" when he portrayed Iraq as an idyllic utopia where children played in parks and families shopped in the streets, and the Saddam Hussein regime was portrayed as no more dangerous than, say, Japan's government. The torture chambers, the mass graves; the 8-year war against Iran; the invasion and brutalization of Kuwait; the defiance of UN resolutions; they were all irrelevant in Moore's twisted tale of Iraqi bliss. Hollywood superstar Sean Penn toured hospitals and elementary schools in Iraq in December 2002 to make the case that Saddam Hussein posed no threat to the world.[16]

After the invasion, as news reports shaped the narrative that no WMD had been found in Iraq, instead of focusing on Hussein's brutality, a disproportionate amount of attention was devoted to the WMD issue. This in spite of the host of other issues Congress cited as justifications for the use of military force. The absence of Iraqi WMD was not viewed as evidence of an intelligence failure; it became evidence that Bush either knew there were no stockpiles, and thus deceived the American people, or Bush was a clueless dolt who blundered the nation into an unjustifiable war. It was the former item that became the preferred narrative. It started with a slogan: "Bush Lied, People Died."

The slogan's roots can be traced to a U.S. Agency for International Development (USAID) contractor named C. Edward Bernier. Bernier was hired by USAID as a media consultant and flown to Kuwait in February 2003 to help propagandize the war effort, as governments are inclined to do for obvious reasons. Since even before the war, Bernier's instincts were that America targeted Iraq solely for its oil. Bernier told friends and colleagues that he was "disgusted" by the warm reactions and open embrace Iraqis gave to U.S. troops in the first few months of Operation Iraqi Freedom (OIF). Bernier quit his $685 per day job after just a few months and returned home to Hilton Head, South Carolina. He told friends that while in Iraq he was able to "dig up stuff" that he could use to make President George W. Bush look bad.

Bernier and his wife, a longtime Democratic Party operative and vocal critic of the war effort, crafted a lengthy email and sent it to his friends in the foreign services. In that email, Bernier wrote that Bush lied about WMD in Iraq, that American men and women and innocent Iraqis were suffering as a consequence of Bush's lies, and that a concerted campaign should be launched nationwide to craft a narrative to that effect. He recommended a bumper sticker: "Bush lies," and recommended a national campaign to raise money to get the word out.[17]

While the Bernier campaign effort was getting underway, news broke that the CIA had sent a "retired U.S. ambassador" to Niger, an African nation known for its robust uranium mines. The former ambassador was sent there to find alleged links between the Hussein regime and uranium yellowcake materials that could be used to build a nuclear bomb. President Bush had made the claim during his 2002 State of the Union Address that Saddam Hussein had tried to purchase uranium from Niger, and former ambassador Joseph C. Wilson IV was sent, so the story went, by the CIA to investigate the Niger story. According to news reports, Wilson conducted his "unbiased" investigation and found that Bush's claim was abjectly false; there were documents in Niger related to uranium yellowcake and Saddam Hussein, Wilson admitted, but they were forgeries. That was the conclusion of the Ambassador's report to the CIA. At least that was the narrative perpetuated by Ambassador Wilson and his comrades in the echo-chamber media.

Wilson was not satisfied with the level of media attention devoted to his story, so he wrote a lengthy *New York Times* op-ed detailing his findings. Wilson argued that the Bush administration knew the documents were forgeries but chose instead to "manipulate intelligence...to justify an invasion of Iraq." Wilson said that Bush administration officials exaggerated the threat posed by Saddam Hussein's weapons and intentionally deceived the American people. The *Times* piece went viral. Combined with the Bernier campaign, the narrative that "Bush Lied" was born.

It wasn't until a year later that the Ambassador's story was exposed as a lie. It turned out that there were documents dating from 1999 that indicated Saddam Hussein did indeed seek uranium yellowcake from Niger, as Bush had asserted, and as Ambassador Wilson testified to during his CIA debriefing and in his official report to the spy agency.[18] Wilson also told the CIA that Iraq and Niger had developed an extensive commercial relationship that most analysts believed included uranium sales and weapons transfers, all of which was in direct violation of several United Nations resolutions. Even more, the CIA reviewed Wilson's report and concluded that his evidence "lent more credibility to the original [CIA] reports on the uranium deal." But, most remarkable, was that Wilson's report was classified "Secret" by the CIA. Yet, Wilson had disclosed the sensitive information in a newspaper article because he wanted to score political points with his echo-chamber Leftist colleagues, and because he wanted to embarrass the Bush administration.[19]

What was hardly ever discussed by media news outlets during this whole affair was the fact that Joe Wilson had been a Democratic Operative for years. He had worked for Al Gore and Tom Foley, both prominent Democrats in Washington. Also, just months before his infamous whistle-blowing op-ed, Wilson signed on to the John Kerry presidential campaign as an advisor. It was his wife, Valerie Plame, a CIA employee and a Democratic operative, who engineered his Niger visit in order to craft a false narrative about the Bush administration. None of these facts were ever discussed while the "Bush Lied" narrative was carefully crafted. Had news of Wilson's political ties with prominent Democrats and history as a party operative been noted, the false narrative may have fallen on deaf ears, or at the very least been scrutinized more closely. The echo-chamber media instead told their readers, listeners, and viewers, a story about a true American patriot, Joe Wilson, who had exposed the Bush administration's lies. It was a simple tale of a president lying and a brave whistle-blower exposing the lie.

However, like most false narratives concocted by the echo-chamber media, the narrative that "Bush Lied, People Died," just does not stand up to scrutiny. For example, if George W. Bush lied about Iraq's WMD programs, as the narrative insists, then he knew something that no one else in the world knew. In fact, all the evidence indicates that, if there were indeed no WMD programs in Iraq, and there were no stockpiles in Iraq before U.S. and coalition forces invaded in March 2003, then everyone had been misled, not just the president of the United States.

For instance, consider the following statements about

Saddam Hussein's WMD programs made by prominent Democrats:

> "One way or the other, we are determined to deny Iraq the capacity to develop weapons of mass destruction and the missiles to deliver them. That is our bottom line." – President Bill Clinton, Feb. 4, 1998
>
> "If Saddam rejects peace and we have to use force, our purpose is clear. We want to seriously diminish the threat posed by Iraq's weapons of mass destruction program." – President Bill Clinton, Feb. 17, 1998
>
> "Iraq is a long way from [here], but what happens there matters a great deal here. For the risks that the leaders of a rogue state will use nuclear, chemical or biological weapons against us or our allies is the greatest security threat we face." – Madeline Albright, Feb 18, 1998
>
> "He will use those weapons of mass destruction again, as he has ten times since 1983." – Sandy Berger, Clinton National Security Adviser, Feb, 18, 1998
>
> "[W]e urge you, after consulting with Congress, and consistent with the U.S. Constitution and laws, to take necessary actions (including, if appropriate, air and missile strikes on suspect Iraqi sites) to respond effectively to the threat posed by Iraq's refusal to end its weapons of mass destruction programs." – A letter to President Clinton, signed

by Democratic Senators Carl Levin, Tom Daschle, John Kerry, and others, Oct. 9, 1998

"Saddam Hussein has been engaged in the development of weapons of mass destruction technology which is a threat to countries in the region and he has made a mockery of the weapons inspection process." – Rep. Nancy Pelosi (D, CA), Dec. 16, 1998

"Hussein has ... chosen to spend his money on building weapons of mass destruction and palaces for his cronies." – Madeline Albright, Clinton Secretary of State, Nov. 10, 1999

"There is no doubt that ... Saddam Hussein has reinvigorated his weapons programs. Reports indicate that biological, chemical and nuclear programs continue apace and may be back to pre-Gulf War status. In addition, Saddam continues to redefine delivery systems and is doubtless using the cover of a licit missile program to develop longer-range missiles that will threaten the United States and our allies." – A letter to President Bush, Signed by Sen. Bob Graham (D, FL), and others, Dec 5, 2001

"We begin with the common belief that Saddam Hussein is a tyrant and a threat to the peace and stability of the region. He has ignored the mandate of the United Nations and is building weapons of mass destruction and the means of delivering them." – Sen. Carl Levin (D, MI), Sept. 19, 2002

"We know that he has stored secret supplies of

biological and chemical weapons throughout his country." – Al Gore, Sept. 23, 2002

"Iraq's search for weapons of mass destruction has proven impossible to deter and we should assume that it will continue for as long as Saddam is in power." – Al Gore, Sept. 23, 2002

"We have known for many years that Saddam Hussein is seeking and developing weapons of mass destruction." – Sen. Ted Kennedy (D, MA), Sept. 27, 2002

"The last UN weapons inspectors left Iraq in October of 1998. We are confident that Saddam Hussein retains some stockpiles of chemical and biological weapons, and that he has since embarked on a crash course to build up his chemical and biological warfare capabilities. Intelligence reports indicate that he is seeking nuclear weapons..." – Sen. Robert Byrd (D, WV), Oct. 3, 2002

"I will be voting to give the President of the United States the authority to use force — if necessary — to disarm Saddam Hussein because I believe that a deadly arsenal of weapons of mass destruction in his hands is a real and grave threat to our security." – Sen. John F. Kerry (D, MA), Oct. 9, 2002

"There is unmistakable evidence that Saddam Hussein is working aggressively to develop nuclear weapons and will likely have nuclear weapons within the next five years ... We also should remember we have always underestimated the progress Saddam has made in development of weapons of mass destruction." – Sen. Jay Rockefeller (D, WV), Oct 10, 2002

"He has systematically violated, over the course of the past 11 years, every significant UN resolution that has demanded that he disarm and destroy his chemical and biological weapons, and any nuclear capacity. This he has refused to do" – Rep. Henry Waxman (D, CA), Oct. 10, 2002

"In the four years since the inspectors left, intelligence reports show that Saddam Hussein has worked to rebuild his chemical and biological weapons stock, his missile delivery capability, and his nuclear program. He has also given aid, comfort, and sanctuary to terrorists, including al Qaeda members ... It is clear, however, that if left unchecked, Saddam Hussein will continue to increase his capacity to wage biological and chemical warfare, and will keep trying to develop nuclear weapons." – Sen. Hillary Clinton (D, NY), Oct 10, 2002

"We are in possession of what I think to be compelling evidence that Saddam Hussein has, and has had for a number of years, a developing capacity for the production and storage of weapons of mass destruction." – Sen. Bob Graham (D, FL), Dec. 8, 2002

"Without question, we need to disarm Saddam Hussein. He is a brutal, murderous dictator, leading an oppressive regime ... He presents a particularly grievous threat because he is so consistently prone to miscalculation ... And now he is miscalculating

> America's response to his continued deceit and his consistent grasp for weapons of mass destruction ... So the threat of Saddam Hussein with weapons of mass destruction is real..." – Sen. John F. Kerry (D, MA), Jan. 23. 2003[20]

Yet, in spite of all of the statements from prominent Democrats regarding Saddam Hussein's WMDs – statements that the echo-chamber never seem willing to discuss on air or write about – the narrative still lives: "Bush Lied, People Died."

Where's the Evidence?

With the "Bush Lied" and the "Bush went it alone" narratives dismantled, let's move next to the other narratives that persist today regarding the Iraq War.

The Bush administration – and 111 Democratic members of Congress – argued that Saddam Hussein had ties to international terrorist organizations, including Osama bin Laden's al Qaeda. They further argued that Saddam Hussein's regime had even harbored international terrorists within his country. They also argued that Saddam Hussein was not allowing free and unfettered inspections of all suspected WMD facilities, as was required by UN sanctions, thus it was reasonable to assume that he possessed WMDs.

First, let's examine the issue of Iraqi WMD, and how the narrative has developed since the invasion of Iraq. Leftists today are fixated on the fact that no chemical or biological weapons stockpiles were discovered in Iraq. They are also fixated on the fact that no WMD programs were discovered. Ask any co-worker, acquaintance, classmate, or person on the street, about the Iraqi WMD issue, and they will tell you that there were none; there were no WMD stockpiles, and there were no WMD programs in Iraq. The reason they will tell you that is because Leftists in the echo chamber have crafted a false narrative that has become the truth.

Leftists point to the report issued by the CIA's Iraq Survey Group (ISG), known as the Duelfer Report, as evidence that Saddam Hussein didn't have any WMDs or a WMD program. Echo-chamber Leftists say the Duelfer Report concluded that Saddam Hussein posed no threat to the United States because his WMD stockpiles and programs were destroyed well before the March 2003 invasion.

Here's the narrative at work in the echo chamber:

- CBS News's program *60 Minutes* reported: "after all this time, questions still remain as to why the United States launched the war in the first place. The Bush administration said it was because of Saddam Hussein's weapons of mass destruction. But there were no such weapons."[21]
- PBS host Tavis Smiley repeated the narrative that "Bush Lied, People Died" while appearing on MSNBC's Morning Joe. Journalist Jon Meacham of *Time* magazine, in a rare moment, actually rejected Smiley's charge.[22]
- Katie Couric suggested that George Bush manipulated intelligence related to Iraq's WMDs. Couric said: "officials knew there was a small chance of actually finding weapons of mass destruction in Iraq." She also pushed the narrative that the WMD issue was the only one used to justify the war, indicating that she and her producers have either completely erased Congress' authorization from their memories – because it just doesn't fit the narrative – or are intentionally deceiving their viewers.[23]

- ABC News' Ann Curry pushed the narrative that Iraq's WMD was the sole reason for going to war. She asked VP Joe Biden: "In a war that was started to protect the world from weapons of mass destruction that were never found, can the United States claim victory?"[24]
- MSNBC's Rachel Maddow vehemently reminded viewers that the ISG "reported six years ago in 2004 that Saddam not only did not have those weapons, he did not have programs to make those weapons, he did not have anyone working on making those weapons. Saddam wasn't pursuing WMDs and we invaded anyway. It is proven, it is empirically known, it is settled, it's in black and white, it's true!"[25]
- Senator Al Franken (D-WI) told MSNBC viewers that President Bill Clinton destroyed Saddam Hussein's WMD stockpiles and programs, and then made the outrageous claim that the ISG report said the same thing; his charge was not challenged.[26]

In March 2006, as the U.S. death toll in Iraq continued to rise and a mid-term election loomed, NBC News' Lisa Myers marked the 3-year anniversary of the invasion with a report that featured information about former Iraqi foreign minister Naji Sabri. According to Myers' sources, Sabri made contact with the CIA in September 2002 via French intermediaries in New York, and told intelligence officials that Saddam Hussein had indeed diverted chemicals marked for use as pesticides to a chemical weapons program, a clear violation of international law and UN resolutions.[27] The NBC News report also noted that the Iraqi foreign minister told the CIA that Saddam Hussein did not have any biological weapons program, but was keenly interested in developing a nuclear weapons program.

That story did not fit the narrative. Leftists wanted the American people to believe that George W. Bush lied about Iraq's WMDs – "Bush Lied, People Died." Thus, a month later, on April 23, 2006, CBS's *60 Minutes* found a former CIA spy who said that President Bush deceived the American people and the world regarding Saddam Hussein's WMD stockpiles and programs. The narrative had been threatened briefly by a reckless NBC News story, but the Leftists in the echo chamber knew they needed to preserve and protect that narrative, thus they dug up a former CIA spy who had the real scoop on the evil Bush administration.

Tyler Drumheller, former head of the CIA's European clandestine office, told Ed Bradley that Iraq's foreign minister, Naji Sabri, told the CIA that Saddam Hussein did *not* have any WMD stockpiles or programs, contrary to what NBC News had reported just the previous month. Drumheller said he informed CIA Headquarters about Sabri's statement. Drumheller later appeared on MSNBC's *Hardball*, CNN's Lou Dobbs, and several other television news programs. He also spoke with Walter Pincus at the *Washington Post*. Drumheller repeated his story over and over again. It went like this: he had warned his superiors at CIA Headquarters that a high-ranking Iraqi source said that Saddam Hussein did *not* have any WMD, but the CIA and the Bush administration ignored him. Then the evil neoconservatives in the Bush administration twisted the truth into a lie to justify an illegal war in Iraq, and poor NBC News was duped by the rabid lunatics at the White House into believing the lie. That was Drumheller's story, and it fit the narrative brilliantly.

Drumheller didn't just sit back, though, and let the lies

go unchallenged, or so he said. He said he "crossed out" a reference to Iraq's mobile biological weapons laboratories in a cable sent to Headquarters. A clandestine source, an Iraqi defector known as CURVEBALL, had told the Germans about Iraq's biological weapons program, but Drumheller and the Germans who spoke with CURVEBALL believed the defector was lying, thus he crossed out the reference to protect the U.S. from being duped by an Iraqi liar. Drumheller was of course portrayed by the echo-chamber Leftist media as a hero – a whistle-blower who knew the truth about Iraq's WMD but was ignored by an administration that was committed to a war in Iraq – a war for oil. Drumheller was the antidote to the lies of the Bush administration – lies that NBC News had been duped into believing, but which the echo chamber was determined to remedy.

However, it was Drumheller who was lying. Subsequent investigations conducted by the Senate Select Committee on Intelligence determined that Drumheller's stories just didn't add up. Drumheller insisted that he warned CIA Headquarters about CURVEBALL, but this was untrue. Investigators reviewed the highly classified cables sent from Drumheller to CIA Headquarters and discovered that, not only did Drumheller *not* warn about CUREVBALL, he urged CIA Director George Tenet to thank the Germans for providing valuable information about Saddam's WMD, specifically the mobile biological weapons laboratories. The Germans who spoke with CURVEBALL also said they believed the Iraq defector's story. Drumheller's whole story was false.

Even more, Drumheller's insistence that Iraqi foreign minister Naji Sabri had said there were no WMD in Iraq was also an abject lie. Cables sent from CIA operatives in New York to Headquarters were reviewed and clearly showed that Sabri actually told the French that Saddam Hussein *did* have chemical weapons stockpiles, as well as other active WMD programs. CIA officials in New York wrote that Saddam Hussein "did not have a nuclear weapon," but "was aggressively and covertly developing such a weapon." The cable also warned that Saddam Hussein had mobile biological labs that were ready to whip up batches of weaponized botulinum toxin or anthrax and unleash them on Israel and U.S forces in theater.[28]

Yet, the echo-chamber Leftists crafted a narrative and ran with it. After one of their own, NBC News, had reported a story that backed up the Bush administration, the echo-chamber media rallied around the narrative like good little soldiers, and used their unique resources and influence to trash the Bush administration and the war effort. They provided a forum for a Democratic Party operative with CIA credentials to lie about his dealings with German sources and lie about his efforts to expose the "truth" about Iraq's WMD, and they did so in order to embarrass President George W. Bush – it was payback for stealing the 2000 election from their guy, Al Gore.

Here are some facts that do not fit the prevailing narrative about Iraqi WMDs, and thus are either ignored or downplayed:

- CNN (and *USA Today*) reported in July 2004: "The departments of Energy and Defense removed '1.77 metric tons of low-enriched uranium and roughly 1,000 highly radioactive sources from [a] former Iraq nuclear research facility ....Radiological sources for medical, agricultural or industrial purposes were not removed, the department said. Less-sensitive materials were repackaged and remained in Iraq....

The material was gathered from around Iraq and taken to the Tuwaitha Nuclear Research Center, 11 miles southeast of Baghdad and the main site for the Iraqi nuclear program before the war."[29]

- *The Washington Post* reported on August 15, 2005: "U.S. troops raiding a warehouse in the northern city of Mosul uncovered a suspected chemical weapons factory containing 1,500 gallons of chemicals believed destined for attacks on U.S. and Iraqi forces and civilians, military officials said Saturday." The lab was built after the invasion, but its existence was proof that Saddam Hussein kept a cadre of WMD experts and precursor agents available as a chemical weapons program hidden from UN inspectors. The key component of any WMD program, and the one that is the most difficult to acquire, is highly trained weapons experts. Saddam Hussein had plenty of them.[30]
- Videotapes were found in Iraq after the invasion, including one that featured Saddam Hussein telling Deputy Prime Minister Tariq Aziz in 1996 that he desired to see a "nuclear explosion in Washington or a germ or chemical" weapon used in the United States. Aziz responded: "The biological is very easy to make…An American living near the White House could do it."
- The infamous Wikileaks documents that were leaked to the world by a disgruntled army sergeant in 2010 revealed that for years after the invasion of Iraq in March 2003, "U.S. troops continued to find chemical weapons labs, encounter insurgent specialists in toxins and uncover weapons of mass destruction."

Containers of mustard gas were found in Iraq in August 2004.[31]

- General Georges Sada, who served as head of Saddam Hussein's air force, said that pilots told him that Iraq's chemical and biological weapons stockpiles – including "sarin 1, sarin 2, and tabun" – were flown to Syria and were shipped by Russian military personnel dressed in civilian clothing from various locations in Iraq to Syria in the months leading up to the coalition invasion. In addition to converted commercial aircraft, convoys of tractor trailers were used to move massive quantities of WMD materials and related equipment out of Iraq. When UN weapons inspectors were finally allowed into Iraq in December 2002, they "confirmed that Iraq had produced more than 8,000 liters of deadly anthrax but could not account for where or how they had gone 'missing'."[32]
- Lt. Gen. James Clapper, Director of the National Geospatial Intelligence Agency, released to the press classified satellite imagery that showed convoys of large trucks headed from Iraq into Syria in the months leading up to the invasion in March 2003. The imagery revealed personnel at an Iraqi military base, al Qaqaa, a "former Iraqi nuclear plant," "loading barrels of explosives into a convoy of 10-ton trucks."[33]
- High-level Ukrainian intelligence officials – Gen. Ihor Smeshko, Gen. Olexander Shipalsky, and Gen. Olexander Sarnatsky – met with Gen. Clapper and Deputy Undersecretary of Defense John A. Shaw at MI-6 Headquarters in London in February 2004 and confirmed that Russian military personnel, Spetsnaz forces, had been in Iraq, posing as civilians while they

oversaw the shipment of WMD stockpiles into Syria. The Russian operation was led by Colonel-General Vladislav Achatov, Colonel-General Igor Maltsev, and was planned by Gen. Yevgeny Primakov, former head of Russian intelligence "who had long-standing ties with Saddam Hussein." The Russian government admitted that it had hundreds of "civilians" in Iraq during the months leading up to the war, but insisted they were there for humanitarian reasons.[34]

- King Abdullah of Jordan informed the world on April 17, 2004, that his intelligence agency had foiled an al Qaeda terrorist attack; the AQ cell "was planning a massive terrorist attack using chemical weapons in Amman," Abdullah said. The intelligence agents "intercepted 20 tons of sarin gas coming into [Jordan] from Syria." Gen. Sada said he believes the sarin gas was part of Saddam's WMD stockpiles that were delivered to the Assad regime in Damascus, Syria, before coalition forces invaded in 2003.[35]
- The ISG's Duelfer Report said the following: "He [Saddam Hussein] sought...to preserve Iraq's intellectual capital for WMD with a minimum of foreign intrusiveness and loss of face.... Saddam wanted to recreate Iraq's WMD capability....Saddam aspired to develop a nuclear capability—in an incremental fashion, irrespective of international pressure and the resulting economic risks—but he intended to focus on ballistic missile and tactical chemical warfare (CW) capabilities....Saddam continued with his public posture of retaining the WMD capability."
- The Duelfer Report also said "there was evidence" related to the "movement of material out of Iraq,

> including the possibility that WMD was involved," and that the evidence was "sufficiently credible to merit further investigation."

Yet the narrative prevails today – "there were no WMD in Iraq!"

Regarding Saddam Hussein's ties to international terrorists, the McClatchy news service informed readers that Pentagon officials speaking "on condition of anonymity" reported: "An exhaustive review of more than 600,000 Iraqi documents that were captured after the 2003 U.S. invasion has found no evidence that Saddam Hussein's regime had any operational links with Osama bin Laden's al Qaida terrorist network."[36] Note the reference to "operational links." Of course there were no operational links. No one said there were operational ties between al Qaeda and the Iraq regime – not the Congress that authorized the use of force, nor the president who approved that authorization. Yet, news reports consistently framed their stories about Saddam Hussein and al Qaeda in a way that suggested the Bush administration said the two entities conspired to attack the U.S. on 9/11.

The echo-chamber media Leftists were committed to crafting a narrative that made the Bush administration look bad. Thus their attention was focused on the absence of "operational ties" between Saddam Hussein and al Qaeda, rather than on the threats that were articulated by Congress and the administration – that is, that Saddam Hussein had ties to terrorist organizations committed to attacking the U.S., and that he had harbored al Qaeda members.

If the echo-chamber media had actually devoted their attention to Saddam Hussein's brutal atrocities and ties to terrorists, they would have discovered that there was an abundance of evidence that indicated terrorist organizations were given safe haven in Iraq, and were ensured protection from outside threats. These facts were buried beneath an avalanche of debris the media had used to divert the public's attention away from Saddam Hussein's brutal history. For instance, beneath that avalanche were these items of interest:

- Documents discovered in Iraq in late 2003 revealed that al Qaeda member Abdul Rahman Yasin had been provided a "house and monthly salary" by the Iraqi regime. Yasin was responsible for creating the explosives that were used in the first World Trade Center bombing in February 1993, which killed 6 American citizens and injured hundreds more.
- Abu Musab al-Zarqawi fled from Afghanistan to Iraq in late 2001 after the Taliban regime collapsed. He had been wounded by coalition forces in Afghanistan. "He received medical care and convalesced for two months in Baghdad." He set up a terrorist training camp in northern Iraq, and formed al Qaeda in Iraq (AQI). In Iraq, Zarqawi trained and funded a terrorist cell that assassinated a U.S. diplomat, Lawrence Foley, in Jordan in October 2002. Zarqawi was the mastermind behind a host of terrorist attacks in Jordan (60 dead), Turkey, and Morocco, as well as several in Europe. He was associated with the foiled chemical weapons attack in Jordan (noted above). Zarqawi was the man who wielded the blade that severed the head of captured American Nicholas Berg in a video released online in May 2004.
- Iraq's ambassador to Pakistan was Abid Al-Karim Muhamed Aswod, whom records obtained in Iraq indicate was a paid operative of al Qaeda.

- Iraq's ambassador to Turkey, Farouk Hijazi, admitted to being appointed by Saddam Hussein as Iraq's representative to al Qaeda in 1994.
- An Iraqi representative from their embassy in Malaysia was linked to the first World Trade Center bombing and al Qaeda's "Operation Bojinka," an al Qaeda plan to blow up a dozen commercial airliners over the Pacific Ocean. He also met with two 9/11 hijackers during their brief stay in Malaysia just months before the terrorist attacks.
- "Abu Nidal Organization, the Arab Liberation Front, Hamas, the Kurdistan Worker's party, the Mujahedin-e-Khalq Organization, and the Palestinian Liberation Front all operated offices or bases in Saddam's Iraq." This was in direct violation of at least one UN resolution, as the bipartisan authorization for the use of force had said.[37]

And the list goes on. The fact that Saddam Hussein had direct ties to al Qaeda and a host of other international terrorist organizations is well-documented and irrefutable.[38] Yet, the prevailing narrative today is that Bush lied about Saddam Hussein and 9/11, and Saddam Hussein was just an inert leader who posed no threat to global peace and national security. But that narrative is based on lies and a complete rejection of well-established facts.

Gitmo and Armed Drones

There are three foreign policy issues that Barack Obama promised he would change to repair America's standing in the world. Candidate Obama promised that as president he would: (1) close the detention facility at Guantanamo Bay, Cuba, also known as "Gitmo"; (2) reduce the use of armed, unmanned drones; (3) end the practice of enhanced interrogation techniques; and (4) halt the practice of extraordinary renditions.

During the last five years of the Bush administration, these four issues were the topic of discussions on Sunday morning talk shows, think tank conferences, and were the central focus of several Hollywood-produced motion pictures.[39] They were also the subject of thousands of magazine and newspaper articles and over a hundred books. Condemning the "atrocities" of the Bush administration, as well as its foreign policy failures, became a cottage industry for Leftists. When not pushing the narratives discussed above ("Bush Lied," etc.), Leftists in the media were directing their attention, and their vast investigative resources, to exploring the atrocities of the Bush administration and how those atrocities were negatively impacting America's standing in the world.

But, beginning in January 2009, after years of condemnations of the wars in Iraq and Afghanistan, and after years of outrage about CIA "black sites," unmanned drones, and Gitmo, a curious silence fell over the echo-chamber media. News coverage of events in Iraq and Afghanistan decreased significantly in the first year of the Obama administration, in spite of spikes in violence in both countries. Anti-war and anti-torture protests all but disappeared. The members of Code Pink and other Leftist anti-war organizations pulled up stakes and returned to their homes, only to very briefly resurface again to protest the National Rifle Association (NRA) after a mass shooting at a Connecticut elementary school.

The difference between 2008 and 2009 was not that the two wars had ended. It wasn't that American military deaths had declined. It wasn't that the U.S. suddenly became loved and adored by everyone around the world. The difference was that a Leftist president was elected into office, and that president needed to be protected from criticism; the echo chamber's task was to ensure that President Obama was viewed as a savior who would rescue the nation from an evil regime that had desecrated America's image in the world.

Shortly after taking office, President Obama declassified and released TOP SECRET memos related to the Bush administration's "enhanced interrogation techniques." Throughout the 2008 campaign, then-Sen. Obama had condemned the Bush administration's use of "harsh interrogation techniques." The techniques, which included waterboarding, were used on three high-level al Qaeda terrorists. President Obama promised the American people that, unlike the previous administration, he would not authorize any harsh treatment of detained terrorists. Such brutal tactics, President Obama said, "undermine our moral authority and do not make us safer."[40]

Throughout the 2008 presidential campaign, Barack Obama promised that, once in the White House, he would redefine America's war on terror. He promised to reach out to the international community in an effort to unite humanity rather than divide the citizens of the world into those who are "for us" and those who are "against us."[41] Barack Obama also told a crowd in Nashua, New Hampshire, that he would significantly alter the way the United States conducted its wars. He said he would increase troop levels in Afghanistan to avoid "air-raiding villages and killing civilians" with unmanned drones. The use of the drones, he said, was "causing enormous problems" for America's relationship with our Afghani and Pakistani allies. The Democratic presidential candidate promised that, unlike his predecessor, he would not use the nation's advanced military hardware to kill civilians and harm the nation's standing around the world, as his predecessor, the cowboy president, had done.[42]

On May 21, 2009, four months after taking office, President Obama spoke to the American people about his commitment to close the detention facility at Guantanamo Bay, Cuba (also known as "Gitmo"). The president told the American people that the facility was "a symbol that helped al Qaeda recruit terrorists to its cause." In fact, the president said that "the existence of Guantanamo likely created more terrorists around the world than it ever detained." Even more, the facility "set back the moral authority that is America's strongest currency in the world." President Obama was unambiguous; Gitmo must be closed to protect the American people from future terrorist attacks:

> Rather than keeping us safer, the prison at Guantanamo has weakened American national security. It is a rallying cry for our enemies. It sets back the willingness of our allies to work with us in fighting an enemy that operates in scores of countries. By any measure, the costs of keeping it open far exceed the complications involved in closing it. That's why I argued that it should be closed throughout my campaign, and that is why I ordered it closed within one year. [...]
>
> We're cleaning up something that is, quite simply, a mess – a misguided experiment that has left in its wake a flood of legal challenges that my administration is forced to deal with on a constant, almost daily basis, and it consumes the time of government officials whose time should be spent on better protecting our country. [...]

> As President, I refuse to allow this problem to fester. I refuse to pass it on to somebody else. It is my responsibility to solve the problem. Our security interests will not permit us to delay. Our courts won't allow it. And neither should our conscience.[43]

As of the writing of this book (September 2012), Guantanamo Bay is still open for business, and there is a remarkable silence from echo-chamber Leftists about it.[44] This silence is rather curious, since Gitmo was the subject of front page stories almost every week during the last three years of the Bush administration. It was, we were told, such an atrocious blight, such a violation of our ideals, such a threat to national security, that it had to be closed. Yet there it is today, open for business. And the echo-chamber media are curiously uncurious about it. It's as if the whole issue was just a handy campaign slogan and today is being intentionally ignored.

The same applies to the practice of rendition. Candidate Barack Obama wrote in the July/August 2007 issue of *Foreign Affairs*, a highly respected journal published by the Council on Foreign Relations:

> People around the world have heard a great deal of late about freedom on the march. Tragically, many have come to associate this with war, torture, and forcibly imposed regime change. To build a better, freer world, we must first behave in ways that reflect the decency and aspirations of the American people. This means ending the practices of shipping away prisoners in the dead of night to be tortured in far-off countries, of detaining thousands without charge or trial, of maintaining

> a network of secret prisons to jail people beyond the reach of the law.[45]

Yet, the practice that candidate Obama promised he would end, and which he characterized as one of the worst possible behaviors our great nation could ever be engaged in, continues today. With the exception of a single *Washington Post* article, no major establishment news outlet has bothered to cover this curious story. Perhaps that's because it would completely undermine the prevailing narrative that the Obama administration has ended the rendition program. Even the American Civil Liberties (ACLU) website continues to insist that the program was terminated by their Messiah Obama when he signed Executive Order 13491, "Ensuring Lawful Interrogations," on January 22, 2009.[46] The Leftist legal organization reported on its website that "President Obama closed the CIA's Detention, Interrogation and Rendition Program" four years ago.[47]

But, according to a solitary *Post* article and an obscure Leftist website article, the rendition program "didn't really end" when the president signed an executive order back in January 2009. Jason Ditz, a writer for Antiwar.com, noted in January 2013: "The executive order shifted the policy somewhat, but it has continued apparently with even more secrecy inasmuch as the continued renditions have mostly escaped scrutiny."[48] The *Post* article noted that "the Obama administration has embraced rendition – the practice of holding and interrogating terrorism suspects in other countries without due process – despite widespread condemnation of the tactic in the years after the Sept. 11, 2001, attacks."[49] Of course, the *Post* article failed to note that one of the most outspoken critics of the program currently sits in the Oval Office.

In addition to Gitmo remaining open and renditions continuing, President Obama's campaign rhetoric about the use of armed drones in foreign countries proved to be just that: hollow campaign rhetoric. In spite of making the case that he would stop "killing civilians" by bombing them from the air, because doing so made Americans less safe and gave the terrorists another issue to rally around, President Obama ramped up the use of armed drones. The *Washington Post* reported that in his first three years in office, his administration had "built an extensive apparatus for using drones to carry out targeted killings of suspected terrorists and stealth surveillance of other adversaries."

Obama's drone "apparatus," the article continued, "involves dozens of secret facilities, including two operational hubs on the East Coast, virtual Air Force cockpits in the Southwest and clandestine bases in at least six countries on two continents." The drone program began under the previous administration, but Obama expanded the program significantly:

> When Obama was sworn into office in 2009, the nation's clandestine drone war was confined to a single country, Pakistan, where 44 strikes over five years had left about 400 people dead, according to the New America Foundation. The number of strikes has since soared to nearly 240, and the number of those killed, according to conservative estimates, has more than quadrupled....[50]

The *Post* article noted further that the increased use of drones was a byproduct of President Obama cancelling the Bush administration's detention and interrogation programs. President Obama painted his administration into a corner by refusing to continue Bush's practice of capturing, detaining, and interrogating al Qaeda operatives. The only alternative was to start killing them all with drones. Which is what he did, and it got almost no attention from the media. The *Post* article was noteworthy due to its rarity. Conversations about the drone program were all but non-existent on the television network news, public radio, and mainstream newspapers and news magazines.

Peter Bergen wrote in the *New York Times*: "The president who won a Nobel Peace Prize less than nine months after his inauguration has turned out to be one of the most militarily aggressive American leaders in decades....He became the first president to authorize the assassination of a United States citizen, Anwar al-Awlaki." Bergen added: "During the Bush administration, there was an American drone attack in Pakistan every 43 days; during the first two years of the Obama administration, there was a drone strike there every four days."

Bergen also looked at the nature of the targets of each president's drone strikes. Bergen noted that "under Bush, al Qaeda members accounted for 25% of all drone targets compared to 40% for Taliban targets. Under Obama, only 8% of targets were al Qaeda compared to just over 50% for Taliban targets... And while under Bush, about a third of all drone strikes killed a militant leader, compared to less than 13% since President Obama took office."

Unlike the previous administration, which used drones mostly to target high-level al Qaeda officials, the Obama administration has developed what are called "signature strikes" that are "based on patterns of merely suspicious activity by a group of men, rather than the identification of a particular individual militant." The drone strikes are not limited to just Pakistan and Afghanistan. Bergen added that "Obama has authorized around 30 drone strikes in Yemen, while Bush only launched one drone attack there during his two terms in office."[51]

The expansion of drone attacks into Yemen is a result of al Qaeda moving its primary base of operations from the borderlands between Pakistan and Afghanistan into the tribal regions of southern Arabia, and also into northern Africa. The number of al Qaeda operatives captured under Obama has significantly decreased as well. This has drawn criticism from intelligence agents at the CIA and other agencies who argue that they've lost insight into terrorist operations. By simply killing operatives rather than capturing them and interrogating them, intelligence services have lost a valuable source of information about the capabilities, plans, and operational and financial infrastructure of America's greatest threat.

Even more, rather than making the U.S. safer, President Obama's increased use of drones actually incited terrorists to attack again. For instance, a *New York Times* article noted: "Drones have replaced Guantánamo as the recruiting tool of choice for militants; in his 2010 guilty plea, Faisal Shahzad, who had tried to set off a car bomb in Times Square, justified targeting civilians by telling the judge, 'When the drones hit, they don't see children'."[52] Al Qaeda has even said that their attack on the U.S. consulate in Benghazi, Egypt, on September 11, 2012, was an act of vengeance in response to the use of drones against al Qaeda operatives.

Yet, in spite of one solitary *New York Times* article – which by the way was heavily slanted towards making Obama look like a strong military leader and statesman rather than a hypocrite – the echo-chamber Leftist media does not seem very outraged about Obama's hypocrisy. In fact, the hypocrisy of the Left, including Barack Obama, was so blatant and obvious that Peter Bergen was compelled to make note of it in his *Times* article.

Candidate Obama condemned Bush's abuses of power. He said using drones was immoral. He said drone strikes make America less safe. He said the same about Gitmo and renditions. But, while condemning the use of harsh interrogation techniques on three high-ranking al Qaeda terrorists, President Obama did not hesitate to order the CIA to assassinate a U.S. citizen in Yemen. Obama's war policy can be summed up thusly: it's immoral and dangerous to national security to capture, detain, and interrogate terrorists; but it is okay to kill an American citizen – not to mention hundreds of civilians – in a foreign country with an armed, unmanned, remote-controlled drone.

"The left," Peter Bergen reminded his readers, "which had loudly condemned George W. Bush for waterboarding and due process violations at Guantanamo, was relatively quiet when the Obama administration, acting as judge and executioner, ordered more than 250 drone strikes in Pakistan since 2009, during which at least 1,400 lives were lost."[53]

Bergen and the tiny handful of journalists that have bothered to address the drone strike and rendition issues are snugly nestled behind a wall of secrecy erected by their fellow Leftists at the nation's major news organizations. Their reporting on these two issues is easily ignored in the cacophony of the Leftist echo-chamber media's overwhelming, wall-to-wall coverage of other vitally important issues, such as which Hollywood celebrity is pregnant or going back into rehab, or both. In fact, as of the writing of this sentence (January 2013), the whole issue of Obama's duplicity regarding drone strikes and renditions has been largely ignored by every major television news organization and all but two major newspapers – that their coverage is spotty and marginal at best.

In fact, the author of the *Post* article on President Obama's continuation of the rendition program, Craig Whitlock, did his level best to downplay the president's role and responsibility for the program. According to Whitlock, the president's hand is being forced into conducting renditions by a stubborn, Republican-controlled Congress. The resulting "impasse and lack of detention options…have led to a de facto policy under which the administration finds it easier to kill terrorism suspects," Whitlock advised his readers. "Renditions, though controversial and complex, represent one of the few alternatives" available for the president to fight al Qaeda.

Nonetheless, even if a tiny handful of journalists are covering the story on the back pages of one or two newspaper, on one cable news network's online site, and at one obscure Leftist, antiwar website, they are still covering for the president by ignoring the story elsewhere – that is, where it matters most, on television. In short, the story is not getting any traction because they don't want it to get any traction; at least not until after the reelection of their emperor in November 2012. Besides, it just does not fit the narrative anyway.[54]

The Surge and General Betray Us

In 2007, after years of increasing death tolls in Iraq, President Bush, against the advice of the majority of military advisors, instituted a "surge" of troops and a dramatic alteration in military strategy. A small contingent of neo-conservative military analysts and a former army general, as well as a handful of active duty military personnel, recommended a complete change in strategy in Iraq. They advised that the war would be lost if the U.S. did not adopt a robust counterinsurgency plan that involved moving U.S. and coalition troops back into the cities and neighborhoods where they would patrol the streets. Initially, the U.S. and coalition death toll increased, due primarily to the fact that troops were confronting insurgents rather than holing up inside bases on the outskirts of cities and towns and venturing into neighborhoods at night only to kick down doors and detain suspected insurgents. However, after just a few months, insurgent attacks began to decline and U.S. and coalition deaths began to decline.

When President Bush first proposed the surge, a prominent young Democratic senator from Illinois became an outspoken opponent. Sen. Barack Obama said a surge of troops into Iraq wouldn't work. In fact, he said it would likely make things worse. Sen. Obama told MSNBC viewers during an interview that he "was not persuaded" that the surge would work, and that he would "actively oppose the president's proposal." He said further: "I think he [Bush] is wrong."[55] Sen. Obama and Sen. Joe Biden both voted against the surge because they believed it would make things worse.

In September, 2007, just days before General David Patraeus was to appear before Congress to testify about the surge and report on the situation in Iraq, the anti-war group MoveOn.org ran a full-page advertisement in the *New York Times*. It featured the headline "General Patraeus or General Betray Us?" The ad accused the general of lying on behalf of the Bush White House. During the hearings, Sen. Barack Obama had an opportunity to speak out against the vile ad, as several senators, both Republican and Democrat, had done that day. But, Sen. Obama used the full seven minutes allotted to him by the committee chair to give a speech, rather than to ask penetrating questions of the witness. He also failed to condemn the Moveon.org advertisement. In fact, when the Senate voted on a resolution in the form of an amendment condemning the MoveOn.org advertisement, Sens. Barack Obama and Joe Biden failed to vote; Sens. Hillary Clinton and Chris Dodd voted against it.[56]

Of note, the *New York Times*, a supposed beacon of neutrality in politics, curiously gave a massive discount to MoveOn.org for their advertisement ($65,000 vice the standard $145,000). Also of note, after Barack Obama was elected to the White House and appointed Gen. Patraeus to command NATO force in Afghanistan, MoveOn.org removed all references to the "Betray Us" advertisement from its website. The echo-chamber media didn't notice, and didn't care.

Ultimately, in spite of all the politicking and nay saying, the surge did work. Violence in Iraq declined precipitously after the additional 20,000 troops arrived and a new strategy was implemented. Neighborhoods that had been plagued with violence began to return to normal. By the time Bush left office in January 2009, things were looking very good in Iraq. In 2007, the worst year for the war, the total number of coalition forces killed was 961. By 2008, it had declined to just 150. In 2010, it had declined to 54.[57] The surge wasn't just successful numerically. The Iraqi population began to side with coalition forces. They started to turn in al Qaeda in Iraq (AQI) operatives and suspected insurgents. The surge, by any measure, was successful.[58]

Here's the context for this issue: Osama bin Laden had repeatedly stated that America's pullouts from Lebanon in

1983 and from Somalia in 1993, as well as its feeble response to the Khobar Towers bombing in 1996 and the U.S. embassy bombings in 1998, and its lack of a response to the USS *Cole* attack in 2000, were all evidence that America was a nothing more than a paper tiger. Osama bin Laden insisted that the American people did not have the will to fight against a superior Muslim army equipped with a faith in the one true god. Had the U.S. followed Sens. Obama's and Biden's plan for withdrawal in 2007, just as the situation in Iraq was at its worst, bin Laden would have had another example of U.S. weakness to highlight. Recruitment of willing terrorists to al Qaeda would have skyrocketed had the U.S. pulled out when things got tough. But, they didn't, because President Bush and a small contingent of patriots rallied to a cause and pushed through the objective, as the army would say.

Curiously, after taking office, President Barack Obama and Vice President Joe Biden, instead of giving credit to the Bush administration for its bold initiative in the face of determined opposition, had the unmitigated gall to take credit for the success in Iraq. In February 2010, Vice President Joe Biden told CNN's Larry King:

> I am very optimistic about – about Iraq. I mean, this could be one of the great achievements of this administration. You're going to see 90,000 American troops come marching home by the end of the summer. You're going to see a stable government in Iraq that is actually moving toward a representative government.
>
> I spent – I've been there 17 times now. I go about every two months -- three months. I know every one of the major players in all the segments of that society. It's impressed me. I've been impressed how

> they have been deciding to use the political process rather than guns to settle their differences.[59]

In December 2011, President Obama echoed his vice president's analysis of the Iraq war and said the following:

> When I took office, nearly 150,000 American troops were deployed in Iraq, and I pledged to end this war responsibly.
>
> Today, only several thousand troops remain there. This is a season of homecomings, and military families across America are being reunited for the holidays. In the coming days, the last American soldiers will cross the border out of Iraq with honor and with their heads held high. After nearly nine years, our war in Iraq ends this month. I'm proud to welcome Prime Minister Maliki, the elected leader of a sovereign, self-reliant, and Democratic Iraq....
>
> Iraq faces great challenges, but today reflects the impressive progress that Iraqis have made. Millions have cast their ballots – some risking or giving their lives – to vote in free elections. The Prime Minister leads Iraq's most inclusive government yet. Iraqis are working to build institutions that are efficient and independent and transparent.[60]

Throughout that remarkable speech, the man who did his level best to ensure that the success he was speaking about would never have happened, without a hint of irony, took credit for that success. Not once has President Obama ever acknowledged that the Bush troop surge succeeded, nor has he ever given credit for that success to his predecessor.

Of course, there's the additional fact that the Obama administration took a success in Iraq and turned it into an unmitigated failure. But, examining that story in detail is beyond the scope of this book.

To this day, no media elitist from the echo chamber has ever confronted President Obama about his duplicity and hypocrisy regarding the Iraq war surge and the success he tried his best to prevent. There was at least one question posed to the White House press secretary the day after VP Biden's claim on CNN,[61] but other than that, there's been no effort to press the issue. The reason the press hasn't done so is because they were committed to ensuring a second term for President Obama, an issue explored further in the next section.

Praetorian Guard

Barack Obama and his wife Michelle attended Trinity Church of Christ in Chicago for nearly 20 years – that's 900 Sundays. Barack and Michelle Obama's relationship with the church's pastor, Rev. Jeremiah Wright, was long and intimate. For instance, Rev. Wright married Barack and Michelle; he baptized their two daughters; and one of Wright's sermons inspired the title to Obama's second autobiography, *The Audacity of Hope*. When video of a fiery sermon by Rev. Wright in which he blamed America for the 9/11 terrorist attacks was aired on Fox News in March 2007, presidential candidate Barack Obama was not compelled to deal with the outrageous comments of his pastor, his "spiritual mentor," for another year, because the majority of the network news organizations ignored the Democratic candidate's pastor, just as they had ignored another Democratic candidate's infidelity and love child.

Rev. Wright said just a week after the terrorist attacks of 9/11, that America was to blame for the attacks: "We bombed Hiroshima! We bombed Nagasaki! And we nuked far more than the thousands in New York and the Pentagon and we never batted an eye. We have supported state terrorism against the Palestinians and black South Africans and now we are indignant, because the stuff we have done overseas is now brought right back into our own front yard! America's chickens are coming home to roost!"

Father Michael Pflegger, another "spiritual leader" praised by Barack Obama, said while speaking at Obama's church: "In America, you have to understand that to say to people of color, 'Well, you gotta get over it', or "It's time to move on,' it's like saying to a woman who has been repeatedly raped over and over and over and over and over, 'You need to get over it.' The *hell* I do! Get the sucker who's been rapin' me and make him pay! America has been raping people of color and America has to pay the price for the rape!"[62]

After snippets from the Rev. Wright sermon were played by a handful of cable news networks, candidate Obama denied he'd ever heard such vile things while he was at Trinity Church – for 900 Sundays. When a video recorded in 2007 surfaced showing Barack Obama heaping praises on Rev. Wright: "I've got to give a special shout-out to my pastor; a guy who puts up with me; counsels me; listens to my wife complain about me. He's a friend and a great leader, not just in Chicago but also around the whole country. So please everybody give an extraordinary welcome to my pastor Dr. Jeremiah Wright, Jr."[63]

Nonetheless, the young Democratic candidate was advised by aides to address, not the hatred that was spewed by his spiritual mentor, but America's troubled history of racism. It would be the first hint that Obama's *modus operandi,* his default position, would be to blame America to distract attention away from his failures and his close ties to radicals. Not surprisingly, his Leftist comrades in the echo chamber stepped up and rendered assistance, because that's their default position too. Inside the echo chamber (and inside the Beltway), maneuvering to blame the victim is called political ju-jitsu, but in the real world it's called a misleading distraction.

Thus Barack Obama gave a speech about racism in America, and it was hailed by his comrades in the echo chamber as groundbreaking – a landmark and extraordinary speech. ABC News's Charlie Gibson said: "It may turn out to be the seminal speech of his presidential campaign....an extraordinary speech." ABC News' George Stephanopoulos called the speech "sophisticated" and "eloquent."[64] In a few short months, the echo-chamber media managed to turn an intimate relationship between a Democratic candidate for president and his angry, America-hating spiritual advisor and pastor of 20 years (900 Sundays!) into nothing more than a casual acquaintanceship. All those outrageous comments from Obama's pastor (and don't forget Father Pflegger, too) were swept under the rug, and the media directed their viewer's, reader's, and listener's, attention to candidate Obama's brilliant speech.

CNN's John Roberts, a devoted and trusted member of the modern-day Praetorian Guard, during an interview with Barack Obama in August 2008, told the prospective Commander-in-Chief: "I want to just stipulate at the beginning of his interview, we are declaring a 'Reverend Wright-free zone' today, so no questions about Reverend Wright. Our viewers want us to move on, so this morning we're going to move on. Is that okay with you?" No worries, sir. We've got your back. The best-trained cohorts of the Roman Praetorian Guards couldn't have done a better job of protecting their emperor than the echo-chamber media did of protecting Barack Obama during the 2008 presidential campaign.

Thus, it came as no surprise that during the 2012 presidential campaign, the Praetorian Guard was reactivated in force. The economy was stagnant and had been since Obama took office in January 2009; "friendly" Afghani troops were turning their weapons on their American allies in Afghanistan; violent anti-American riots were raging across the Middle East; a U.S. ambassador and three embassy staffers had been murdered by an al Qaeda-affiliated terrorist group in Libya; violence was erupting again in Iraq (a war that was supposed to have been "ended" by the Obama administration); and polls were indicating that GOP candidate Mitt Romney was making inroads in key battleground states. As the election drew near, the White House called in the Praetorian Guard to protect the emperor once again, and they willingly stepped up to serve.

On September 11, 2012, the eleventh anniversary of the 9/11 terrorist attacks, al Qaeda-affiliated terrorists attacked the U.S. consulate in Benghazi, Libya. The terrorists, armed with mortars, rocket-propelled grenades, and AK-47s, infiltrated the compound where U.S. Ambassador Christopher Stevens was visiting from the main U.S. Embassy in Tripoli. They swarmed in and laid waste to the facility. They killed two Americans, including Ambassador Stevens. Five hours later they attacked a second time killing two more Americans.[65] Witnesses on the scene reported that the attack was not an outgrowth of a protest. It was a well-coordinated attack by a contingent of terrorist agents positioned at key locations throughout the city. Most importantly, it was a terrorist attack scheduled to coincide with the anniversary of the 9/11 attacks, and was retribution for the killing earlier in the year of a key al Qaeda operative, Abu Yahya al-Libi.[66] It was an act of war, and a stark reminder that America's number one enemy remained a determined foe and still posed a threat.

Earlier that day (the eleventh anniversary of 9/11), a mob gathered outside the U.S. embassy in Cairo, Egypt, to protest an obscure anti-Islamic film on Youtube. The 14-minute video was unknown outside a small audience until Muslim leaders in Egypt began to promote it in order to stir up anti-American hatred. The efforts, as usual, were effective. As the crowd grew to an unmanageable size, embassy officials issued a statement early in the morning condemning the film's insults of Islam. The embassy statement was intended to quell the growing unrest and to distance the American government from a film produced in America. But the angry mob had grown large and unruly and showed no signs of dispersing. At approximately 6:00 a.m. Cairo time, embassy officials released the following statement:

> The Embassy of the United States in Cairo condemns the continuing efforts by misguided individuals to hurt the religious feelings of Muslims – as we condemn efforts to offend believers of all religions. Today, the 11th anniversary of the September 11, 2001 terrorist attacks on the United States, Americans are honoring our patriots and those who serve our nation as the fitting response to the enemies of democracy. Respect for religious beliefs is a cornerstone of American democracy. We firmly reject the actions by those who abuse

> the universal right of free speech to hurt the religious beliefs of others.

Later in the day, the Cairo mob breached embassy walls and entered sovereign American territory. They tore down the American flag and raised the black flag of al Qaeda in its place. The embassy's statement had failed to appease the angry mob.

When news of the Cairo embassy's statement reached back home in America, the campaign of Republican presidential candidate Mitt Romney issued a press release. They condemned the U.S. embassy's apparent appeasement of Muslim violence against sovereign U.S. territory. The embassy's statement, the Romney campaign said, was an apology for free speech. The default position of the Obama administration, it seemed, was not to defend freedom of speech, but rather to sympathize with radical Muslims who were attacking the American embassy. Of note, the Romney campaign's statement was issued before news broke of the death of the ambassador in Libya. As expected, and as usual, the death of Ambassador Stevens proved to be the opening the Praetorian Guard needed to craft a misleading distraction.

By the next morning, Americans were waking up to videos of violent anti-American protests at U.S. embassies around the world. Barack Obama's determination to heal the rift between the United States and Muslims in the Middle East was in danger of being undermined. Even worse, with Election Day looming large on the horizon, and polls showing a virtual dead heat between the president and his GOP opponent, the chances of a reelection were in danger as well. In the rapidly evolving environment of Washington politics, a cadre of pool reporters covering Mitt Romney's campaign quickly rallied to the defense of the emperor. A coordinated attack on the GOP candidate was devised on the fly. The goal of the press that morning was to craft an ad hoc narrative that would divert attention away from what was clearly a foreign policy crisis. The president's administration had just issued what amounted to a "hostage statement," as noted conservative columnist Charles Krauthammer aptly called it, and combined with the death of a U.S. ambassador and three embassy staffers in Libya, things were looking very bad for the emperor, or President Obama as those outside the echo chamber know him.

Typically, the echo chamber meets in closed forums online and plans their attacks via emails or teleconferences. Their coordination is usually done via online forums or behind closed doors. For instance, when the Rev. Wright story broke in 2008, a journalist for the *Washington Independent* posted instructions to his fellow journalists on the online Leftist-only journalist forum JournoList. Participants in the forum included "Richard Kim of the *Nation*, Michael Tomasky of the *Guardian*, Thomas Schaller of the *Baltimore Sun*, Holly Yeager of the *Columbia Journalism Review*, *Slate* magazine contributor David Greenberg, columnist Joe Conason, Chris Hayes of the *Nation*." Spencer Ackerman posted the following directions to his colleagues in the echo chamber: "If the right forces us all to either defend Wright or tear him down, no matter what we choose, we lose the game they've put upon us. Instead, take one of them – Fred Barnes, Karl Rove, who cares – and call them racists....find a right winger's [sic] and smash it through a plate-glass window. Take a snapshot of the bleeding mess and send it out in a Christmas card to let the right know that it needs to live in a state of constant fear. Obviously, I mean this rhetorically."[67]

Things were moving quickly the morning after the

ambassador and three other Americans were killed in Libya – the election loomed large and the Praetorian Guard needed to act swiftly to protect their emperor. There was no time to rally the troops online. The echo-chamber media had to pounce immediately – to smash Romney's head through a plate glass window, so to speak. They needed to prevent the Romney campaign and the GOP from framing the narrative. An open microphone captured the Praetorian Guard's pre-attack coordination that morning.[68] The press corps aimed the vast arsenal of their influential media war machine on the emperor's political enemy, Mitt Romney.

The open mike recording of the echo chamber that day offered an insightful glimpse of the inner workings of the Praetorian Guard as they concocted a false narrative designed to distract the American public's attention away from an administration's failure. It went like this: Romney's condemnation of the Cairo embassy's statement was politically-motivated and clumsy and un-statesman-like. Romney "jumped the gun" and "should have waited" before making the "strongly issued statement." One reported asked: "So what did the White House do wrong then, Governor, Romney?"[69] The Praetorian Guard closed ranks and formed an impenetrable shield around their emperor. The shield consisted of a false narrative composed of two misleading distractions: (1) Romney's so-called "gaffe" and (2) the anti-Islam film.

On the morning after the attack, ABC News' George Stephanopoulos told viewers waiting for the president to speak about the attack that "it was all sparked by an anti-Muslim film produced by an Israeli living in California." He continued: "That film also sparked protests and attacks on the U.S. embassy in Cairo." When the president appeared in the

Rose Garden outside the White House alongside Secretary of State Hillary Clinton, he pushed the narrative that it was the film that sparked the attack that killed Ambassador Stevens. He said: "Since our founding, the United States has been a nation that respects all faiths. We reject all efforts to denigrate the religious beliefs of others. But there is absolutely no justification to this type of senseless violence."[70]

When a member of the White House press corps – someone apparently outside the echo chamber (probably Ed Henry of Fox News, based on Jay Carney's calling him "Ed") – dared to suggest that the attack in Libya may have been a terrorist attack timed to mark the 9/11 anniversary, and therefore may have been pre-planned, Press Secretary Jay Carney reprimanded him for straying from the narrative: "I think that you're conveniently conflating two things, which is the anniversary of 9/11 and the incidents that took place, which are under investigation."[71] With that, the echo chamber had received their instructions from their emperor. The storyline would be that the Benghazi attack was not terrorism, but was a spontaneous outburst sparked by an outrageous anti-Islam film produced by a Jew in California.

During first week after the attack, U.S. Ambassador to the United Nations Susan Rice became the key representative for the White House regarding the Benghazi attack. She appeared on every Sunday morning talk show and pushed the narrative that the attack was not a terrorist attack, but rather was a spontaneous riot sparked by the anti-Islam film. It was curious to see Susan Rice rather than Hillary Clinton representing the Obama White House in discussions about the death of a major State Department figure, since the embassies are all part of the State Department. Sources in the administration reported that the White House knew they were pushing a false narrative – in fact, reports indicated that President Obama and his national security staff knew within 24 hours of the attack that it was the work of al Qaeda.[72] Thus they threw Susan Rice – a black female – under the bus, and she dutifully took the heat and diverted criticism away from key policymakers (i.e., the president, vice president, and secretary of state).

On November 14, 2012, eight weeks after the 9/11 Benghazi terrorist attack, President Obama held his first press conference after winning reelection – it was his first press conference in eight months. He spoke about the impending fiscal cliff and other issues. Jonathon Carl of Fox News was called on and asked the president to comment on the Republican's call for a special investigation into the Benghazi attack; and investigation that was being led by three Republican senators: John McCain, Lindsay Graham, and Kelly Ayotte. Mr. Carl also inquired about the White House's narrative about the attack being a response to the anti-Islam film. The president responded:

> As I've said before, she made an appearance at the request of the White House in which she gave her best understanding of the intelligence that had been provided to her. If Senator McCain and Senator Graham and others want to go after somebody, they should go after me. And I'm happy to have that discussion with them. But for them to go after the U.N. Ambassador, who had nothing to do with Benghazi, and was simply making a presentation based on intelligence that she had received, and to besmirch her reputation is outrageous....But when they go after the U.N. Ambassador, apparently because they think she's

> an easy target, then they've got a problem with me.[73]

Note that the president referred to the two male Republicans by name, but referred to Sen. Ayotte as "others." By selectively citing only the two male senators and intentionally leaving out the female Republican's name, the president tipped his hand. Remember, during the Democrat's national convention just a week before the Benghazi attack, and during the entire campaign of 2012, the Democratic Party had pushed a theme that the Republicans were waging a "war on women." Dozens of speakers at the convention pushed the narrative. The overriding theme of the whole convention consisted of reminders that women needed to be protected from Republicans. Caroline Kennedy, daughter of President John F. Kennedy, told the crowd that President Obama "has been a champion for women's rights." She warned that Republicans would "roll back" the clock and return the nation to the days of back alley abortions and starving children on the streets.[74]

The president of the National Abortion Rights Action League (NARAL) spoke at the convention and warned that "women in America cannot trust Mitt Romney. We cannot trust Mitt Romney to protect our health." She continued: "[Romney] would repeal Obamacare, taking away our access to better maternity and prenatal care, and the law's near universal coverage of birth control. And we cannot trust Mitt Romney to respect our rights. He would overturn Roe v. Wade and sign into law a wave of outrageous restrictions on a woman's ability to make decisions about her pregnancy. Mitt Romney would take away our power to make decisions about our lives and our futures."[75]

Lilly Ledbetter, an equal-pay advocate, also spoke at the

convention. She warned women that a vote for Romney was a vote for discrimination against women.[76] Three female Representatives spoke to the convention and warned that a vote for Mitt Romney was a vote to allow violence against women, including rape, to allow unfair wages, and to force sick and pregnant women out on the streets. Rep. Nancy Pelosi (D-CA), Rep. Caroline Maloney (D-NY), and Rep. Rosa DeLauro (D-CT), pushed the narrative that the GOP was waging a "war on women."[77]

The media pushed the "war on women" narrative, as well. MSNBC political analyst Karen Finney said that if Mitt Romney is elected, women would "be in the grave by [their] mid-30s."[78] A *New York Times* editorial warned that if Romney became president, "Some women would die."[79] CBS News' Nancy Giles said Republicans are waging a "war on women."[80] NBC News featured a segment about Republican efforts to "limit women's access to contraceptives and abortion," and Brian Williams wondered aloud, "Who woke up in the Republican Party one day recently and said, 'I know what, let's go after, let's go after reproductive rights in the United States'? What was that about?"[81]

Thus, when the White House sought to push a false narrative about the Benghazi attack, the most appropriate person to take the lead and appear on national television had to be a woman. By sending a woman out to the five Sunday morning talk shows to push the false narrative, the White House was making a very calculated maneuver to make it much harder for anyone to criticize the narrative. It was ambush politics, and the trap was set when they tasked Susan Rice with becoming the face of the administration.

But why did the White House craft a false narrative about the root cause of the Benghazi attack in the first place?

One reason was that the White House had been running a reelection campaign since 2011 that included the remarkably optimistic assertion that al Qaeda was being "decimated" and was on the run. The false narrative that terrorists were losing to Obama in his administration's struggle against "man-made disasters" was pushed hard in the weeks prior to the Democratic National Convention. For instance:

- On September 6, 2012, just one week before the Benghazi attack, President Obama told a cheering crowd at the Democratic National Convention that "al Qaeda is on the path to defeat, and Osama bin Laden is dead." The crowd shouted "USA! USA! USA!"
- A day later in Portsmouth, New Hampshire, President Obama told a crowd: "We have decimated al Qaeda leadership and Osama bin Laden is dead."
- Later that same day, President Obama told a crowd in Iowa City, Iowa, that "al Qaeda is on the path to defeat, and Osama bin Laden is dead."
- The next day, President Obama told a crowd in Kissimmee, Florida, that "as we come up on September 11th, we know that al Qaeda is on the path to defeat and Osama bin Laden is dead."
- That same day, in Seminole, Florida, the president said "A new tower rises above the New York skyline; meanwhile al Qaeda is on the path to defeat and Osama bin Laden is dead."

The president repeated the claim for weeks before September 11, 2012, that "al Qaeda is on the path to defeat," that "we have decimated al Qaeda leadership," and that "Osama bin Laden is dead." Thus, when al-Qaeda-affiliated terrorists attacked the consulate in Benghazi, of course he wanted the whole episode to just go away. But, four Americans were dead, including the ambassador, so a lie had to be spun, and a scapegoat fingered and held accountable. And the crazy anti-Islam video maker was put in jail, and the White House sent a black female out to deceive the American public.

Also of note is the fact that there hadn't been a successful terrorist attack on a U.S. embassy since 1998, and there hadn't been a successful attack on the U.S. by al Qaeda since 9/11 – and the last time a U.S. ambassador was killed was in 1979, during the miserable Carter administration. The false narrative about the motives of the Benghazi terrorists was crafted in order to divert attention away from the fact that all of President Obama's bluster about destroying al Qaeda was exposed as false and at the most inopportune time – just two months before the election. Unfortunately, President Obama's whole foreign policy *bona fides* rested on the notion that he had made America safer during his "apology tour" in 2009; President Obama had insisted that the Arab Spring was a sign that his policies were working.

In May 2011, President Obama hyped the success his policies were having in the Middle East. He told the American people:

> For six months, we have witnessed an extraordinary change taking place in the Middle East and North Africa. Square by square, town by town, country by country, the people have risen up to demand their basic human rights. Two leaders have stepped aside. More may follow....In Afghanistan, we've broken the Taliban's momentum, and this July we will begin to bring our troops home and continue a transition to Afghan lead. And after years of war against al Qaeda and its affiliates, we have dealt

al Qaeda a huge blow by killing its leader, Osama bin Laden.

Regarding President Obama's insistence that his efforts in Afghanistan had "broken the Taliban's momentum," one story that got overshadowed by the Benghazi attack was the attack on an airbase in Afghanistan on September 14, 2012. Just three days after the Benghazi attack, and after numerous anti-American protests around the world were still occurring, fifteen Taliban insurgents dressed as U.S. soldiers breached a wall surrounding Camp Bastion in Helmand province in southern Afghanistan. The terrorists killed two U.S. Marines and injured nine others. They destroyed six Harrier jump-jets assigned to Marine Attack Squadron 211, and seriously damaged two others. The story was covered by a small contingent of media, including one writer at the online tech magazine *Wired*, who wrote that "the death and destruction wrought on a heavily-defended NATO base by just 15 determined attackers is a chilling reminder of the insurgency's enduring potency." The attack came in the shadow of several instances of so-called "green on blue" attacks – that is, supposedly allied Afghani soldiers turning their weapons on their U.S. counterparts. The deadly green-on-blue attacks prompted a halt to joint patrols, a clear victory for the Taliban, and the attack on Camp Bastion was a capstone for their newfound momentum. And the story was almost entirely overlooked by America's major news outlets. Again, it undermined the White House's narrative, thus it had to be buried.

The events of September 2012 were a clear sign that the Obama administration's foreign policies were failing. Thus, with Afghanistan sliding into the abyss, new violence erupting in Iraq, riots at dozens of U.S. embassies across the globe, and an ambassador and three embassy staffers dead, the Praetorian Guard rushed into action. The echo chamber focused their attention on several of Mitt Romney's so-called "gaffes" to distract attention away from President Obama's catastrophic week:

- NBC News' Chuck Todd said Romney's remarks about the Cairo embassy's appeasement statement looked "crass and tone deaf." He asked rhetorically: "Now here's what we don't get. Why the Romney campaign didn't wait until it had all the facts." The finger-sniffing adolescents at NBC News couldn't resist including as part of their news coverage a short clip to mock Sarah Palin.[82]
- *Newsweek*'s Christopher Dickey defended Emperor Obama's handling of the crisis and highlighted the "difficult position" the president was in after the violent protests erupted around the world. He further noted that "Those out of office don't need to show the same restraint as those who are in, and those backing the Republican ticket, predictably, show even less."[83]
- Howard Kurtz defended the emperor and condemned Romney's "ill-timed assault on President Obama." He reminded readers of Romney's previous foreign policy "blunders" in order to frame the narrative: Romney bad, Obama good.[84]
- Time magazine's Rana Foroohar condemned Romney's statement and compared Glenn Beck to the radical Muslims who attacked the U.S. embassies.[85]
- *New York Times* reporter Ashley Parker framed the whole episode in terms of Romney's failure to mention the military during his GOP convention speech.[86]
- CNN's Don Lemon pushed the narrative when he

questioned Romney campaign foreign policy advisor Richard Williamson. Lemon asked: "Is this the time for a candidate for the presidency to speak out in a way that is critical of the government? It couldn't wait?" He also asked: "Don't you think that this makes Romney look like he is trying to use a crisis to his own political advantage rather than thinking about what is best for the situation, being pragmatic about it, standing back, getting the facts, and then commenting?"[87]

- NBC News' Andrea Mitchell suggested that Romney was merely "injecting politics into a national tragedy."[88]
- ABC News' Diane Sawyer, in the days following the deadly Benghazi attack, focused her viewers' attention to a hidden-camera recording from a Romney fundraiser. The video, she told us, was a "bombshell" that sent out "shockwaves" and would cause a "political earthquake" across the electorate. Yet, the death of an ambassador at the hands of al Qaeda-affiliated terrorists, and a concerted effort by the Obama administration to lie and cover it up, were overshadowed by the hidden-camera Romney video.[89]
- NBC devoted their resources in the days after the deadly Benghazi attack to analyzing the Romney "gaffe" and how it would completely alter the political landscape.[90]
- CBS's Norah O'Donnell barely noticed the Benghazi attack and the Obama administration's lies, and instead discussed whether Romney insulted GOP voters in the hidden-video, and pushed a new and

false narrative about dissention within the Romney campaign.[91]

- Reuters pushed the narrative that the Romney camp was "reeling" from having to deal with a "gaffe-prone" Romney.[92]
- CNN hyped a "tsunami" of Romney campaign problems.[93]
- NBC's Nightly News charged that Romney was losing Ohio after the hidden-video "gaffe."[94]
- NPR did their best to distract attention away from the deadly attack and spoke with guest David Brooks about whether "the wheels just [fell] off the GOP campaign."[95]

In short, the echo chamber formed a Praetorian Guard around the president to deflect criticism, and then went into attack mode and leveled criticism after criticism against Mitt Romney. During the first three days after the September 11, 2012, Benghazi terrorist attack, the three big networks spent 20 minutes talking about Romney's so-called "gaffe" for every one minute spent talking about the terrorist attack.[96]

CBS News' Norah O'Donnell cross examined a Romney surrogate just days after the terrorist attack in Libya, and sent a clear signal to the White House that she could be counted on as a key member of the Praetorian Guard. She leveled a bayonet at the heart of Romney campaign advisor Rob Portman and charged right through him.[97] In fact, the Leftists in media were in such a tizzy defending their emperor that one liberal commentator – a Fox News contributor – was compelled to call their behavior "insane."[98]

Even six weeks after the attack, the Praetorian Guard was still at work. With four dead Americans, and a White House intentionally deceiving the American public, echo-chamber

Leftists were forced to downplay the Benghazi attack. Instead of highlighting the fact that the president's campaign rhetoric about "decimating al Qaeda" was misplaced and naïve, the media erected a shield around the White House.

A new false narrative was crafted: Four dead Americans? No big deal:

- *New York Times* White House correspondent Helene Cooper said on NBC News' Meet the Press that the Benghazi attack was "peripheral to what's going on right now."[99]
- *Time* magazine's Joe Klein said that the Benghazi attack was "like the October mirage – it really isn't an issue."[100]
- *New York Times'* foreign affairs correspondent Thomas Friedman said the Benghazi attack issue was mere politics, something "contrived" by conservatives to harm President Obama's foreign affairs *bona fides.*[101]
- NPR's Nina Totenberg said: "It seems obvious to me that there was a screw-up at relatively low levels. I am not clear about what the intelligence said right away to the President. Certainly the Vice President suggested in his debate that they had been told initially something different. And there'd be no reason to send Susan Rice out to lie if she was going to get exposed immediately."[102]

Curiously, the same Leftists who were condemning Romney for clumsily commenting on foreign policy while Americans were dying overseas were curiously silent when then-presidential candidate and Democratic Party nominee Barack Obama used the deaths of Americans overseas to criticize President Bush's foreign policy in July 2008. Barack

Obama criticized the wars in Afghanistan and Iraq, said the surge was a failure, and noted that a brazen attack on U.S. service men in Afghanistan was evidence that Bush's war effort was failing.[103] But, because he was echoing what the press corps already believed to be true, his words were not deemed to be "crass and tone deaf," but rather were seen as noble and statesman-like.

Additionally, the president who Leftist echo-chamber media figures were trying to portray as a first-class statesman, even as they did their level best to portray his opponent as a clumsy fool on foreign policy, said just two days after the Cairo and Benghazi attacks that Egypt was not an ally of the United States. It was viewed by many as an inadvertent signal that America's relationship to its Arab ally in the Middle East had somehow changed.[104] The State Department was forced to issue a correction later to diffuse what could have become an even larger mess in Cairo.[105] Also, President Obama referred to the Benghazi attack as a "bump in the road,"[106] and told comedian Jon Stewart that the death of four Americans was "not optimal."[107] But those "gaffes" slipped through the sieve and fell into obscurity, as do all such gaffes by Democrats. Again, those gaffes just didn't fit the false narrative.

Throughout the whole embassy violence affair, two outrageous and revealing truths about the Obama administration were exposed. The first is related to President Obama's priorities. The day after the embassy attacks, as the bodies of the four dead Americans were being gathered up in Benghazi, and the embassy in Cairo was removing the black flag of radical Islam from its flag pole and painting over the anti-US graffiti from inside the embassy compound, President Obama was on Air Force One headed to Las Vegas to attend a campaign event.[108] Getting reelected was paramount for the president that day, as it had been for months prior. In fact, as the anniversary of 9/11 approached, President Obama reportedly skipped every daily intelligence briefing from September 5 until after the attacks on September 11.[109] But that wasn't unusual; he had skipped almost half of all the intelligence briefings during the first three and a half years of his presidency. Yet, during that same time he managed to play over 100 rounds of golf and set a record for a sitting president's campaign events while in office. Priorities!

The second truth that was revealed during the crisis is that President Obama's instincts were to blame America and disregard the importance of the U.S. Constitution. When the anti-Islam film's usefulness for distracting the public's attention away from their foreign policy failures became apparent, the administration unleashed its full wrath on the filmmaker. Nakoula Basseley Nakoula, an Egyptian-born Coptic Christian, was taken into custody for questioning amidst a media circus just days after the terrorist attack. Until that time, the filmmaker's identity was unknown. But, Obama's attorney general diverted Department of Justice resources away from terrorists and drug smugglers and embezzlers and a host of other dangerous criminals, and unleashed them on the man who dared to insult Islam – to hell with freedom of speech! Thus, when a Pakistani member of parliament placed a $100,000 bounty on the head of the filmmaker for the crime of blasphemy, aspiring jihadis were provided a breadcrumb path right to his front door courtesy of President Obama's Department of Justice.

Finally, regarding the "jumping the gun" meme of the distraction narrative, President Obama commented on Romney's apparent misstep during an interview: "It's important for you to make sure that the statements that you make are backed up by the facts. And that you've thought through the ramifications before you make them." He added that Romney demonstrated "a tendency to shoot first and aim later."[110] Does anyone recall President Obama's "the police acted stupidly" remark?[111]

In short, a Democratic administration's foreign policy failure was turned into a failure for a GOP presidential candidate. A terrorist attack in Libya was turned into an isolated protest inspired by an obscure Coptic Christian filmmaker in Los Angeles. And the first successful assassination of an American ambassador overseas since 1979 was turned into a meditation on the First Amendment. And the successful destruction of an important CIA/FBI safe house and surveillance facility in Libya by al Qaeda-affiliated terrorists was turned into a mere bump in the road. And it was all the work of a devoted Praetorian Guard media committed to ensuring the reelection of Barack Obama.[112]

Just one week after this whole affair, a Rasmussen poll noted that less than one in four Americans were buying the echo chamber's false narrative that the Benghazi attack was a response to the anti-Islam film, as the White House had suggested for over two weeks. Of note, the group that most subscribed to the echo chamber's false narrative was, of course, the echo chamber. Hot Air's Ed Morrissey noted: "A peek at the internals [of the polling] is instructive. Only one demographic has a majority which backs the Obama administration's original spin on this story – the political class, with 50% agreeing that the embassy attacks are spontaneous and prompted by the video."[113]

Sometimes, the echo chamber's narrative falls flat. Apparently, this was one time it did so – but, not for a lack of trying. As of two weeks after Ambassador Susan Rice pushed the false narrative that the Benghazi attack was a response to an anti-Islam film, ABC News' Good Morning America and NBC's Today both neglected to inform their viewers of the fact that the Obama administration lied (and was still lying) about the true nature of the attack.[114]

To contrast the way the echo chamber treated the Obama administration versus the way they treated the Bush administration, recall that the *New York Times* ran front page stories about the Abu Ghraib prisoner abuse outrage for 32 days straight in April, May, and June 2004.[115] The president of the newspaper felt compelled to write a lengthy article to defend his paper's month-long, blatant anti-Bush drumbeat.[116] Four months later, in October 2004, the *New York Times* contrived a controversy about stolen explosives from a weapons cache in Iraq. For the week leading up to the November 2004 presidential election, readers were treated to a series of front page headlines about the al Qaqaa weapons depot, and the newspaper concocted a false narrative about a White House cover up. The whole story was a big nothing and most of the details were either false or misleading. But the paper's editors did their level best to embarrass the Bush administration on the eve of the election.[117]

In stark contrast to the Abu Ghraib and al Qaqaa fiascos, just two weeks before the 2012 presidential election, internal government emails were leaked to the press that indicated the State Department and the White House both knew within a few hours after the attack in Benghazi that the motive behind the terrorist attack was not an anti-Islam film, but was the work of a local terrorist group, Ansar al-Sharia – yet the White House and State Department pushed the "anti-Islam film" narrative for over two weeks after the attack. Also, emails released by government officials indicated that during the attack, CIA operatives in Benghazi requested assistance three times, but all three requests were denied, even though military forces were standing by and ready to defend U.S. personnel.[118] President Obama refused to answer any questions about where he was during the attack, why requests for assistance were denied, and why he neglected to cancel a Las Vegas campaign event the day after the deadly attack.[119]

Both the *New York Times* and the *Washington Post* buried the breaking story deep within their newspapers, and four of five hosts of Sunday morning talk shows completely ignored it (only Fox News' Chris Wallace breached the subject of the White House cover up).[120] The blackout of the story represented the Praetorian Guard's last ditch effort to protect their emperor.

CHAPTER FOUR – FEAR AND ENVY

Echo-chamber Leftists in the media have created a new sort of sacrament in modern politics. Everyone who runs for the White House must produce tax returns, and lots of them. Beginning in the 1970s, presidential candidates, as well as incumbents, have been pressured by their political opponents and the media to disclose their tax returns. The transparency of public office holder's finances has been the justification. The public deserves to know about the finances of elected officials, the argument goes.

However, tax returns used to be considered a private matter between the filer and the Internal Revenue Service, which is bound by law to seal every citizen's records. It used to be understood that the IRS was responsible for keeping tabs on the legality of every citizen's tax returns. Career accountants at the IRS, as opposed to elected officials or talking heads on television, were expected to be neutral arbiters of a citizen's tax records. They would analyze them to determine if any irregularities existed, and then make a case for an audit to further explore the veracity of the individual's finances.

But today, an individual's income and tax rates are

a measure of their moral goodness. Thus, they must be subjected to review by Leftists in the echo chamber who subscribe to the false narrative that the accumulation of wealth comes at the cost of the less fortunate. The Leftist narrative regarding wealth and charity consists of the following elements: (1) wealth is a zero sum game – that is, when one person earns a dollar, another person loses a dollar; (2) rich people accumulated their wealth on the backs of the poor; (3) the federal government must eliminate any existing gaps between rich and poor; (4) all wealth belongs first to the government, which should distribute it to those citizens deemed most deserving of it; and (5) raising taxes on the rich is patriotic and a moral obligation.

All of these elements appear to varying degrees in the narratives crafted by Leftist politicians and their comrades in the echo-chamber media.

The Decline of Private Charities

Since the passage of FDR's New Deal, and LBJ's Great Society, the federal government has significantly displaced traditional, local charities such as churches, civic groups, and non-profits as a major source of support for needy, low-income families. Prior to the 1930s, the federal government was rarely involved with charities.

In fact, when Congress passed legislation to provide assistance to Texas farmers suffering under a severe drought in 1887, President Grover Cleveland vetoed the bill and wrote a letter of explanation to Congress:

> I can find no warrant for such an appropriation in the Constitution and I do not believe that the power and duty of the general government ought to be extended to the relief of individual suffering

> which is in no manner properly related to the public service or benefit. A prevalent tendency to disregard the limited mission of this power and duty should I think be steadfastly resisted to the end that the lesson should be constantly enforced that though the people support the government the government should not support the people.
>
> The friendliness and charity of our countrymen can always be relied upon to relieve their fellow citizens in misfortune. This has been repeatedly and quite lately demonstrated. Federal aid in such cases encourages the expectation of paternal care on the part of the government and weakens the sturdiness of our national character while it prevents the indulgence among our people of that kindly sentiment and conduct which strengthen the bonds of brotherhood.[1]

However, during the first half of the twentieth century, federal officials determined that they could use the massive funds in the federal treasury as a source of charity. As a consequence, churches and other local aid organizations became marginalized and hard pressed for funds. For instance:

> Jonathan Gruber of MIT and Daniel Hungerman of the National Bureau of Economic Research have demonstrated that as government aid expenditures skyrocketed during the New Deal (increasing more than sixfold from 1933 to 1939), church-based private charity to the needy declined precipitously—by an estimated 30 percent.[2]

The decline in charitable giving to churches and other local organizations that had traditionally rendered assistance to the poor declined further in the 1960s under Democrat Lyndon B. Johnson's Great Society, which expanded the welfare state to include programs like Medicare and Medicaid. (Of note, in 1966, Medicare cost $3 billion. That year, the House Ways and Means Committee estimated that Medicare would cost $12 billion in 1990, allowing for inflation. The actual cost of Medicare in 1990 was $107 billion – that's a $95 billion or 89 percent underestimation of the costs of the program.[3] A reasonable person could be forgiven for suspecting that the federal government intentionally lied to the American people about the cost of a major new entitlement so as to dismiss the program's critics. Nonetheless, federal programs have never cost what their defenders say they will cost, and in every case throughout the nation's history, bureaucracies inevitably expand into bloated monstrosities that suck more and more federal tax dollars into their bottomless coffers.)

Prior to the displacement of charities by the federal government, poor families often turned to local community organizations for assistance. Sometimes it was a church, other times it was an ethnic organization. For example, Polish immigrants arriving in Baltimore during the turn of the 19th century formed organizations to assist new arrivals. This was true also for the Irish, Jews, Italians, etc., in New York City and elsewhere. These organizations loaned money at low interest rates, and helped new arrivals find housing and work. But nothing was free or easy. Recipients were required to find work within a reasonable amount of time, stay sober, stay out of jail, and become independent citizens who could begin contributing to the neighborhood. The goal often was to empower people to eventually begin giving back to the community by earning a living and investing in their neighborhood. They were inspired by other successful immigrants to create a business, open a store or factory, and hire other immigrants. Everyone was expected, if they received assistance, to contribute to an environment of self-reliance. There was little room for drunkards and slackers. If you didn't work, you didn't get help. The constant threat of living in the streets loomed large, and it sharpened people's minds and compelled an ethic of hard work, thrift, and responsibility.

Within one or two generations, Poles, Italians, Irish, Greeks, Asians, and other ethnic groups were flourishing. Neighborhoods in American cities bustled with economic activity, and crime rates were relatively low. Decent housing was available for anyone who worked hard, lived within their means, saved money, stayed sober and out of jail. For young women, getting pregnant before marriage was condemnable because it placed an undue burden on the families of both the girl and the reckless young man. The ethics of hard work and responsibility were very effective. Studies of immigrant populations in the first half of the twentieth century reveal that each generation was often much better off than the previous generation. And they did this by practicing thrift, hard work, personal responsibility, and self-control.

The Great Depression hit these neighborhood's especially hard. Unemployment rates, which hovered near 3 percent or below throughout the 1920s, jumped to 5 percent in October 1929, and then skyrocketed to nearly 18 percent by 1931. By the presidential election in November 1932, the unemployment rate was over 22 percent nationwide and approaching 50 percent in some cities. Unemployment rates stayed at or above 14 percent through 1940.

In 1932, American citizens and companies donated

massively to struggling Americans, through "community chest drives, benefit performances by movie theater owners, and exhibition games by sports teams." Food was donated as well, including by such noted food magnates as Oscar Mayer and Will Kellogg, who donated significant amounts of food to struggling families. The American Red Cross, the nation's leading relief organization, "opposed federal intervention in feeding the poor." They warned that if "government relief occurred, sources of support for private charities would dry up."[4]

President Herbert Hoover, under pressure from Congress, increased the top marginal income tax rate from 25 to 63 percent in order to fund a massive relief package to states. Millionaires Oscar Mayer, Will Kellogg, and a host of others significantly decreased donations of food and other goods and services to the needy. The Red Cross's warning proved correct.

Federal spending rose precipitously in 1932, as Congress entered into the charity service. A $300 million grant to states for aid relief was passed in Congress and signed by President Hoover. Ten states took the money, but Illinois received the most ($55.4 million). Massachusetts, "a state almost comparable to Illinois in population, neither asked for nor received any of the federal money." Gov. Joseph Ely and most of the Massachusetts legislature "believed that relief should be a local and state function." They passed on the federal government's offer, but paid in the end anyway.

During those first few years of the Great Depression, officials in Massachusetts coordinated with private businesses and organizations to raise millions of dollars in relief money. They held charitable concerts, baseball and football games, wrestling matches, and even city employees (teachers, police, etc.) in Boston donated $2.5 million to feed the hungry in their home state. Most of the other New England states, as well as several others across the country, followed suit, and raised tens of millions of dollars for charitable services to the people of their respective states. These states all refused the federal government's aid package.

But, here's the irony, and the outrage. While citizens of these states cut back on expenses in order to donate to local charities, they also were compelled by threat of force to contribute to the citizens of Illinois and the other states who received the federal grant (a large chunk of which was never paid back). "The $300 million was largely raised by taxes on businesses and personal income, and by excises on cars, cigarettes, and movie tickets," says Burton Folsom in his book, *New Deal or Raw Deal?* Thus, "the federalizing of relief shifted funds from the frugal and thrifty states like Massachusetts, Nebraska, and Maryland, to the inefficient and manipulative states like Illinois, Pennsylvania, and West Virginia." Those latter states, to some degree, provided false or misleading data to the federal government in order to receive a portion of the grant money. Citizens of these states also were not compelled to be as thrifty or frugal with their money as the citizens of the states that didn't take the federal handout. Thus, citizens of Illinois, etc., were not double-taxed like the citizens of Massachusetts, etc. An added bonus for the politicians in these recipient states was that their citizens were more likely to reelect them, seeing as they brought home the bacon, so to speak.[5]

The lesson of the Great Depression for frugal and self-sufficient Americans was crystal clear: Don't bother saving your money to contribute to local charities; you're just going to have to contribute to the federal government for relief efforts anyway. As long as Congress can be sold on the idea of federal relief by state legislators and governors (and CEOs can convince them to subsidize or bailout their failing business), federal taxes are going to be raised, and that money is going to be given away regardless of whether one contributes to a local charity or not. Thus, the federal government became in the 1930s the largest charitable organization in the nation's history. And it only got bigger in the 1960s.

The twentieth century witnessed the near wholesale displacement of private charities with bloated bureaucracies in Washington, D.C. As a result, beneficence is no longer measured by one's donations to private charities, but rather by the amount of federal taxes an individual pays and by their support for politicians who will campaign and legislate for higher taxes. That's why, during presidential elections, such great emphasis is placed on candidates releasing their federal tax returns. It's a test of their charitableness, their moral character.

Leftists demand that candidates release their tax returns. Wealthy people must be publicly shamed if they have not paid "their fair share" to the nation's largest charity. Today, what a person earns and pays in taxes has become a handy political tool that Leftists use to provoke citizen's basest and most destructive emotions: Envy!

One of the narratives that echo-chamber Leftists have concocted to inspire envy is that Republicans are the party of the rich and greedy, while Democrats are the party of the poor and working class. In recent years, the narrative has become a common theme in the media, particularly regarding tax policy – because, remember, taxes to the Left are the equivalent to charitable giving. *Rolling Stone* columnist Tim Dickins crafted a propaganda piece that informed readers that

"Republicans [had] abandoned the poor and middle class."[6] The British-based weekly *The Economist* warned its readers that Republicans were "Obstructive, reckless, extreme, [and] willing to dismantle the whole edifice of the New Deal" in their efforts to lower taxes for the rich. They concluded that, if Republicans took control of Congress and the White House, they would craft "tax proposals that look bound to squeeze the poor and reward the rich even more." They also noted how the evil billionaire brothers Charles and David Koch, big contributors to Republican candidates, were behind efforts to give tax dollars to the rich and stick it to the poor and middle class.[7] One pundit wrote that the policies of presumptive GOP vice-presidential candidate Rep. Paul Ryan (R-WI) will certainly "hurt the poor."[8]

President Obama has echoed these sentiments. He told a crowd in Kansas in December 2011, that Republicans "want to return to the same practices that got us into this mess." He continued:

> In fact, they want to go back to the same policies that stacked the deck against middle-class Americans for way too many years. And their philosophy is simple: We are better off when everybody is left to fend for themselves and play by their own rules.

The president insisted that Republicans want to return to the days when the government stood aside while "our citizens and even our children" worked "ungodly hours in conditions that were unsafe and unsanitary." He said Republicans: (1) want to "restrict education to the privileged few"; (2) believe that "massive inequality and exploitation of people [is] just the price you pay for progress"; (3) will grant the rich a "free license to take whatever [they] can from whomever [they] can"; and (4) want to "turn back technology or put up walls around America."[9]

The President also frequently warns the American public that a vote for Republicans is a vote for the fat cats on Wall Street. However, a rare and remarkably candid *Los Angeles Times* article from 2008 informed readers that Democrats "are the darlings of Wall St."

> Concern is rising that "no matter who the Democratic nominee is and who wins in November, Wall Street will have a friend in the White House," said Massie Ritsch of the nonprofit Center for Responsive Politics, which tracks campaign donations. "The door will be open to these big banks."[...]
>
> Sen. Clinton of New York is leading the way, bringing in at least $6.29 million from the securities and investment industry, compared with $6.03 million for Sen. Obama of Illinois and $2.59 million for McCain, according to the Center for Responsive Politics. Those figures include donations from the investment companies' employees and political action committees.[10]

In 2008, Reuters informed readers that "Wall Street is putting its money behind Democrat Barack Obama for president."[11] Nonetheless, the prevailing narrative remained entrenched in the American conscience, and voters chose Obama because they believed that he was an enemy of big money and a friend of the downtrodden and needy.

However, a cursory examination of the president's administration reveals that Barack Obama is no enemy of big money interests. For example, President Obama has invited a litany of Wall Street executives to taxpayer-funded meet-and-greets with White House staffers and administration officials. Over one dozen Wall Street executives have been guests at the Obama White House, and some of them have been guests at least ten times in just the first three years of his administration![12] Yet, we're told that Obama is an enemy of Wall Street and a friend of the poor and middle-class. How many poor folks have been invited to the Obama White House to meet and greet the President and First Lady and top-level administration officials?

Factcheck.org further notes that President Obama hired "Wall Street executives to serve in the White House – including White House budget director Jacob Lew (Citigroup) and former chief of staff William Daley (J.P. Morgan Chase). He also has appointed some long-time investment bankers – including ex-Goldman Sachs executives Gary Gensler, who chairs the Commodity Futures Trading Commission, and Phil Murphy, U.S. ambassador to Germany."[13] Also of note, several officials have left Obama's White House to work for top Wall Street firms as high-salaried executives.[14] Does that sound like a White House that's an enemy of Wall Street?

President Obama's Treasury Secretary, Timothy Geithner, has become the center of attention in a probe into malfeasance regarding the decline of one of Wall Street's biggest corporations, Lehman Brothers. According to PBS's Frontline:

> [Federal] Regulators, including Geithner, who would later become [President Obama's] Treasury secretary, claim they did the best they could with the information that they had at the time. But FRONTLINE interviews with key officials and documents, including internal Federal Reserve

> Bank of New York emails, reveal another side to the story: a trail of missed warnings and evidence that regulators declined to pursue information that might have helped them to understand the systemic risk posed by Lehman.[15]

Thus, while trillions of dollars in investments were misused, Geithner looked the other way to ensure his buddies on Wall Street would profit from the economic bubble. Then, after the bubble collapsed and an economic crisis shook the world, President Obama decided that Mr. Geithner was the best person to oversee the nation's economy as his Secretary of Treasury. Even more, President Obama consistently argues that more financial regulation is required to prevent another crisis, in spite of the fact that his very own Treasury Secretary neglected to enforce the regulations that were on the books when the crisis hit in 2007-2008. Besides Frontline, no major news organization even cares about this news story. It should be a front page headline, but it just does not fit the narrative.

In spite of these facts, most Americans still subscribe to the notion that Republicans are the friends of the rich and the enemy of the poor and middle class. People still believe that Republican policies favor the rich and harm the poor and middle-class. "Asked separately which candidate will do more to help the middle class, 52 percent pointed to Mr. Obama… Thirty-eight percent cited Romney," said CBS News.[16] When asked which candidate, Romney or Obama, would "do more to advance the economic interests of wealthy Americans," 65 percent said Romney versus 24 percent who said Obama.[17] The false narrative is working.

According to echo-chamber Leftists in the media and their colleagues in the Democratic Party, Republicans are indeed the party of the rich. According to the vast majority of editors at the nation's leading newspapers and television news organizations, Republican policies do more harm to the poor and middle class and favor the wealthiest Americans. Democrats are the champions of the poor and middle-class. That's the narrative that dictated the media's coverage of the heated debates surrounding the Bush tax cuts of 2001. Across the nation, media outlets both large and small informed their viewers, readers, and listeners, that the Bush tax cuts were a gift to the rich and would harm the poor and middle class.

Even more, echo-chamber Leftists insisted that Bush's tax cuts were responsible for the massive debt and budget shortfalls that culminated in the economic crisis of 2008. When combined with two unfunded wars in Afghanistan and Iraq, the echo chamber media told us, the Bush administration is to blame for the massive debt crisis the nation is still experiencing in 2013. The narrative regarding Bush's tax cuts consisted of the argument that Bush and his Republican allies in Congress cut taxes for the rich and squeezed the middle class for money to pay for Bush's illegal wars.

However, Professor Groseclose examined the Bush tax cuts debate and discovered something very interesting. Both parties made arguments for and against the tax cuts that appeared on the surface to be contradictory, but which were both true. Groseclose discovered that each party emphasized two separate but equally true facts about the tax cuts. However, while one fact was friendly to conservatives, the other was friendly to Leftists. The two facts, as articulated by *New York Times* columnist David E. Rosenbaum, are: (1) "President Bush's tax-cut plan would result in a windfall for the wealthy," while (2) "the wealthy would wind up paying a bigger share of the national tax burden."[18]

Both facts, it turned out, were true. But, as Groseclose's study shows, the fact about the tax cuts that Democrats preferred was cited far more frequently on television and radio news programs and in newspaper articles. Using 19 news media outlets, Groseclose counted the instances where each fact was highlighted, and discovered that on average, the fact about the Bush tax cuts that supported Democrats' criticism was used 562 times while the fact that supported Republicans' take on the tax cuts was used a mere 135 times. In other words, media outlets used the Democrat-friendly fact 80.6 percent of the time in their reports on the tax cuts, yet both facts were equally true.

Thus, the narrative that Bush's tax cuts rewarded the rich was crafted by echo-chamber Leftists by simply emphasizing the Democrats' talking point while either deemphasizing or completely ignoring the Republicans' talking point. Just as Soledad O'Brien uses only Leftist talking points, so too do most of her colleagues in the echo-chamber media. As a consequence, the Leftist narrative about Bush's tax cuts took hold and is today viewed as the truth.

Here's another fact that is ignored by echo-chamber Leftists: Of the ten wealthiest Senators, eight are Democrats and two are Republicans, as of 2010. In fact, the combined wealth of the top eight Senators totaled over $1.1 billion versus a measly $113 million combined for the number eight and number nine Senators on the list, the two Republicans. In the House, the top ten wealthiest consists of six Republicans and four Democrats; the combined wealth for the top four Democrats is $665 million and $1.1 billion for the richest six Republicans. Democratic Senators topped the chart on average ($13.2 million versus $7 million for Republican Senators).[19]

Yet, somehow Democrats are given a pass when it comes to moral outrage about wealth. The reason is simple: Leftists have convinced voters that they feel their pain; that they have struggled just like the rest of us; and are thus the champions of the poor. Republicans, on the other hand, want to let the rich keep all their money and thus burden the middle-class with having to fund the federal government. At least that's what we're told by the Democratic Party and their colleagues in the echo-chamber Leftist media.

Leftist echo-chamber media elites provide a valuable service to their masters in public office; they protect the Democratic Party from any facts that do not comport with the narrative. For instance, with the nation's economy reeling under the worst recovery since the Great Depression, CNN's Ashleigh Banfield opened her Friday night, Aug. 17, 2012, news program, not with a report about the fact that 44 states had just experienced unemployment increases over the previous month. Instead, she and her staff felt it was important to craft a 12-minute dialogue centered on GOP presidential candidate Mitt Romney's tax returns.

Ms. Banfield and a guest speculated on the possibility that Romney was refusing to release his returns from 2009 because that's the year President Obama offered amnesty for anyone who may have failed to properly disclose certain financial data, like tax-free offshore accounts. After twelve minutes of speculating about the Republican's undisclosed tax returns, Ms. Banfield said: "We do not know anything about whether the Romneys have taken any advantage of any kind of amnesty program."[20]

Never mind the fact that 23 million Americans were

unemployed and looking for jobs. That little fact just didn't fit the narrative. Instead, Mitt Romney is rich! Evil and rich!

Be Thankful and Vote Democrat!

Not nearly as much scrutiny and scorn and speculation is ever devoted to the taxes of Democratic candidates as is devoted to those of Republican candidates. For instance, during the 2012 presidential campaign, news organizations discussed GOP candidate Mitt Romney's tax returns incessantly for months, because the man earned $13 million in 2011, and paid taxes at an average rate of 13 or 14 percent. However, it turned out the Romneys gave 29.65 percent of their income to charities (that's over $4 million), while claiming for tax deduction purposes only 16 percent. News organizations paid little attention to the charity portion of the Romney's tax returns, and instead focused their attention on his income tax rates. Leftists in the echo chamber beat the drum over and over again – Romney didn't pay his fair share in taxes![21]

But, unlike the case of the Bush tax cuts, the reason for the unbalanced reporting about the GOP candidate's taxes is not to concoct a false narrative. The reason that Leftist are fixated on and outraged about tax returns is rooted in their ideological belief that taxes are a measure of morality. For instance, in September 2008, just two months before the presidential election, *USA Today* noted:

> Democratic vice presidential candidate Joe Biden and his wife gave an average of $369 a year to charity during the past decade....The Bidens reported earning $319,853 last year, including $71,000 in royalties for his memoir....The Bidens reported giving $995 in charitable donations last

> year — about 0.3% of their income and the highest amount in the past decade. The low was $120 in 1999, about 0.1% of yearly income.[22]

There was absolutely no outrage from the Left regarding the fact that a husband and wife making over six times the average yearly income of a typical American family contributed a measly $369 to charity. Charitable giving by the Obamas, Barack and Michelle, was equally miserable. In 2002, they gave only 0.4 percent; in 2003, they gave 1.4 percent; 2004, they donated 1.2 percent; 2005, after Barack Obama took office as a senator for Illinois, charitable donations from the Obamas leapt to a whopping 4.6 percent. Only after deciding to run for higher office did Barack Obama and his wife begin contributing more than 2 percent of their income to charity, as if it actually mattered.[23] Echo-chamber Leftists in the nation's newsroom voted overwhelmingly for Obama and Biden, and likely would have if the Obamas gave nothing to charity.

The reason there is never any outrage about these low figures is because giving to private charities is not, in the minds of Leftists, real charity. Remember, echo-chamber Leftists live, eat, sleep, and work in places where few of their colleagues and friends attend church or volunteer for religiously-based charities. Thus, they don't see the important charitable services that churches provide every day in neighborhoods around the country. To the secular Leftist – who believes that opposing same-sex marriage is the equivalent of gassing Jews during the Holocaust – donating money to a religious institution is akin to subsidizing the Nazis (for instance, Chik-fil-A, a Christian-owned restaurant chain, was labeled a hate-group, several restaurants were vandalized, and several cities and colleges tried to get them forcefully removed from their neighborhoods and food courts, all because CEO and president Dan Cathy dared to express support for traditional marriage, and because the restaurant donated some of their profits to religious-based charities). Leftists clearly prefer increased tax rates over donations to private charities because to them, the government is their charity; government is their church; and their religion is Progressivism/Leftism.

Raising taxes, for Leftists, is the moral equivalent of the Sunday morning tithe. For instance, a group calling themselves "Patriotic Millionaires for Fiscal Strength" lobbied on Capitol Hill in 2011. They wanted tax rates for millionaires – including themselves – increased so the federal government could pay down the nation's debt and continue to fund bureaucratic monstrosities like Social Security, Medicare, Medicaid, and the hundreds of other social programs.

One of the group's leaders, Garret Gruener, made his wealth via venture capital in the 1990s and 2000s. He was one of the founders of an online search engine, Ask.com, and is a committed Leftist ideologue – he ran for public office in California as a liberal Democrat.[24] His campaign contributions over the last 12 years were made exclusively to liberal Democrats.[25] In short, Garrett Gruener, like his comrades in "Patriotic Millionaires," is a Leftist Democratic money machine. He donates to charities, certainly, but only to those that promote his ideological beliefs; and there's nothing wrong with that. That's freedom of association.

However, because most, if not all, of the so-called "Patriotic Millionaires" are Leftists, their charitable donations likely go to Leftwing causes like PETA, Greenpeace, etc. That's none of my business, though – it's their business. But, when they lobby Congress to use the extraordinary power of the federal government to take other people's money by threat of force, and then redistribute it, and then try to label it as "charity," then we've got a serious problem.

First, we must remember that few, if any, of these "Patriotic Millionaires" ever turned a wrench, or swung a hammer, or bagged groceries, or waited tables, or poured cement, or pressed shirts, in order to make ends meet. Few, if any, of them mortgaged their homes to meet payroll. The vast majority of them either inherited their massive wealth, or tapped a keyboard and pushed a mouse for a few hours each day while they raked in the cash; all while sitting comfortably in big, leather chairs in air conditioned offices somewhere high above the noisy streets and unwashed masses below. There's nothing wrong with living high above the dirty streets of the city. But, it is certainly wrong to lobby Congress to treat every wealthy person as if they are all alike; that is, bored billionaires with soft, chubby, pink hands. When they do that, they're marginalizing many small business owners who may earn a large income, but who reinvest their earnings back into the company, either by expanding and hiring, or perhaps with generous healthcare packages and bonuses.[26]

The "Patriotic Millionaires," unlike the wrench turner or welder, more than likely earned his money the "easy way" – venture capital, inheritance, software development, etc. Therefore, as they travel around the world in cozy First Class accommodations, or on their own private jets, and stay in the best hotels, and are chauffeured around town behind tinted windows, they perhaps begin to feel a bit guilty. Living in extravagance while their neighbors struggle to make ends meet does that sort of thing – rubbing soft, pink hands together in the back of an air-conditioned SUV while zipping past sweaty men laying pavement tends to inspire some guilt; at least, one would hope it does. Thus, in response to feeling particularly guilty for having such tremendous wealth without sweating or freezing outside every weekday to pay the electric bill and feed the kids and make payroll, "Patriotic Millionaires" are compelled to mitigate that guilt by donating to their favorite charity: the federal government.

These so-called "patriots" see no harm in raising taxes for other millionaires. In fact, not only do these wealthy Leftists believe that every millionaire should pay higher taxes, and see no harm in doing so, they make sure that everyone knows just how charitable they are. The "Patriotic Millionaires" went to Capitol Hill on a socialist Hajj, of sorts. They informed the media that they would be in town, and if anyone wanted to see real charity in action, they should bring their lights and cameras for a big display of superior morality and beneficence. They wanted everyone to know about their role in solving the nation's problems. They appeared on television, insisting that the nation's economic crisis could be repaired by raising taxes on the wealthiest one percent of Americans – those earning over $1 million a year. (Of note, a *Washington Post* editorial admitted that "it's impossible to tackle the federal debt by taxing only the wealthy," but still insisted that taxes on the rich should be raised regardless, for purposes of fairness, of course.[27])

Leftists in the echo chamber media fell over themselves to cover the "Patriotic Millionaires." However, one journalist from outside the echo chamber decided to test the beneficence of these "patriotic" men and women. Michelle Fields of the *Daily Caller*, an online conservative news organization, took an iPad and a videographer to Capitol Hill and approached several "patriotic millionaires." She challenged them to donate directly to the federal government. Here's part of that exchange:

FIELDS: Can you tell me what you're doing here today?

PATRIOT #1: So, I'm here arguing in favor of higher taxes on the wealthy. I'm one of the wealthiest one percent. In fact, I'm considerably higher in the hierarchy than that, and I think we need to – we should be paying more of our fair share. There's a lot of talk about shared sacrifice, but I haven't actually seen anybody asking the people who've benefitted the most from the policies that led to the deficit – the wealthy – to contribute.

FIELDS: Well, now is your chance. I have the Department of Treasury right here [holds up the iPad]; the donate page. Would you like to donate a few thousand dollars? Ten thousand?

PATRIOT #1: No, I wouldn't.

FIELDS [to a group of "patriots"]: Would you guys be willing to donate to the Department of Treasure?

PATRIOT #2: Individually?

FIELDS: Yes.

PATRIOT #2: No. We believe… [At this point, his voice trails off and he looks desperately to a fellow "patriotic millionaire" for help].[28]

The video runs for several minutes as "patriotic millionaires" refused to contribute directly and individually to the federal treasury. Every so-called "patriotic millionaire" who was asked to donate directly to the federal treasury that day balked. Remember, they were urging our elected officials in the federal government to raise theirs and every millionaire's taxes in order to save the nation from impending doom. Yet, they all balked when given the chance to do so individually.

Most of them refused to donate with a certain degree of noticeable shame, an indication that they knew deep down inside that they were engaging in mock beneficence. Thus, they were shamed into admitting that they did not really want to contribute directly and individually to the federal government. In fact, some even admitted that their contributions likely wouldn't help the nation's deficit problem. It was pure magic – a sight to behold – watching clichés and grand gestures of artificial charity falling meekly under the glare of non-echo-chamber scrutiny. They fully expected to be greeted only by fellow Leftists, and they cannot be blamed for that expectation. However, it's a new day in journalism, and conservatives are making their presence known, one tiny step at a time.

What was exposed in that fine video was this truth: Leftists are not necessarily beneficent. They are not necessarily moral people. Those so-called "patriots" want the federal government to confiscate under threat of force other people's money, so that they can feel better about themselves. They were seeking to use the power of the federal government to rehabilitate their feelings of guilt. Remember that the federal government compels by threat of force. You can test this truth yourself by simply not paying your taxes. In fact, in 2008, Actor Wesley Snipes tested it, and was sentenced to three years in prison for failing to file his tax returns. Do you know of anyone who's serving time for not dropping a tithe in the Sunday morning collection plate?

These so-called "patriotic millionaires" are opposed to

individuals willingly donating to the federal government. Freedom of conscience, freedom of action, does not fit with their concept of charity. They, like Joe Biden and Barack Obama, do not give their wealth to the federal government willingly as individuals; they only give as part of a collective, comfortable in the fact that their contributions are matched by contributions from their neighbors. As we noted above, Obama and Biden, for several years, only grudgingly gave to private charities, and sometimes it was less than one penny on the dollar. They, like the "patriotic millionaires," would rather use the coercive power of the federal government to take by force the wealth of other American citizens across the nation, to redistribute that wealth the way they see fit, and then congratulate themselves for being "charitable" and "beneficent."

In the months prior to the "patriotic millionaires" going to Washington, the nation's debt and deficit were skyrocketing to record levels. A serious crisis was fast approaching. Two camps, two schools of thought, emerged. Leftist Democrats believed that raising taxes on the wealthiest Americans would solve the nation's debt crisis and reduce deficits. Conservative Republicans said taxes should remain low, and some even suggested that tax rates be lowered for the wealthiest Americans as well as the middle class. There were two competing visions; two competing narratives. Leftist Democrats, to make their case, crafted a narrative consisting of class warfare. It's an old narrative that dates back centuries. During the debt and deficit debate, though, it was pushed by echo-chamber Leftists in media, and echoed by their colleagues in government.

For instance, Sen. Claire McCaskill (D-MO) held a press

conference and spoke to the American people about the differences between the Republican and Democratic plans:

> Now, they [the Republicans] want to say this is class warfare. Well, you know, in a way, it is, because we're fighting for the middle class. We are fighting for the middle class. Frankly, the middle class hasn't had enough champions in America.
>
> Seventy percent of Americans don't itemize deductions. So that big, old tax code – it's been written for wealthy America – the ones that itemize deductions. And then you get to the very, very top [of the tax bracket], where a lot of these people's incomes are about dividends and capital gains, and not even ordinary income, they have all kinds of ways that they can use the tax code to avoid paying taxes.
>
> This is about leveling the playing field for what has always made our country different from everyone else. That is, as strong, vibrant middle class. And I will tell you this, if [the Republicans] think it's okay to raise taxes for the embattled middle class, because they're gonna pout if we don't give more money to millionaires, it really is time for the people of America to take up pitch forks.[29]

Sen. McCaskill's statement is rich with hyperbolic rhetoric, particularly when considering the fact that she's consistently refused to reform the tax code to eliminate the very loopholes she loves to demonize. But, what's most intriguing about her comments is what they reveal about how she thinks about wealth and taxes. Note this key phrase: Republicans, she said, are "gonna pout if we don't give more money to millionaires."

Did you catch that? Republicans want to lower taxes for the rich, which is, according to her, the same as giving "more money to millionaires." She's talking about tax cuts as if they're government handouts. The federal government, in the mind of the Leftist, is a beneficent grantor of wealth. You don't earn your wealth. You're not entitled to the money in your checking account, or the money you've invested, or the money you've earned by providing a service or developing a product. It belongs first to Sen. McCaskill and her Leftist comrades in Washington, D.C., who have empowered themselves with the ability to let you keep some portion of your wealth – your "fair share." To the Leftist, that's charity.

Unfortunately, Sen. McCaskill is technically correct. Since the passage of the income tax, the federal government has a claim, a lien, first dibs, on the money you earn. Yes, you receive a check from your employer; but only after the federal government has withdrawn its share and deemed what's left your "fair share" to use as you please. So, Leftists like Sen. McCaskill are correct. The federal government does have first claim to your earnings, and you're compelled by threat of force to acquiesce to their demands. You are, in essence, a subject, a serf, whose masters in Washington have granted you a brief reprieve from the totalitarianism of bygone days.

But, Leftists like Sen. McCaskill are not satisfied with having a lien on your income and wealth. They want us to believe that when they raise our taxes, they're doing something moral, something patriotic. They raise taxes on the "wealthiest" Americans, and then call themselves "champions" of the middle-class for having done so. Therefore, because they are our "champions," they believe they should have the power to decide how much each citizen gets to keep of their own money. They decide who deserves and who doesn't deserve. They have the power to reward and penalize.

For instance, President Obama's White House Press Secretary Joe Gibbs said the following in 2009:

> [The] President...said that the strength of our fundamentals should be measured as to whether the middle class is getting a fair shake – are we taking steps to create jobs; are we taking steps to prevent home foreclosures; are we taking steps to put money back in people's pockets who most deserve it, rather than to continue tax cuts that reward those that have done just fine over eight years.
>
> Remember the backdrop of this entire debate was: action versus inaction. There was a great debate about the exact financial regulatory structure that we have discussed throughout today's briefing. The question was, were we going to move forward in a plan that would create jobs, a plan that would stem home foreclosures, a plan that would reward the middle class with tax cuts, and a plan that would re-regulate our financial industry – or were we not?[30]

Note the use of phrases like "put money back in people's pockets who most deserve it," and "tax cuts that reward," and "reward the middle class with tax cuts." That's your money he's talking about, yet he talks about it as if it's his to give away, and then only to those who "most deserve" it. Presumably, the people who most deserve money are those who are friendliest to the president and his administration. After all, Leftists are speaking directly to a segment of the population that begrudges other people's wealth. If you listen closely to a Leftist, you suddenly realize that they believe your neighbor's wealth is your concern. If your neighbor has more than you – a better car, a bigger car, a bigger house, high-speed internet and a DVR, an in-ground swimming pool, a raised deck and shiny gas grill – then you're likely being cheated somehow. Therefore, your neighbor's wealth is undeserved and illegitimate. The Leftist politician who uses this language wants you to enter the polling booth and pull the lever based on envy and greed – to pull the lever and vote for the politicians who believes you neighbor doesn't deserve his wealth. The Leftist politician who says these things wants you to grant him the power to take your neighbor's wealth and redistribute it to you and everyone else who you and they believe really deserves it.

Rep. Rahm Emanuel, former White House Chief of Staff for President Obama, frequently used the language of envy when discussing taxes. Emanuel said the following to CNN's Wolf Blitzer during the 2008 presidential campaign:

> An economy cannot grow if the middle class is weakened. And we have to strengthen them by having a jobs agenda that basically starts to reward the middle class and put them at the center of our economic policies. That is a strategy that makes sure the middle class are strong and has been missing the last seven years....First of all, Wolf, there is going to be a tax cut. John McCain has a plan to reward the wealthiest one percent in America which has led us to this economic crisis in our country. Barack Obama has a tax cut to the middle class. There will be a tax cut. The question is who will benefit and who won't.

> And Barack Obama's tax cuts will help the middle class....[Obama's plan has] a tax cut to reward the middle class.[31]

For the Leftist, it's all about the benefits; it's about which candidate will give you what you believe you deserve; which candidate will promise you the wealth that your neighbor currently enjoys; which candidate feels your pain; which candidate will be your champion. Once, a long time ago, it was about which candidate will get the hell out of the way so you can succeed or fail on your own. If you succeed, it's yours to enjoy and do with as you please. If you failed, then you struggled to recover and continue reaching for success. Today, Americans vote for the candidate who inspires envy and greed and covetousness. Yet, we're told it's patriotic and charitable to do so.

Today, we're told to be thankful and vote Democrat!

Corrupting Charity and Scripture

While Leftists argue that what they are doing is charitable, and that they are the real champions of the American people, the real patriots, the sad fact is that their concept of charity is the exact opposite of true charity.

Our word "charity" is derived from the Latin "caritas," which means "love."[32] Love is an act of the will, compelled by the conscience, whether by a belief that a Creator demands we love one another, or by a humanistic compulsion to behave decently towards our fellow man. In either case, both love and charity cannot be coerced – to compel love or charity corrupts their very meaning. Yet, coercion is the hallmark of Progressivism/Leftism.

For example, the so-called "patriotic millionaires" who lobbied Congress to raise taxes on all wealthy Americans were insisting that the government use its coercive powers to take more money from wealthy Americans. Yet, they refused to act individually when offered the opportunity. When given the chance to demonstrate true charity, they balked and pushed for coercion and force instead.

Leftists are so confident that they are morally correct, so justified in stealing other people's money, that they are willing to distort ancient, Holy Scriptures in order to make their case. For instance, as the debt crisis debate heated up in Washington, echo-chamber Leftists, the vast majority of which, according to their own admissions, never attend church, started citing Biblical scriptures to justify the actions of the "patriotic millionaires." Jesus was a socialist, they said, and they cited from scripture to make their case.

The most cited biblical scripture can be found in Matthew Chapter 19, where Jesus is confronted by a rich young man who insists that he's doing everything right to please God. The rich young man presses Jesus for instructions on what he needs to do to be perfect and to be accepted into heaven when he dies. Jesus tells him: "If you want to be perfect, go, sell your possessions and give to the poor, and you will have treasure in heaven. Then come, follow me."

According to Leftists, this quote is proof that Jesus, if he were alive today, would support higher taxes for the wealthy, universal healthcare, and other redistributionist, socialist federal government programs. For instance, MSNBC host Lawrence O'Donnell tried to make the case that Jesus was a socialist, and he intentionally misquoted the scriptures in order to do so. O'Donnell said that based on the words of Jesus, while he "may not have specified specific tax brackets, he was the first recorded advocate of a progressive income tax."[33]

The actual message that Jesus was conveying was that we should not be so committed to earthly treasures that we forget that it is nothing that we own or anything that we do here on earth that gets us into heaven. Jesus told his disciples:

> Truly I tell you, it is hard for someone who is rich to enter the kingdom of heaven. Again I tell you, it is easier for a camel to go through the eye of a needle than for someone who is rich to enter the kingdom of God." They asked him "Who then can be saved?" He responded: "With man this is impossible, but with God all things are possible."

Note that Jesus said it is "hard for someone who is rich to enter the kingdom of heaven." He didn't say it was impossible. The "eye of a needle" that Jesus referred to was a small opening in the walls of ancient cities. There were usually several of these openings spaced around the city to accommodate traffic into and out of the city. They were designed to prevent armies from swarming in and conquering the city while allowing individual citizens to enter and exit without having to walk all the way to the main entrance. They were large enough for a man, and even perhaps his camel. But, the camel had to be unpacked first before passing through the eye of the needle. Thus, Jesus was suggesting that when we die, we don't take our earthly possessions with us. We must unpack them and leave them behind. He warned about becoming too attached to, even covetous of, earthly possessions.

Jesus' instructions were for us to not envy our neighbor's wealth, but rather to focus on serving and worshipping God. Yet, the message of Leftists is to covet your neighbor's wealth. In fact, the entire message of the Democratic Party is one of envy and greed. They want us to covet our neighbor's possessions, in complete contradiction to the scriptures.[34] Remember, covet means "to desire wrongfully, inordinately, or without due regard for the rights of others."[35] Leftists want us to desire other people's wealth so much, that we are willing to empower the federal government to take their wealth under threat of force, and then redistribute that wealth into our bank accounts. That's a complete corruption of the scriptures and the teachings of Jesus.

It is absolutely plain and clear that Leftists must either corrupt or completely rewrite the Bible in order to make their case that Jesus was a socialist. Based on the party platform and rhetoric of the Democratic Party, here is how a Leftist Jesus would have spoken to the wealthy young man in Matthew Chapter 19:

> If you want to be perfect, I'm sending a centurion guard to your home to take your possessions and bring them to me, so that I may then redistribute them to the poor; and you can share in the credit for the charity that we've both shown; and you can vote for me so that I may obtain greater power and control over the organs of earthly government; so that I may gather greater power and continue to take by force from your wealthy neighbors; so that I may entrench my power over all the people; so that I may call anyone who opposes my efforts a greedy capitalist who cares not for the poor among you; so that I may continue to inspire envy and greed among you; then come, vote for me again and again.

No one, regardless of their faith, would suggest that Jesus would say these things. Yet, Leftists want us to believe that he would if he were alive today. Leftists must arrogantly rewrite scriptures in order to make their case. That arrogance was demonstrated again when *Washington Post* columnist Gregory Paul tried to make the case that Jesus was a Marxist and that all true Christians must be communists (or collectivists). Mr. Paul cited from the book of Acts, chapters 4 and 5. Here's his take on the scriptures:

> To get just how central collectivism is to Christian canon, consider that the Bible contains the first description of socialism in history. Anti-socialist Christians also claim that the Biblical version was voluntary. Aside from it being obvious that the biblical version of God was not the anti-socialist Christian capitalists commonly proclaim he was, some dark passages in Acts indicate how deeply pro-socialist the New Testament deity is. Chapter 5 details how when a church member fails to turn over all his property to the church "he fell down and died," when his wife later did the same "she fell down... and died... Great fear seized the whole church and all who heard about these events."
>
> Dear readers, does this not sound like a form of terror-enforced-communism imposed by a God who thinks that Christians who fail to join the collective are worthy of death? Not only is socialism a Christian invention, so is its extreme communistic variant. The claim by many Christians that Christ hates socialism is untrue, while no explicit description of capitalism is found in the Bible - not surprising because it had not yet evolved.[36]

However, the biblical passage Mr. Paul provides to his readers is incomplete and misleading, as expected. Mr. Paul wanted his readers to believe that the wealthy couple in the story, Ananias and Sapphira, died because they failed to turn over all their property to the church, the collective. However, a thorough reading of this passage indicates clearly that the couple died because they promised to turn over all their property, and then lied in order to keep a portion of it. They died because they lied to the church, not because they didn't share everything. Nor did they die because, as Mr. Paul suggested, they failed "to join the collective."

In fact, if one reads the previous chapter of Acts together with the one from which Mr. Paul cherry-picked, you realize that the men who formed the small collective did so in defiance of a centralized authority. Apostles Peter and John, the two founders of the collective that Mr. Paul seemed so infatuated with, had been imprisoned by Jewish elders in Jerusalem. The Sanhedrin arrested them for preaching that Jesus was the Messiah, in direct conflict with orthodox doctrine – remember, the Apostle Paul was a Sanhedrin sent to Damascus to arrest followers of Christ. That's who was in power in Jerusalem, the Sanhedrin, with the approval of the ruling Roman Empire.

Keep that in mind as you read the actual scripture in its entirety. Notice how Mr. Paul cherry-picked choice fragments in order to make his case that Christians were the first communists (Acts 4:32-37, and Acts 5:1-11):

> All the believers were one in heart and mind. No one claimed that any of their possessions was their own, but they shared everything they had. With great power the apostles continued to testify to

the resurrection of the Lord Jesus. And God's grace was so powerfully at work in them all that there were no needy persons among them.

For from time to time those who owned land or houses sold them, brought the money from the sales and put it at the apostles' feet, and it was distributed to anyone who had need. Joseph, a Levite from Cyprus, whom the apostles called Barnabas (which means "son of encouragement"), sold a field he owned and brought the money and put it at the apostles' feet.

Now a man named Ananias, together with his wife Sapphira, also sold a piece of property. With his wife's full knowledge he kept back part of the money for himself, but brought the rest and put it at the apostles' feet.

Then Peter said, "Ananias, how is it that Satan has so filled your heart that you have lied to the Holy Spirit and have kept for yourself some of the money you received for the land? Didn't it belong to you before it was sold? And after it was sold, wasn't the money at your disposal? What made you think of doing such a thing? You have not lied just to human beings but to God."

When Ananias heard this, he fell down and died. And great fear seized all who heard what had happened. Then some young men came forward, wrapped up his body, and carried him out and buried him.

About three hours later his wife came in, not knowing what had happened. Peter asked her,

> "Tell me, is this the price you and Ananias got for the land?" "Yes," she said, "that is the price."
>
> Peter said to her, "How could you conspire to test the Spirit of the Lord? Listen! The feet of the men who buried your husband are at the door, and they will carry you out also." At that moment she fell down at his feet and died.
>
> Then the young men came in and, finding her dead, carried her out and buried her beside her husband. Great fear seized the whole church and all who heard about these events.

This passage is intended to draw a stark contrast between a true follower of Christ, Joseph, a Levite from Cyprus, and the wealthy couple who died when confronted with their deceit. Joseph sold one of his fields and brought the money to the apostles for distribution to the needy. The couple also sold land, but lied about how much money they received, thus they deceived the church and betrayed the trust of their fellow believers. More importantly, the message of the passage is intended to warn against lying to God by withholding from him, and then expecting to be praised by your fellow man for your beneficence. The couple sold their land, not to give all the proceeds to people in need, but to enjoy a portion of it themselves while reaping praises from their colleagues for being beneficent.

Note also this key passage: "From time to time those who owned land or houses sold them." This indicates that members of the collective were permitted to own private property – in contrast to what the Leftist *Washington Post* writer wanted us to believe. In fact, classical historian Richard Bauckham, Ph.D., noted: "This verse may suggest that there existed within the community of believers an inner group which practised community of property, but that the practice did not extend to all. Ananias and Sapphira were under no compulsion to enter this inner group...."[37]

Dr. Bauckham examined extra-biblical records from the period, particularly those related to Roman property laws, and concluded:

> Those who sought to join the property-sharing arrangements will still have...retained their own premises, but made them available for the community's use.... It is most likely that major events of the sale and surrender of real estate would only occur when a member had property which could not be usefully employed.... Poorer converts will not have been expected to sell their land and livelihood, but rather work it and put the proceeds at the service of the community.[38]

Bauckham also notes that such property-sharing communities were not unusual in the first century. Therefore, the Christian doctrine did not dictate or inspire the establishment of the collective community. It's most likely that the collective living arrangement was rooted in cultural traditions that predated Christ's teachings, which contradicts and undermines Mr. Paul's assertion that Christians were the first communists. In other words, the property-sharing collective described in the Book of Acts was not a byproduct of a faith in Jesus Christ. It likely was a cultural practice for believers ostracized from the society at large. For instance, the Essenes, a minority Jewish group that was marginalized and forced to live outside of orthodox Judaism, also practiced property-sharing, as did several other ancient societies in other parts of the world. Thus, an examination of the actual biblical text reveals that Mr. Paul's analysis is not just wrong, but intentionally misleading. That is, of course, assuming that he bothered to read the book and examine the works of classicists and historians in order to understand what was written 2,000 years ago.

If any parallel can be drawn between the two biblical characters, Ananias and Sapphira, and a modern equivalent, it is with the so-called "patriotic millionaires." It is the Leftist who is most like the lying couple in the Book of Acts. The "patriotic millionaires" are the ones who withheld from the collective – they refused to give individually to the Treasury. They are the ones who are comfortable lobbying their comrades in Congress to take by force the wealth of their neighbors. They are the ones who sought public accolades and congratulations for their so-called beneficence. The "Patriotic Millionaires" are today's Ananias and Sapphira.

In light of these facts, it is clear that every argument Mr. Paul made is false. He completely distorted scripture to make his case for big government socialism. He was wrong when he wrote that the couple died because they failed to give everything to the collective. He was wrong when he wrote that they died because they refused to join the collective. The scriptures tell us that Ananias and Sapphira died because they sought glory without actually doing what was necessary to receive it. They wanted to be congratulated for their charity, but their hearts were deceptive. They lied to the Holy Spirit, and that is a deadly sin.

Mr. Paul needs to brush up on his bible skills before trying to preach from it. For instance, had he bothered to actually pick up a bible, he just may have come across Jesus' instructions for donating to charities (Matthew 6:1-4):

> Take heed that you do not do your charitable deeds before men, to be seen by them. Otherwise you have no reward from your Father in heaven. Therefore, when you do a charitable deed, do not sound a trumpet before you as the hypocrites do in the synagogues and in the streets, that they may have glory from men. Assuredly, I say to you, they have their reward. But when you do a charitable deed, do not let your left hand know what your right hand is doing, that your charitable deed may be in secret; and your Father who sees in secret will Himself reward you openly.

The "patriotic millionaires" would find Jesus' directive counterproductive, even counterintuitive. After all, they appeared on Capitol Hill and were interviewed on television so that everyone would know just how charitable they were. They were seeking the spotlight to draw attention to themselves so everyone was aware of just how deserving they were of our praise and congratulations and thanks. They wanted everyone to hear their trumpets. They wanted everyone to fall on their knees in praise.

A recent study by the *Chronicle of Philanthropy* concluded that the more religious a person is, the more likely they are to give to private charities. The findings were based on data obtained from the Internal Revenue Service. It comes as no surprise that people who attend church are more likely to give to charity, probably to their church or an organization sponsored by their church. But, there was also a correlation between income and charitable giving. The higher an individual's income, the lower the percentage of that income they give to charity. Thus, "households earning between $50,000 and $75,000 year give an average of 7.6 percent of their discretionary income to charity," while those earning over $100,000 a year give on average 4.2 percent, and those earning over $200,000 a year give on average 2.8 percent.[39] Of particular interest is this finding from the study: "The eight states that ranked highest in *The Chronicle*'s analysis voted for John McCain in the last presidential contest while the seven lowest-ranking states supported Barack Obama."[40]

The Leftist tendency to distort Christian doctrine in order to achieve political ends was demonstrated clearly during the vice presidential debate between Vice President Joe Biden and Rep. Paul Ryan in October 2012. Moderator Martha Raddatz noted that both candidates were devout Catholics. She then asked how their religion shapes their views on the issue of abortion. VP Biden responded:

> My religion defines who I am, and I've been a practicing Catholic my whole life. And has particularly informed my social doctrine. The Catholic social doctrine talks about taking care of those who - who can't take care of themselves, people who need help. With regard to - with regard to abortion, I accept my church's position on abortion as a - what we call a (inaudible) doctrine. Life begins at conception in the church's judgment. I accept it in my personal life. But I refuse to impose it on equally devout Christians and Muslims and Jews, and I just refuse to impose that on others, unlike my friend here, the - the congressman. I - I do not believe that we have a right to tell other people that - women they can't control their body. It's a decision between them and their doctor. In my view and the Supreme Court, I'm not going to interfere with that.

The vice president insisted, as do all Leftist Christians, that he did not want to impose his religious beliefs on other Americans by interfering with a woman and her physician regarding the issue of abortion. Biden said his religion teaches that life begins at conception, but he did not think that terminating an unborn child is murder. That position alone is rather hypocritical, but there's more to the story.

On the issue of abortion, Joe Biden told the American people that, in spite of his religious belief, "I just refuse to impose that on others." However, regarding taxes, Joe Biden has never once hesitated to impose his religious views on others.

For instance, in February 2012, the vice president told union members in Akron, Ohio, that his religious beliefs inform his tax policies:

> Catholic social doctrine as I was taught it is, you take care of people who need the help the most. Now it'd be different if you could make the case to me that by giving this tax cut to the very wealthy, everybody else was going to be better off. We saw what happened the last eight years when we gave that tax cut.

Back during the 2008 campaign, then-Sen. Biden insisted that he and then-Sen. Obama "want to take money and put it back in the pocket of middle-class people."[41] Not only was raising taxes on the wealthiest American the "patriotic" thing to do, but it was also the Christian thing to do. Yet, while Joe Biden insists one day that he doesn't want to impose his Christian views on other Americans, he turns around and votes in support of legislation which actually imposes his Christian views on other Americans.

Conservative blogger Ed Morrissey noted that the catechism, the doctrine of the Catholic Church, is very clear about the religious obligations of the individual, and also the obligations of individuals to their government. Morrissey noted that "in only one instance does Church doctrine talk about paying tax, when Paragraph 586 [of the catechism] notes the significance of Jesus paying the temple tax, which also has nothing to do with acts of charity."

Morrissey continued:

> In the most well-known Biblical passage on taxpaying, Jesus tells the Pharisees to "Render therefore to Caesar the things that are Caesar's, and to God the things that are God's." Paragraph 2242 [of the catechism] instructs that this makes clear the separation of taxation from religious duty, "the distinction between serving God and serving the political community."[42]

Thus, Vice President Joe Biden lied when he said he doesn't want to impose his religious beliefs on others. He imposes them on the American people every time he votes on tax policies in the Senate, as he himself admitted. But his ideological worldview insists that Jesus actually said "render under Caesar the things that are God's." In other words, Biden and the other Leftists who call themselves Christians actually are saying: "I'll raise your taxes and then congratulate myself for being charitable."

But, it would be a mistake to believe that Joe Biden votes for higher taxes on the wealthy because of his Christian faith. That's just a convenient excuse. He does it because he subscribes to an ideology that is based upon envy. Leftist doctrine instructs its adherents that their wealthier neighbors don't deserve their wealth. It teaches that it's the government's responsibility to take the wealth from the rich and redistribute it to anyone with less wealth. It removes any distinctions between church and state. In the Leftist mind, the state and the church are one in the same. God is government, and the government is god. And, the fundamental religious doctrines of Leftism are fear and envy.

Just a reminder: Joe Biden and his wife have consistently given less than one percent of their income to charity. Thus, they clearly are rendering unto Caesar that which belongs to God – a clear distortion of the biblical text.[43]

Fear and Envy Rule

On July 13, 2012, (Friday the13th), President Obama spoke at a campaign stop in Roanoke, Virginia:

> Look, if you've been successful, you didn't get there on your own. You didn't get there on your own. I'm always struck by people who think, 'Well, it must be because I was just so smart'. There are a lot of smart people out there. 'It must be because I worked harder than everybody else'. Let me tell you something, there are a whole bunch of hardworking people out there. If you were successful, somebody along the line gave you some help. There was a great teacher somewhere in your life. Somebody helped to create this unbelievable American system that we have that allowed you to thrive. Somebody invested in roads and bridges. If you've got a business, you didn't build that. Somebody else made that happen. The Internet didn't get invented on its own. Government research created the Internet so

> that all the companies could make money off the Internet. The point is, that when we succeed, we succeed because of our individual initiative, but also because we do things together.[44]

The audience in that small Appalachian community hooted and hollered and swooned like a church congregation under a spell. The president spoke like a preacher. His cadence mimicked the Southern Gospel preacher. The audience responded in kind. The president preached that day, and his sermon was about envy and covetousness. But, rather than condemning those two evils, President Obama's homily was designed to inspire them. His disciples were told that they are entitled to the wealth of their more successful neighbors, who he reminded everyone "didn't get there" on their own. The president preached to the congregation, and led them to believe that they deserve credit for the success of their neighbors – the car mechanic, the baker, the restaurant owner, the electrician, the plumber, the HVAC technician, the carpenter, or the dry cleaner.

President Obama's disciples, by virtue of voting for President Obama, believe that they are sanctified, blessed, crowned in glory, and a saint in the Kingdom of Collectivism.[45] His surrogates in the echo-chamber media took up the mantle and defended their leader's comments. The *New York Times*' political reporter, Peter Baker, in a so-called "news" article, spun President Obama's "you didn't build that" comment into an innocuous statement about how everyone contributes to the collective good. So, too, did a journalist from the Associated Press.[46] They knew that what the president said was becoming a campaign tool for the Republicans, thus they attempted to spin the meaning into something digestible to the general public.

President Obama's statement was an articulation of the fundamental ideology of the Democratic Party. For instance, Rep. Barney Frank (D-MA) said in December 2011:

> There is nobody in this country who got rich on his own. Nobody. You built a factory out there, good for you. But I want to be clear, you moved your goods to market on the roads the rest of us paid for. You hired workers the rest of paid to educate. Now look, you built a factory and it turned into something terrific or a great idea. God bless. Keep a big hunk of it. But part of the underlying social contract is you take a hunk of that and pay forward for the next kid who comes along.[47]

The fact is that Americans, regardless of recent trends, remain primarily a people committed to individual success and responsibility. Outside the echo chamber, Americans admire their wealthy neighbors. They see their wealthy neighbors' charity at work in their communities. They see true beneficence. And when they hear Barack Obama and other Leftists speak, they know they are disingenuously manipulating the electorate; inspiring greed and envy; grasping for power; fundamentally transforming the nation into a socialist collective.

Economist Peter Schiff traveled to the Democratic Party's national convention in August 2012 and asked party delegates whether they would support a federal law to ban corporate profits. Corporations like Apple, Exxon, UPS, Sony, Ford, Merck, Bayer, Eli Lilly, McDonald's, Sears, Motorola, General Electric, Wal-Mart, Target, Microsoft, Google, General Mills, Starbucks, Mattel, Verizon, etc., would all have their profits taken by threat of force, and the money would be laundered through the labyrinth of bureaucracies in Washington. It would eventually be distributed to campaign donors and cronies around the nation, as was done with the $831 billion Obama stimulus.[48]

Schiff asked over two dozen Democratic Party officials whether they'd support a ban on corporate profits, and not surprisingly many of them said they would support a ban or a cap on corporate profits. Schiff's video reveals the abject greed and envy that simmers inside the hearts of Leftists.[49] Their hatred of anyone who is better off than they are has distorted their conscience and has twisted their minds so much, rational ideas are rejected and irrational ideas are lovingly embraced.

On the campaign trail in 2012, GOP presidential candidate Mitt Romney commented on President Obama's infamous "you didn't build that" statement. Mr. Romney used a metaphor to demonstrate the fallacy of Mr. Obama's ideology. Imagine a child in public school, he said, who works hard and makes the honor roll. Of course the child was driven to school each day by a public employee – a public school bus driver. Of course the bus was paid for by tax payer money. Of course the bus used roads built and maintained by public service employees. Of course the teacher is paid with tax payer money. But, in spite of all that, no rational person would suggest that those people should get equal credit for the child's success. That is, no one outside the echo chamber, where the collectivist mentality rules, would make such an assertion.

The whole concept of everyone being a part of a collective was articulated with absolute clarity and without ambiguity in a Democratic Party video aired during their party convention in August 2012. As images of average Americans going about their business in small town USA flashed on the big screen above the stage, a voice-over said the following: "Government's the only thing we all belong to. We're in different churches, different clubs. But we're together as a part of our city, or our county, or our state – or our nation."[50] The Marxist hostility to religion oozed out of that statement. Doing good for others, says the collectivist and the Leftist, is best accomplished via the government, not by fragmented factions of sectarians sitting in pews across the nation. Government! Not God!

It was the collectivists in Mao Zedong's Communist China who insisted that everyone wear the same clothing; no one was to be higher in status or prestige or fashion than anyone else. They were viewed equally expendable, too, as Mao masterminded the largest manslaughter in human history – over 80 million Chinese dead at the hands of their own government. In fascist Italy, the collectivists compelled groupthink, and no one was permitted to claim success on their own. Dissenters were executed wholesale. Such has been the case everywhere collectivism is practiced. Today, the Democratic Party is doing their best to reshape the American conscience into a collectivist utopia, and nothing, not even sacred scriptures or the immorality of envy and greed and covetousness, will stand in their way. They are moral and all others are evil.

Leftists have cornered the market on political violence since the rise of the Jacobins of the French Revolution. Leftist revolutionaries in France established the Committee of Public Safety which oversaw the imprisonment and execution of tens of thousands of citizens believed to be a threat to the new regime. The ancient religions – that is, Christianity and Judaism – were officially banned, and two new cults, one embracing deistic beliefs and the other atheistic beliefs, emerged and struggled for power. Ultimately, with the execution of the deist's chief defender, Maximilien Robespierre, the atheists gained the upper hand and established a Cult of Reason. All religious buildings were converted into temples of Reason, and the government became the focus of all power and worship.

The worshippers of Reason were Leftists. They subscribed to the notion of an all-powerful state, and they subscribed to the notion of collectivism over individuality. They are the ancestors of the modern liberal, the modern secular Leftist, the modern Democratic Party. Their legacy can be traced through the rise of Marxism in the 19th century, through the rise of Progressivism in turn-of-the-century America, through the rise of fascism in early 20th century Europe, and through the rise of communism in Russia, China, and elsewhere after World Wars One and Two.

Since the end of World War Two, revisionist historians have succeeded in erasing all evidence of the fact that the Nazis were Leftists. Today, you'll hear cries that the Tea Party protesters are fascists and Nazis. George W. Bush was called Hitler, as are any critics of President Obama's radical agenda to nationalize various facets of American society. When Obama says the rich must "pay their fair share" and calls for raising their taxes, critics raise the possibility that the president is a socialist. Those critics are immediately labeled racists, and even called Nazis.

Curiously, when one compares the rhetoric of today's Democratic Party to that of Adolf Hitler, it is very hard to differentiate between the two. For instance, in 1927, Hitler said: "We are socialists, we are enemies of today's capitalistic economic system for the exploitation of the economically weak, with its unfair salaries, with its unseemly evaluation of a human being according to wealth and property instead of responsibility and performance, and we are determined to destroy this system under all conditions."[51]

History is littered with the victims of violent Leftists. This is even true of American history. For instance, there have been twenty attempted assassinations of sitting, former, and presidents-elect in the United States, four of which resulted in the victim's death. While some of them were carried out by deranged lunatics and psychotics, most of the others were committed by radicalized Leftists who were outraged by the economic inequality of the Industrial Revolution, or by Leftists who were devoted to mythical utopian ideals or merely seeking notoriety.

Republican President Abraham Lincoln's assassin, John Wilkes Booth, was a stage actor and the equivalent of today's Hollywood star. He was adored by crowds all across the nation, and committed himself to the arts and fashionable society, as well as to pretending to be a great and noble man by virtue of his acting talent alone – like Matt Damon, but with actual talent. He fancied himself a tyrant killer, like the Roman senator Brutus, assassin of Julius Caesar.

Booth was a Democrat, a Confederate sympathizer, and hated the Republican president. His love of the Confederacy was rooted in his adoration of romantic myths of a utopian society foisted upon the masses by the elite class. The audiences of the South reciprocated the adoration of a fine gentleman of the arts, being the aristocrats that they were. Fine dining, fine clothing, fine housing, and fine everything could be found in the Confederate States. In fact, the vast amount of wealth that was accumulated by a tiny minority of citizens of the antebellum South was one of the singular greatest concentrations of material wealth in the history of mankind. The excesses of southern culture were very much like that of today's Hollywood.

During the Civil War, the Confederate navy petitioned their government to sequester the South's massive cargo ships for use in the war. However, many of their requests were denied because the aristocracy insisted on using the ships to continue importing highly coveted and expensive products from Europe, such as rare antiquities, wine, and other fineries. And, like today's glitterati, who jet around the world from gala to gala while preaching to middle America about their apocalyptic carbon footprints,[52] antebellum aristocrats enjoyed banquets and balls and wore expensive gowns and reveled in their wealth and privilege while their neighbors suffered in abject poverty. Lincoln's assassin was just as infatuated with the idea of a utopian socieity as are today's talking heads in media who ingratiate themselves to Hollywood royalty with as much enthusiasm as a tween girl swooning over Justin Bieber.

Similarly, just as today's Democratic Party cozies up to today's social elites in Hollywood, the Democratic Party of the 19th century cozied up with the antebellum aristocracy. One contemporary of Booth's noted: "I have never wondered why many actors were strongly predisposed toward the South. There, their social status is nine times as big as with us [Northerners]. The hospitable, lounging, buzzing character of the southerner is entirely consonant with the cosmopolitanism of the stage."[53] Lincoln's assassin was a devout utopian who fancied himself a revolutionary. He would have found himself today an admired figure in Hollywood, and among the chattering classes that fill the echo chambers of Leftist ideology.

Republican President William McKinley's assassin, Leon

Czolgosz, was an anarchist, not unlike the masked protesters of the Occupy Wall Street (OWS) gangs. Czolgosz was a Leftist radical by all measures of the characterization. He adored the socialists and anarchists of the age, and admired their anti-capitalist rhetoric and opposition to authority. He railed against the wealthy for their exploitation of the poor, as do today's Democrats, including President Obama. Czolgosz was a great admirer of Emma Goldman, a noted anarchist, anti-capitalist, and friend of Planned Parenthood founder Margaret Sanger. After the assassination, Goldman defended Czolgosz's actions by arguing that he had merely killed the "president of the money kings and trust magnates." The similarities between early 20th century anarchists and today's Democrats, with their demonization of Mitt Romney – or any wealthy person, for that matter – are striking. Note, also, the admiration of Planned Parenthood, a much-favored organization by today's Leftists in the Democratic Party.

When Italy's King Umberto I was assassinated in 1900 by an anti-capitalist anarchist, Czolgosz decided to emulate the act. While Czolgosz wasn't opposed to big government per se, he was opposed to a big government that failed to redistribute the nation's wealth from the rich to the poor. His last recorded words were: "I killed the president because he was the enemy of the good people; the good working people."[54] Czolgosz was the quintessential OWS protester – or Democratic Party operative and talking head on MSNBC.

Samuel Byck attempted to hijack a commercial airliner and fly it into the White House to kill Republican President Richard Nixon in 1974. He was intent on overthrowing the government because he believed it was oppressing poor people, and fancied himself a champion of the little guy. He was outraged by the Watergate scandal, the gasoline lines, his helplessness, as well as his weight and absence of self-control. He was an angry man who would have found comfort in the tent cities of Occupy Wall Street.

Lee Harvey Oswald was a radical Leftist, from the same mold as many of today's college professors. Even as a child growing up in Louisiana, Oswald described himself as a Marxist and a socialist. He enlisted in the United States Marine Corps in 1956 as a way of escaping his overbearing mother. He was granted a security clearance to handle classified government documents and operate sensitive military equipment, in spite of his pro-Soviet views and determination to learn to speak Russian. After a court-martial and demotion for shooting himself in the arm, fighting with a sergeant, and illegally discharging his rifle into the jungle in the Philippines, Oswald was temporarily sent to the brig. He received a discharge from the marines in September 1959.

In October 1959, Oswald defected to the Soviet Union where, after being refused citizenship, he attempted suicide. He was placed under psychiatric observation, but eventually landed a job at a factory in Minsk. He soon realized that the Soviet Union was not the paradise he had read about in Soviet propaganda – that is, the poetry, novels, plays, and films beloved today by the likes Alan Alda, Ed Asner, Ed Begley, Jr., etc., and the vast majority of the Democratic Party. Before leaving the USSR and returning to the US, Oswald married a Russian woman, Marina.

Oswald became an outspoken supporter of Communist revolutionary Fidel Castro, and joined a pro-Castro organization in New Orleans in April 1963. He spent his days handing out pro-Castro leaflets on the streets. However, within a few months, Oswald left New Orleans and traveled to Mexico City where he visited the Cuban embassy and requested a visa so he could travel to Havana and meet with Soviets at their embassy.

Curiously, Oswald's name was discovered among papers obtained by the FBI in New York City one year before the Kennedy assassination. Federal agents had foiled a terrorist plot to bomb several major department stores, the bus terminal, and several subway stations in Manhattan, as well as oil refineries in New Jersey. When they stormed a New York City jewelry store owned by two Cuban agents, they discovered, in addition to bombs and weapons, a list of American citizens associated with the pro-Castro organization behind the terrorist plot. Oswald's name was among them, as were a CBS News correspondent, a Hollywood filmmaker (who today teaches at a university in California), a future Clinton administration appointee, and the co-owner of *The Nation* magazine, a Leftist monthly that can be found in the offices of nearly every Democratic member of Congress. Of note, the terrorist bombing was planned to occur on November 23, 1962.[55]

And the list goes on and on. From Robert F. Kennedy assassin Sirhan Sirhan, to terrorists Sacco and Venzetti, the instances of Leftists engaging in political violence are legion. Yet, the consistent narrative that is pushed in media today is that it's the Republicans and conservatives who are violent and a danger to civilized society. Of note, the National Socialist German Worker's Party, or Nazis for short, were committed Leftists who nationalized industry and pushed for a redistribution of wealth for the greater good of the German people.

Republicans are Evil Incarnate

Democratic strategist and former governor of Vermont,

Howard Dean, said: "In contradistinction to the Republicans, we [Democrats] don't think children ought to go to bed hungry at night."[56] At the time, Dean was the Chairman of the Democratic National Committee. In December 2012, Rep. Jan Schakowsky (D-Ill) said Republicans were "literally tak[ing] food out of the mouths of hungry babies,"[57] and Rep. Steny Hoyer (D-MD) likened Republicans to parents holding guns to their children's heads and demanding everyone agree with them, or else.[58]

A Democratic Party official said that anyone voting for GOP presidential candidate Mitt Romney was doing so because they do "not like to see people other than a white man in the White House or in any other elective position." "Let's be real clear about it," she said. "Mitt Romney is speaking to a group of people out there who don't like folks like President Barack Obama in any elective or leadership position. We know what's going on here. And some people may be afraid to say it, but I'm not....He's speaking to that fringe out there who do not want to see anybody but a white person in a leadership position."[59] Virginia Senator Louise Lucas is on President Obama's "Truth Team," representing the administration's issues for Virginians. She told her children, after listening to Mitt Romney, that racism is alive and well in the United States. Her message is that whenever her constituents and her own children underachieve and fail, their failure is not their fault. It's the fault of some racist white, wealthy "cracker."

The vice-chairman of the House Democratic Caucus, Rep. James Clyburn (D-SC), said: "What we've gotten from a lot of my Republican friends has been a lot of recitations of their faith, but when it comes time to fulfill what we find in Matthew 25 – do 'unto the least of these' – to them there's something wrong with feeding people when they're hungry.

This is not the Christian way that you do things."[60] The *modus operandi* of the Democratic Party is to make the American people believe that Republicans actually want children to starve to death.

Not only are Republicans evil brutes who want children to starve, they're also white – and that alone is a bad thing, say the Leftists. When Mitt Romney chose Rep. Paul Ryan (R-WI) as his vice presidential running mate, MSNBC panelists devoted several hours to discussing the fact that the GOP presidential and vice presidential candidates were both "white guys." They used the phrase dozens of times that morning, and used it repeatedly throughout the presidential campaign. You see, for echo-chamber Leftists, "white guys" is a moral characterization, not a description of skin color. "White guys" is Leftist-speak for "morally inferior," or just plain "evil."[61] Here's how one blogger summed up the Leftist view on race:

> Since progressivism is largely a status game, in which people compete for social prestige by repeating a set of approved phrases and opinions to other status-seeking mandarins, it's not surprising that some will go to sado-masochistic lengths to remain part of the alpha group. By now, the increasingly creepy tendency of using the word "white" as a glib insult has become well established in left-wing commentary.[62]

Remember, the Progressive movement never embraced the idea expressed by Dr. Martin Luther King, Jr., that individuals should be judged by the content of their character rather than the color of their skin. Beginning in the 1960s, Progressives in the Democratic Party have crafted a federal government that places individuals into partitioned boxes labeled by race, class, sex, and religion. Quotas have been in place for over forty years, and billions of dollars are spent every year by both government and private entities to ensure that their workforces are "representative" of the American public at large.

MSNBC's Chris Matthews likes to believe that he's not like those evil, racist Republicans. Of course he's white, but he's a Progressive, thus he hates the fact that he's white. He therefore fantasizes about how morally superior he is to conservatives – and, seemingly, his fantasy contains some level of racial agnosticism. During his coverage of the RNC convention in August 2012, Chris Matthews said the following:

> But I go back to living in D.C. all these years. I've lived there 40 years, a black-majority city, and anybody who wants to get up early in Washington and drive down North Capitol (Street) and drive past Florida Avenue, sees nothing but young... black people up at 6:30 in the morning going to work. That's where they're going, to work, and not at big-wage jobs and not to get a welfare check, they're out working hard all day and not coming home with a fantastic paycheck. So this notion of blacks live on welfare and whites live on work is a brilliant political ploy but it's not true.[63]

Chris Matthews wants his audience to believe that he lives right downtown in the ghetto with the poor blacks of the District – right down there with all those hard-working, blue-collar blacks. That's what he wants his viewers to think, but in reality Matthews lives in Chevy Chase, Maryland, which has a black population of less than one percent, and is among the most affluent cities in America. Drive through

Chris Matthew's hometown and witness the disproportionate number of Mercedes, Lexus, Range Rovers, and other high-end automobiles on the streets. Drive through Chevy Chase and count the million-dollar mega-houses. Perhaps Chevy Chase's six black citizens live across the street from Chris Matthews, thus he just thinks he's in a ghetto. Leftists like Chris Matthews see blacks and think "ghetto," yet they are the enlightened ones among us. They hear the words "welfare" and "food stamps," and think "blacks," yet they're the anointed ones.

Now, either Matthews is lying to his audience, or he's lying to himself. Either way, he's a liar and a deceiver. Either he lives in some self-imposed fantasy where he's just a regular guy like everyone else, or he's intentionally deceiving his audience. Based on the network's track record, it's likely the latter. Curiously, the very same day Matthews made the above comments, he also suggested that the Republicans speaking at their party convention may be exposing their racism by saying "Chicago" too much. You see, Chicago is populated with black people, thus by reminding Americans that President Obama was once a senator from Chicago, conservatives are reminding Americans that he's black, thus conservatives are playing the race card when they say the word "Chicago."[64]

Inside the echo chamber, I suppose Chris Matthews sounds like a reasonable man. But, out here in the real world, he sounds like a certifiable lunatic.

Hostage Takers and Terrorists

In 2010, members of Congress debated the federal budget. Republicans insisted that any budget proposal should include an extension of the so-called "Bush Tax Cuts," and Democrats insisted that any budget proposal should extend only the portion of the tax cuts for anyone earning less than $250,000/ year. When Republicans stood firm, and Democrats stood firm, CNN's Eliot Spitzer likened Republicans to terrorists and hostage takers. Spitzer said: "Republicans in the Senate are holding us hostage. Every major piece of every issue that needs to be addressed for this nation is being held hostage to the one issue of tax cuts for the rich. Is that any way to govern right now?"[65]

In late 2012, as the nation approached the so-called "fiscal cliff," the Democratic Party pushed a narrative that Republicans were holding the nation hostage by refusing to allow the "Bush Tax Cuts" to expire for citizens earning more than $250,000/year. A White House report noted: "There is no reason to hold the middle-class hostage while we debate tax cuts for the highest income earners." The Obama administration report repeated the word "hostage" at least three more times, and warned that unless a deal was reached there would be "psychological" damage to the middle-class when retail sales were affected during the Christmas shopping season.[66]

Rep. Sheila Jackson Lee (D-TX) compared Republicans to the Iranians who took Americans hostage in 1979, because they opposed allowing tax rates for the "rich" to rise again to their pre-Bush levels.[67] NPR's Dave Davies said members of Congress were "terrorizing" the American people by refusing to compromise on a "fiscal cliff" deal. Mr. Davies pointed his readers to a humor columnist who labeled Republicans in Congress "evil" geniuses and compared them to al Qaeda terrorists.[68] Leftists in several media outlets pushed the narrative that Republicans in Congress were holding the nation hostage by refusing to raise taxes on the "rich."[69]

The "fiscal cliff" was the most covered story of the last two months of 2012, interrupted only briefly by a mass shooting in Connecticut. Actually, the story took on new prominence once President Obama was reelected. News outlets tasked their graphic design teams to create the most hyperbolic visuals warning viewers of an impending catastrophe if Congress failed to compromise and pass a new budget. Newsreaders and commentators hyperventilated about the looming economic crisis. News channels offered their viewers onscreen clocks that mimicked a countdown to a dramatic space launch or deadly atomic explosion.

Throughout the last few weeks of December 2012, television news and most major newspapers pushed the narrative that the Republicans would be responsible for the apocalypse following a trip over the "fiscal cliff." However, no one – not even conservative Republicans – ever challenged the narrative by raising the following questions: How did the federal government grow into such a gargantuan monstrosity that Congress can hold the American people hostage? How did the federal government become empowered with the ability to "terrorize" American citizens? How did Congress acquire the power to threaten the very livelihoods of taxpayers?

The reality of the situation was inadvertently expressed by Leftist Georgetown University law professor Louis Michael Seidman: "Why should a lame-duck House, 27 members of which were defeated for re-election, have a stranglehold on our economy? Why does a grotesquely malapportioned Senate get to decide the nation's fate?" Of course, Professor Seidman's solution is "constitutional disobedience" and "constitutional infidelity," to free "ourselves from constitutional bondage so that we can give real freedom a chance."[70] Rather than highlighting the outrageous expansion of federal influence into the lives of American citizens, and the increasing dependency of citizens on the federal government, the Leftist's instincts are invariably to disobey the law, including the "supreme law of the land," and abandon the wisdom and knowledge of the Framers of the U.S. Constitution.

American citizens – who felt comfortable putting their retirement and healthcare into the hands of a distant, centralized government – were being treated to the frightening prospect of having their very livelihoods endangered by the very same distant, centralized government. No political commentator was able to highlight the most obvious irony: that the federal government was specifically designed to be a glacial entity ill-equipped and unworthy of being entrusted with the care and maintenance of individual American citizens.

But, Leftists have intentionally, over many decades, enabled a vast growth in federal power and influence. Curiously, they've done so by adopting the philosophy of a "living constitution," which means that they can make the document mean whatever they want it to mean. The great irony of the whole episode is that, the tendency of Progressives to disregard the original meaning of the Constitution is the root cause of the fact that the federal government has become a bloated monstrosity, and further, that the citizens have become dependent upon distant, centralized bureaucracies for their well-being, a development that runs contrary to the original intent of the Framers.[71]

CONCLUSION

Everyone has a moral framework – the atheist as well as the fundamentalist Christian – and believing that one is a moral person is a fundamental requirement for living a reasonable life. No rational person walks around looking for an opportunity to behave immorally in order to simply experience the feeling, and to demonstrate to the world, that they're less moral than the next person. For instance, the "patriotic millionaires" went to Capitol Hill to experience a feeling of moral superiority, not moral inferiority.

But the moral framework of the "patriotic millionaires" and other Leftists is corrupted. The very idea that patriotism or charity can be compelled is counterintuitive to anyone willing to give it a minute of thought. But Leftist ideology corrupts the conscience and distorts the mind. For example, President Obama's campaign released a television ad featuring Mitt Romney being interviewed by Scott Pelley on CBS News' *60 Minutes*. The discussion topic was tax rates on capital gains and fairness. Here's the exchange as it appeared in the Obama campaign ad:

> SCOTT PELLEY: You made on your investments personally about $20 million last year and you paid

14 percent in federal taxes. That's the capital gains rate. Is that fair to the guy who makes $50,000 and paid a higher rate than you did?

[Jump: Portion edited]

PELLEY: So you think it is fair?

MITT ROMNEY: Yeah, I think it's the right way to encourage economic growth.

VOICEOVER: Lower tax rates for him ... than us. Is that the way to grow America?

Never mind that the Obama campaign artfully and deceptively edited the exchange to deceive viewers.[1] What's most revealing about the narrative in which the conversation is framed is the "fair" aspect of the tax issue. Why is "fairness" an issue with respect to taxes? It's rather simple: taxes are coercive. That is, taxes are taken under threat of force or compulsion by the government. Thus, it's unfair that the compulsive force of the government treats one person differently than another. No person argues that it's "not fair" that Romney gave millions of dollars to charities every year for the last decade while the president and vice president gave a mere fraction of a percent of their money to charity. Just as no person argues that it's "not fair" that the guy making $50,000 didn't give millions of dollars to charities, or failed to employ a hundred people last year. But, it is unfair that an individual is taxed at a greater rate than his neighbor – unless, that is, that neighbor is wealthier than you, and you envy their wealth enough to desire it be confiscated by force, laundered through bloated bureaucracies in Washington, and then a fraction of what's left is returned or redistributed to the American public at large.

Yet, that's the dirty little secret of Leftist ideology. It's feelings-based, not rational, as I noted in Chapter Three, thus it's empowered by envy and fear, as I noted in Chapter Five. If the viewer of the Obama campaign ad feels slighted because the evil Romney paid a lower tax rate, then Leftist ideology has prevailed. However, if the viewer explores the issue, even only for a minute, he may conclude that: (1) perhaps Romney's wealth was taxed twice (first at the corporate level, 35 percent, and then at the capital gains rate, at 13.9 percent); (2) the business-owning Romney may better understand how to reinvest earnings back into his successful enterprise and grow the business; and (3) Romney has a payroll to meet, meaning that he's got a lot of guys earning $50,000 to pay (you know, the poor guy that Scott Pelley was so concerned about). If the viewer of the campaign ad bothered to explore those issues, then Leftist ideology would fail and the viewer would recognize the campaign ad as nothing more than pure envy-mongering. But enough viewers often do not stop to ask those questions because the sources of information – the news outlets, the echo chamber – have failed in their duty to inform the public.

That's why you'll never hear a Scott Pelley or another establishment journalist challenge the envy narrative – a narrative that is used very effectively by Leftists. You'll never hear an echo-chamber Leftist in media dissect the prevailing narratives about wealth and taxes. Either they've never heard an alternative viewpoint, or they just completely reject it because they see it as extreme or out-of-the-mainstream. Either way, the public is not well served by an echo-chamber media that refuses to acknowledge alternative ideas merely because of their desire to maintain a sense of moral superiority.

The Core Issues

But, that's what the Left does with respect to every issue discussed in this book. All of the narratives that the Left offers are secondary to the issues. That's why they want to manipulate the conversation away from the core issue at hand. That's why they want to craft false narratives that focus attention on secondary and tertiary elements of the issue rather than the core issue.

For instance, with respect to the economy, the core issue is whether taxes are compulsory, and therefore not the same thing as charity. With respect to guns, the core issue is whether civilized, law-abiding citizens are entitled to use a weapon to protect themselves from armed criminal thugs. With respect to war, the core issue is whether a Democratic president should be held to the same standards as a Republican president.

In each chapter of this book, the case was made that Leftists in the echo chamber are determined to divert attention away from the core issues, and instead focus the public's attention toward ancillary elements. Journalists should ask why the Brooklyn subway rape victim was forced to fend for herself while elected officials and Hollywood celebrities enjoy the protection of armed security guards. Journalists should be asking President Obama and Vice President Biden why they gave less than one percent of their wealth to charity while condemning Mitt Romney, who gave nearly 30 percent of his wealth to charity, for being "greedy." Journalists should be asking President Obama why he thinks it was morally reprehensible and a threat to national security for President Bush to order the waterboarding of three al Qaeda detainees responsible for the 9/11 terrorist attacks, while he himself ordered the execution, via unmanned drones, of an American citizen in Yemen (as well as hundreds of other suspected terrorists, and perhaps even hundreds of innocent civilians in various nations).

Most importantly, media should be encouraged to examine the morality of Leftist ideology, which consists of the idea that individual citizens should expect the government to do what they are capable of doing themselves. Regarding self-defense – that is, the protection of oneself and one's family from criminal thugs – the government has declared, correctly, that it is the responsibility of the individual, not the government, to secure oneself and one's family from harm (see Chapter Three). This, in stark contrast to Leftist ideology, which says that citizens cannot be trusted to defend themselves in public, and therefore must remain disarmed and dependent on government for their personal security. Regarding charity, Leftists believe that material and economic inequality is of utmost moral importance, and that it should be remedied with the redistribution of wealth via the coercive force of government – which they then categorize as a form of charity. This, in stark contrast to conservative ideology, which recognizes that charitable giving cannot be compelled, nor can it be attributed to another person or entity vicariously.

If the core issues were addressed by media, and if Leftist's assumptions about morality were examined, then journalists would demonstrate their commitment to revealing the true landscape of American politics, rather than their distorted representations of it. But they don't ask those questions because they live inside echo chambers of Leftist ideology. The American public deserves far better from the "fourth estate."

The Media's Influence

As the title of this book suggests, the prevalence of Leftist narratives in media reporting can and has severely altered the landscape of American politics. This has been demonstrated, for instance, with respect to the issue of abortion. When the infamous Supreme Court case *Roe v. Wade* was decided in January 1973, Gallup polling indicated that among 18-29 year olds, 26 percent believed that abortion should be legal under any circumstance, and 18 percent believed it should be illegal in all circumstances. By the mid-1990s, support for abortion-on-demand had increased to its highest levels – among the same age group, 36 percent believed that abortion should be legal under any circumstance, and 14 percent believed it should be illegal in all circumstances.[2]

The reason for the increased support (a 10 percent jump) can be attributed partly to the efforts of the establishment media. For one thing, while television programs often feature violence on an epic scale (see, for instance, AMC's The Walking Dead, fine program that I watch myself), and even cable health channels show graphic images of surgical procedures, abortions are never featured on television. Also, the word "abortion" is rarely used in media; instead, words like "choice," "women's health," or "contraception" are used in its place. Thus, the language is altered and the graphic images are hidden. That's propaganda, plain and simple, and it represents a concerted effort by the echo chamber to shape the American public's views about abortion. And it has worked – until recently, that is.

Professor Tim Groseclose of UCLA conducted a thorough examination of the way media influences public opinion. Details of his efforts are available in his book *Left Turn: How Liberal Media Bias Distorts the American Mind*. Based on the works of economists Stefano DellaVigna and Ethan Kaplan, as well as political scientists Alan S. Gerber and Donald P. Green, Groseclose developed a tool to measure the way media affects public opinion. His conclusion is that because the media are overwhelmingly Leftist, their narratives distort the way the news is reported,[3] as this book demonstrated very clearly. As a consequence, the narratives developed by the media have influenced voting trends, and that influence can be measured.

The way the media portrayed the Bush tax cuts issue (see Chapter Five), for instance, measurably influenced the opinions of the American public. One of the studies cited by Groseclose discovered that the presence of Fox News on certain cable providers in the 1990s measurably affected voting patterns by slightly altering the electorate towards a more conservative viewpoint. Of note, the researchers accounted for any endogeneity problems, thus the data were a reliable and truthful reflection of the change in political views.[4]

Any suggestion that media bias has no effect on the opinions of readers, viewers, and listeners runs contrary to logic and reason. Advertising firms have made their fortunes on the idea that they can influence people's opinions. NBC charged $3.5 million for a thirty-second spot during the Super Bowl in February 2012, and many spots were sold – clear evidence of the fact that opinions can be influenced. Political campaigns spend millions of dollars to affect public opinion. Thus, the question is not *whether* opinions can be affected. The question is *how much* can they be affected.

Professor Groseclose answers the second question. But that answer is not what this book is about. This book merely presents the false narratives and concomitant biases in the hope that readers will recognize them and become more aware of them in the future. I've also included the opposing view, the conservative view, about each issue in order to put things in context.

Full Disclosure

"So, the media's biased," a friend said to me. "What's the solution?" he asked.

The short answer is that no one outside the media can solve the problem. Individuals within the media, within the echo chamber even, must first acknowledge that there is a problem. There are a host of individuals from within the media establishment who've openly admitted that the vast majority of journalists are biased to the Left of the political spectrum.[5] Nonetheless, as long as a majority leans Left, and as long as a majority refuses to admit that their ideology affects their reporting, then the "echo chamber" problem will remain.

Former NBC News and CNN anchor Campbell Brown married a Bush administration official, Dan Senor, in 2006, and apparently faced accusations of being biased in favor of the Bush administration because of her marriage. Senor was also a Romney campaign advisor during the 2012 campaign, and apparently this did not sit too well with some of Brown's comrades in the echo chamber. She defended her ability to remain an independent thinker, in spite of her marriage to a "Romney guy." In this modern age, it's highly dubious and ironic to suggest that someone is incapable of subscribing to a different ideology than their spouse, yet echo chamber Leftists are eager to adopt nineteenth-century Victorian views about women when it serves their interests.

As I discussed in Chapter One, it makes sense for

journalists to be open about their biases. After all, not everyone has government-issued credentials that grant them access to the halls of power. They should not, however, be compelled to disclose their ideological views. However, they should want to. Campbell Brown wrote: "Failing to disclose gives your intellectual opponents a means of distraction, a way to create a diversion so that your arguments go unheard. It is an effective strategy."[6] If for no other reason than that, journalists should be open about their politics.

Professor Groseclose's remedy for the problem is the same. First, journalist must admit that they are biased, and the American public must demand transparency of journalists. *Slate* magazine, for example, offered readers some insight into its journalist's political views, and readers responded positively. Second, journalist must get outside the echo chamber. They must venture out into those regions of America where people see the world differently than they do in Manhattan or Washington, D.C.[7]

Trust in the media has declined significantly over the last couple decades. A Gallup survey taken in 2012 indicated that distrust in media had reached record levels. Six in ten Americans said they have "little or no trust" in media.[8] Who can blame them? A number of journalists have been busted in the last decade for contriving stories, plagiarizing, manipulating photographs, omitting key information, and even accepting bribes.[9] This explains why more and more people are seeking sources beyond the establishment media for their news.

In fact, a *Time* magazine survey indicated that comedian Jon Stewart may be the most trusted source for news.[10] The reason likely has to do with the fact that viewers know where he stands; he doesn't hide his bias and he doesn't pretend to be objective, which most rational people understand is nearly impossible. When people turn on his program, they know who they're watching and where he stands politically. There's no subterfuge or pretense, though there is plenty of arrogance.

The decline in trust of the media has mirrored an increase in cynicism. That's bad news for the country. The less people feel they can affect change, the less likely they are to get involved, and the less likely they are to get informed about important issues that affect their lives. Nothing good can come from these trends. It's up to the public to demand more transparency from the echo-chamber media elitists and take back the power that's been centralized in the editorial boards of America's major news outlets and the hallowed halls of government. It is my belief that the future of our great nation depends upon people challenging the narratives and taking back power from the arrogant, shameless elitists in the echo chambers of Washington, D.C., and Manhattan.

BIBLIOGRAPHY

Books:

Bauckham, Richard. *The Book of Acts in Its Palestinian Setting.* Grand Rapids, MI: Wm. B. Eerdmans Publishing, 1995.

Dutton, Kevin. *The Wisdom of Psychopaths: What Saints, Spies, and Serial Killers Can Teach Us About Success.* New York: Farrar, Strauss and Giroux, 2012.

Ferguson, Niall. *Civilization: The West and the Rest.* New York: Penguin Group, Inc., 2011.

Folsom, Burton. *New Deal or Raw Deal? How FDR's Economic Legacy Has Damaged America.* New York: Simon & Schuster, Inc., 2008.

Fontova, Humberto. *Fidel: Hollywood's Favorite Tyrant.* Washington, D.C.: Regnery Publishing, Inc., 2005.

Gaddis, John Lewis. *The Landscape of History: How Historians Map the Past.* New York: Oxford University Press, 2002.

Goldberg, Bernard. *A Slobbering Love Affair.* Washington, D.C.: Regnery Publishing, Inc., 2009.

Goldberg, Jonah. *Liberal Fascism: The Secret History of the American Left from Mussolini to the Politics of Meaning.* New York: Random House, Inc., 2007.

Groseclose, Tim. *Left Turn: How Liberal Media Bias Distorts the American Mind.* New York: St. Martin's Press, 2011.

Harris, Lee. *Civilization and its Enemies: The Next Stage of History*. New York: Simon & Schuster, Inc., 2004.

Medved, Michael. *The Ten Big Lies About America: Combating the Destructive Distortions About Our Nation*. New York: Random House, Inc., 2008.

Muravchik, Joshua. *Heaven on Earth: The Rise and Fall of Socialism*. San Francisco, CA: Encounter Books, 2002.

Newton, Michael E. *The Path to Tyranny: A History of Free Society's Descent into Tyranny*. Eleftheria Publishing, Kindle Edition, 2010.

Ricks, Thomas E. *The Gamble: General Patraeus and the American Military Adventure in Iraq*. New York: Penguin Books, 2009.

Riessman, Catherine Kohler. *Narrative Methods for the Human Sciences*. Thousand Oaks, CA: Sage Publications, Inc., 2008.

Seibert, Jeffrey W. *I Done My Duty: The Complete Story of the Assassination of President McKinley*. Bowie, MD: Heritage Books, 2002.

Sowell, Thomas. *A Conflict of Visions: Ideological Origins of Political Struggles*. New York: Basic Books, 2007.

Timmerman, Kenneth R. *Shadow Warriors: The Untold Story of Traitors, Saboteurs, and the Party of Surrender*. New York: Random House, Inc., 2007.

Twenge, Jean M. and W. Keith Campbell. *The Narcissism Epidemic: Living in the Age of Entitlement*. New York: Simon & Schuster, Inc., 2009.

Online Resources:

http://dailycaller.com/
http://drudgereport.com/
http://hotair.com/
http://newsbusters.org/
http://pjmedia.com/instapundit/

http://www.breitbart.com/
http://www.salon.com/
http://www.slate.com/
http://www.theblaze.com/
http://www.thedailybeast.com/

ENDNOTES

INTRODUCTION

1. A Joke.
2. Jacqueline Howard, "Psychopathic Personality Traits Linked With U.S. Presidential Success, Psychologists Suggest," *The Huffington Post*, Sep. 13, 2012: http://www.huffingtonpost.com/2012/09/13/psychopathic-personality-traits-president_n_1874567.html.
3. Jim Kouri, "Serial killers and politicians share traits," *The Examiner*, Jun. 12, 2009: http://www.examiner.com/article/serial-killers-and-politicians-share-traits. See also, Melanie Kruvelis, "Study: Politicians and Psychopaths Aren't So Different," *Reason*, Aug. 1, 2012: http://reason.com/blog/2012/08/01/breaking-news-politicians-and-psychopath.
4. Kevin Dutton, *The Wisdom of Psychopaths: What Saints, Spies, and Serial Killers Can Teach Us About Success* (New York: Farrar, Strauss and Giroux, 2012), p. 162.
5. Kathleen Maher, "By the Numbers: the jobs of the First Congress vs. the 112th Congress," Constitution Daily, February 2012: http://blog.constitutioncenter.org/2012/02/by-the-numbers-the-jobs-jobs-jobs-of-the-first-congress-vs-the-112th-congress/; (accessed Jan. 6, 2013).
6. R. Eric Peterson, "Representatives and Senators: Trends in Characteristics Since 1945" (Cornell University Publications,

Feb. 17, 2012), p. 10. Available online: http://digitalcommons.ilr.cornell.edu/cgi/viewcontent.cgi (accessed Jan. 6, 2013).

7. Jeam M. Twenge and W. Keith Campbell, *The Narcissism Epidemic: Living in the Age of Entitlement* (New York: Free Press, Inc., 2009), p. 59.
8. Twenge and Campbell, p. 5. For instance, "In 2004, 74% of high school students admitted to cheating, up from 61% in 1992" p. 206.
9. Twenge and Campbell, p. 136. Of note, today the United States government is more than $16 trillion in debt, primarily the result of a massive expansion of federal spending on so-called entitlements.
10. Niall Ferguson, "The World; Why America Outpaces Europe (Clue: The God Factor)," *New York Times*, Jun. 8, 2003: http://www.nytimes.com/2003/06/08/weekinreview/the-world-why-america-outpaces-europe-clue-the-god-factor.html.
11. Niall Ferguson, *Civilization: The West and the Rest* (New York: Penguin Group, Inc., 2011), p. 265.
12. See, for instance, "America's European moment," *The Economist*, Jan. 5, 2013: http://www.economist.com/news/leaders/21569024-troubling-similarities-between-fiscal-mismanagement-washington-and-mess.
13. The most recent example (as of the writing of this sentence) occurred in Louisiana: Erica Ritz, "Police Force to Evacuate Louisiana Mall After Enormous Teen Brawl Breaks Out in Food Court," *The Blaze*, Jan. 6, 2013: http://www.theblaze.com/stories/police-forced-to-evacuate-louisiana-mall-after-enormous-teen-brawl-breaks-out-in-food-court/.
14. Corey Dade, "Flash Mobs Aren't Just For Fun Anymore," *NPR*, May 26, 2011: http://www.npr.org/2011/05/26/136578945/flash-mobs-arent-just-for-fun-anymore. See also, Annie Vauhan, "Teenage Flash Mob Robberies on the Rise," Fox News, Jun. 18, 2011: http://www.foxnews.com/us/2011/06/18/top-five-most-brazen-flash-mob-robberies/.

15. Thomas Sowell, *A Conflict of Visions: Ideological Origins of Political Struggles* (New York: Basic Books, 2007), pp. 11-17.
16. For two remarkable surveys of the Leftist attempt to usher in a utopia on earth, see Joshua Muravchik, Heaven on Earth: The Rise and Fall of Socialism (San Francisco, CA: Encounter Books, 2002); and Jonah Goldberg, Liberal Fascism: The Secret History of the American Left from Mussolini to the Politics of Meaning (New York: Random House, Inc., 2007).
17. Catherine Kohler Riessman, *Narrative Methods for the Human Sciences* (Thousand Oaks, CA: Sage Publications, Inc., 2008), p. 3.
18. John Lewis Gaddis, *The Landscape of History: How Historians Map the Past* (New York: Oxford University Press, 2002), pp. 136, 140-141.

CHAPTER ONE

1. "Exhibit 1-10: Newspaper Journalists of the 1990s," *Media Research Center*: http://www.mrc.org/media-bias-101/exhibit-1-10-newspaper-journalists-1990s.
2. "Media Bias 101: What Journalists Really Think -- and What the Public Thinks About Them," *Media Research Center*: http://www.mrc.org/media-bias-101/media-bias-101-what-journalists-really-think-and-what-public-thinks-about-them
3. See "How the media vote," at the *Media Research Center* website: http://archive.mrc.org/biasbasics/biasbasics3.asp. See, also, Tim Groseclose, *Left Turn: How Liberal Media Bias Distorts the American Mind* (New York: St. Martin's Press, 2011), p. 99.
4. Groseclose, p. 106.
5. Groseclose, p. 141. Groseclose notes that Manhattanites voted for Obama over Bush by 84-13 percent. Also of note, actress Kyra Sedgwick told PBS's Tavis Smiley that people in L.A. and New York "have a narrower view of the way people behave, of what's important to people." See Noel Sheppard, "Kyra Sedgwick: 'People in NY and LA Have Narrower

View' of Race, Abortion and Women's Rights," *Newsbusters*: http://newsbusters.org/blogs/noel-sheppard/2012/09/01/kyra-sedgwick-people-ny-and-la-have-narrower-view-rape-abortion-and-w#ixzz25GwYfLD6.

6. Groseclose, p. 112.
7. Groseclose, p. 252. Ms. Raddatz was a guest on C-SPAN's *Washington Journal*, on May 11, 2007 when she made these comments.
8. Noel Sheppard, "Soledad O'Brien Caught Reading Liberal Blog During Heated Debate With Romney Adviser," *Newsbusters*: http://newsbusters.org/blogs/noel-sheppard/2012/08/13/soledad-obrien-caught-reading-liberal-blog-during-heated-debate-romne#ixzz23hAs2mHu.
9. "Echo Chamber: Soledad 'Round Table' on Gun Control Has No Opposing Views," *Breitbart*, Dec. 20, 2012: http://www.breitbart.com/Breitbart-TV/2012/12/20/Echo-Chamber-Soledad-Round-Table-On-Gun-Control-Has-No-Opposing-Views.
10. Dylan Byers, "ABC draws possible Tea Party connection with alleged Aurora shooter," *Politico*: http://www.politico.com/blogs/media/2012/07/aurora-abc-draws-possible-tea-party-connection-129568.html.
11. Matthew Balan, "CBS's Bill Plante Minimizes Pro-Gun Rights Voices; Slants 3 to 1 In Favor of Gun Control," *Newsbusters*, Dec. 19, 2012: http://newsbusters.org/blogs/matthew-balan/2012/12/19/cbss-bill-plante-minimizes-pro-gun-rights-voices-slants-3-1-favor-gun#ixzz2Fcc1uGE3.
12. I can hear journalists who read these words making the case that I'm insulting their readers, viewers, and listeners by suggesting that they are unable to discern bias from truth. To the contrary; I'm suggesting that readers, viewers, and listeners are capapble, thus should be privy to journalist's ideology. Why all the secrecy?
13. Brent Baker, "Flashback: Reacting to MRC, ABC News Chief Westin Apologized for 'No Opinion' on Whether

Pentagon Was 'Legitimate' 9/11 Target," *Newsbusters*: http://newsbusters.org/blogs/brent-baker/2010/09/07/flashback-reacting-mrc-abc-news-chief-westin-apologized-no-opinion-whet#ixzz25oNCpTjS.

14. Bernard Goldberg, *Arrogance: Rescuing America from the Media Elite* (New York: Time Warner, 2003), pp. 201-202.
15. See, for instance, Brad Wilmouth, "On PBS, Liberal Columnists Slam Biden for 'Chains' Gaffe," *Newsbusters*: http://newsbusters.org/blogs/brad-wilmouth/2012/08/18/pbs-liberal-columnists-slam-biden-chains-gaffe#ixzz24MoAARSQ. See also: Scott Whitlock, "Once Again, Only CBS Spotlights Racial Overtones in Biden 'Chains' Attack," *Newsbusters*: http://newsbusters.org/blogs/scott-whitlock/2012/08/15/only-cbs-spotlights-racial-overtones-bidens-chains-attack#ixzz24MoZpv6Z.
16. Scott Whitlock, "Frenzied Media Give Four Times More Coverage to Akin Flap Than Biden's 'Chains' Smear," *Newsbusters*: http://newsbusters.org/blogs/scott-whitlock/2012/08/22/frenzied-media-give-four-times-more-coverage-akin-flap-bidens-chains#ixzz24Mli3ujB.
17. Brad Wilmouth, "MSNBC's Halperin: 'Media Is Very Susceptible to Doing What the Obama Campaign Wants'," *Newsbusters*: http://newsbusters.org/blogs/brad-wilmouth/2012/08/19/msnbcs-halperin-media-very-susceptible-doing-what-obama-campaign-want#ixzz24MnTbqlo.
18. Jeff Poor, "Newt Gingrich blasts Thomas Friedman on abortion, Biden on race, Rove on Todd Akin remarks," Daily Caller: http://dailycaller.com/2012/09/02/newt-gingrich-blasts-thomas-friedman-on-abortion-biden-on-race-rove-on-todd-akin-remarks/#ixzz25MVEhT3k.
19. Ibid.
20. Clay Waters, "GOP Convention 'Colossal Hoax.' Party 'Trades in Human Horridness,' *New York* Times Columnists Say," *Newsbusters*: http://newsbusters.org/blogs/clay-waters/2012/09/03/gop-convention-colossal-hoax-party-trades-human-horridness-new-york-tim#ixzz25WLpBgmX.

21. Clay Waters, "Obama's '57 States' Gaffe Finally Makes the New York Times News Page," *Newsbusters*: http://newsbusters.org/blogs/clay-waters/2011/11/18/obamas-57-states-gaffe-finally-makes-new-york-times-news-page#ixzz24Mt7V0zo. See, also: Tom Blumer, "Old Media Ignores Obama's '57 States,' Obsessed Over Quayle's 'Potatoe'," Newsbusters: http://newsbusters.org/blogs/tom-blumer/2008/05/11/old-media-ignores-obamas-57-states-obsessed-over-quayles-potatoe#ixzz24MtJNyRf.
22. Associated Press, May 9, 2012. See: "Obama: '10,000 People Died' in Kansas Tornado," *Fox News*: http://www.foxnews.com/story/0,2933,270852,00.html.
23. President Obama also suggested during an address to a joint session of Congress that Abraham Lincoln founded the Republican Party, which is false; see, Timothy Birdnow, "PBS alters transcript to hide Obama gaffe," *American Thinker*: http://www.americanthinker.com/blog/2011/09/pbs_alters_transcript_to_hide_obama_gaffe.html He also referred to Hawaii as Asia and offended the entire nation of Poland by saying there were Polish concentration camps during World War Two (see, for instance, Tim Graham, "Networks Bury Obama's 'Polish Death Camp' Gaffe, But ABC and NBC Find Time to Mock a Romney Misspelling," *Newsbusters*: http://newsbusters.org/blogs/tim-graham/2012/05/31/networks-bury-obamas-polish-death-camp-gaffe-abc-and-nbc-find-time-mock-#ixzz24Mzde1Yc). President Obama referred to Hawaii as Asia. To see more Obama gaffes, try these sites: http://newsbusters.org/forum/topic-discussion/handy-reference-guide-obama039s-gaffes-and-goofs; http://politicalhumor.about.com/od/barackobama/a/obama-isms.htm.
24. Groseclose, p. 112.
25. See, Groseclose, pp. 123-135.
26. "Abortion," Gallup, Aug. 23, 2012: http://www.gallup.com/poll/1576/abortion.aspx.
27. This is a common metaphor, and has been used by other media

critics: See, for instance, Bernard Goldberg, *A Slobbering Love Affair* (Regnery Publishing, Inc., 2009), p. 66.

28. Arthur S. Brisbane, "Success and Risk as The Times Transforms," *New York Times*, Aug. 25, 2012: http://www.nytimes.com/2012/08/26/opinion/sunday/success-and-risk-as-the-times-transforms.html. See also: Noel Sheppard, "Outgoing Public Editor: Progressivism 'Bleeds Through the Fabric of the New York Times'," Newsbusters: http://newsbusters.org/blogs/noel-sheppard/2012/08/26/outgoing-public-editor-progressivism-bleeds-through-fabric-new-york-t#ixzz24hP0eRlw; also:
29. Patrick B. Pexton, "Will The Post be about news or opinion?" *Washington Post*, Sep. 28, 2012: http://www.washingtonpost.com/opinions/patrick-pexton-is-it-news-or-is-it-politics/2012/09/28/fac19242-097c-11e2-858a-5311df86ab04_story.html. See also, Ed Morrissey, "WaPo ombud: Say, there aren't many conservatives in our 'news' section, huh?" *Hot Air*: http://hotair.com/archives/2012/09/29/wapo-ombud-say-there-arent-many-conservatives-in-our-news-section-huh/.
30. Lucy Madison, "Poll: Distrust in media hits new high," *CBS News*, Sep. 21, 2012: http://www.cbsnews.com/8301-503544_162-57517656-503544/poll-distrust-in-media-hits-new-high/.

CHAPTER TWO

1. "REPORT: Gun Homicide is the Leading Cause Of Death Among Black Teens," *Black Youth Project*, Mar. 28, 2012: http://www.blackyouthproject.com/2012/03/report-gun-homicide-is-the-leading-cause-of-death-among-black-teens/.
2. The implication of this syllogism is that opponents of private gun ownership, at their core, have some degree of negative feelings about the United States of America. That's not to say that they hate America, but that they either believe we're not exceptional, or that other nations are superior, particularly those that restrict private gun ownership.

3. Jason Howerton, "Ed Schultz's Anti-Gun Argument: People Who Wrote the Second Amendment 'Owned Slaves, Oppressed Women and Were Short on Tolerance,'" *The Blaze*, Dec. 14, 2012: ed-schultzs-anti-gun-argument-people-who-wrote-the-second-amendment-owned-slaves-oppressed-women-were-short-on-tolerance.
4. Dan Gainor, "MSNBC's Ed Schultz Talks Gun 'Confiscation'," *Newsbusters*, Dec. 16, 2012: http://newsbusters.org/blogs/dan-gainor/2012/12/16/msnbc-s-ed-schultz-talks-gun-confiscation.
5. Erica Ritz, "Michael Moore Goes on Anti-American Twitter Rant After Sandy Hood: 'We Began American [With] Genocide'," *The Blaze*, Dec. 17, 2012: http://www.theblaze.com/stories/michael-moore-goes-on-anti-american-twitter-rant-after-sandy-hook-we-began-america-with-genocide/.
6. Louis Michael Seidman, "Let's Give Up on the Constitution," *New York Times*, Dec. 30, 2012: http://www.nytimes.com/2012/12/31/opinion/lets-give-up-on-the-constitution.html.
7. Jeffrey Goldberg, "The Case for More Guns (And More Gun Control)," *The Atlantic*, December 2012: http://www.theatlantic.com/magazine/archive/2012/12/the-case-for-more-guns-and-more-gun-control/309161/.
8. Rich Noyes, "20 Years of Bias: Evil America," *Newsbusters*: http://newsbusters.org/blogs/rich-noyes/2007/10/25/20-years-bias-evil-america.
9. John Avlon, "Don't let this moment pass without acting on gun control," CNN, Dec. 18, 2012: http://www.cnn.com/2012/12/18/opinion/avlon-gun-politics/.
10. Glenn Reynolds, Instapundit blog post, Dec. 18, 2012: http://pjmedia.com/instapundit/159956/.
11. Julie Pace, "White House ramping up gun violence discussions," *Yahoo News* (Associated Press), Jan. 8, 2013: http://news.yahoo.com/white-house-ramping-gun-violence-discussions-110136366--politics.html.

12. Herschel Smith, "High Magazine Clips And The Shoulder Thing That Goes Up," *Captain's Journal*, Dec. 21, 2012: http://www.captainsjournal.com/2012/12/18/high-magazine-clips-and-the-shoulder-thing-that-goes-up/.
13. Christina Boyle, "Subway rape victim comes forward after suit tossed against MTA workers who ignored her cry for help," *The New York Daily News*, April 3, 2009: http://www.nydailynews.com/news/subway-rape-victim-suit-tossed-mta-workers-cry-article-1.359180.
14. "Mother Sues Cops For Failing to Protect Kids," *Fox News*, March 30, 2005: http://www.foxnews.com/story/0,2933,151860,00.html.
15. Linda Greenhouse, "Justices Rule Police Do Not Have a Constitutional Duty to Protect Someone," *New York Times* (June 28, 2005): http://www.nytimes.com/2005/06/28/politics/28scotus.html.
16. See, for instance, John R. Lott, *More Guns Less Crime* (Chicago: University of Chicago Press, 1998). Professor Lott's work and the work of other academics can be found at http://www2.lib.uchicago.edu/~llou/guns.html.
17. Sumathi Reddy, "A Thin Line on Skirts," *The Wall Street Journal*: http://online.wsj.com/article/SB10001424052970204262045766011742409523328.html. More: http://www.theblaze.com/stories/nypd-warns-women-not-to-wear-short-skirts-because-they-could-get-raped-poll/.
18. Joyce Lee Malcolm, "Self-Defense: An Endangered Right," *CATO Policy Report*, Vol. XXVI No. 2, March/April 2004: http://www.cato.org/sites/cato.org/files/serials/files/policy-report/2004/3/cpr-26n2-1.pdf.
19. "Newton's horror: Only drastic gun control could make a big difference," *The Economist*, Dec. 22, 2012: http://www.economist.com/news/leaders/21568735-only-drastic-gun-control-could-make-big-difference-small-measures-can-help-bit-newtowns.
20. Tom Blumer, "WSJ Op-Ed: Gun-Banning Efforts in the

UK, Australia 'Haven't Made People Safer' (In Fact, They're Less Safe)," *Newsbusters*, Dec. 27, 2012: http://newsbusters.org/blogs/tom-blumer/2012/12/27/wsj-op-ed-gun-banning-efforts-uk-australia-havent-made-people-safer-fact.

21. Jeremy Gorner and Peter Nickeas, "Chicago police confirm 'tragic number' of 500 homicides," *Chicago Tribune*, Dec. 28, 2012: http://www.chicagotribune.com/news/local/breaking/chi-chicago-2012-homicide-toll-20121228,0,5456581.story.
22. Jeffrey Goldberg, "The Case for More Guns (And More Gun Control)," *The Atlantic*, December 2012: http://www.theatlantic.com/magazine/archive/2012/12/the-case-for-more-guns-and-more-gun-control/309161/.
23. Scott Whitlock, "Elderly Man Saves a Café Full of People By Shooting Gun-Wielding Robbers; NBC, CBS Skip," *Newsbusters*: http://newsbusters.org/blogs/scott-whitlock/2012/07/18/elderly-man-saves-cafe-full-people-shooting-gun-wielding-robbers-nbc.
24. Becket Adams, "How Bad Is Detroit? This Shock Video Shows One Woman Who Tried To Report a Crime Waiting 4 hours for Police," *The Blaze*: http://www.theblaze.com/stories/how-bad-is-detroit-this-shock-vid-shows-one-woman-who-tried-to-report-a-crime-waiting-4-hrs-for-police/.
25. Erica Ritz, "Some California 'Meter Maids' Are Making Nearly $100K a Year," *The Blaze* (Aug. 14, 2012): http://www.theblaze.com/stories/some-california-meter-maids-are-making-nearly-100k-a-year/.
26. See "City of Bell scandal," at Wikipedia: http://en.wikipedia.org/wiki/City_of_Bell_scandal.
27. Larry Gabriel, "How Corrupt is Detroit?" *Metro Times* (March 14, 2012): http://metrotimes.com/columns/how-corrupt-is-detroit-1.1285299.
28. Ed Morrissey, "Video: When open carry is your only option," *Hotair*: http://hotair.com/archives/2011/08/10/video-when-open-carry-is-your-only-option/.
29. Jason Howerton, "Lock Your Doors & Load Your Guns: Calif.

City Attorney Tells Residents to be Self-Reliant Following Cuts to Police Force," *The Blaze*, Nov. 30, 2012: http://www.theblaze.com/stories/lock-your-doors-and-load-your-guns-city-attorney-tells-san-bernardino-residents-to-be-self-reliant-following-police-downsizing/.

30. Becket Adams, "President Obama Cites Sandy Hook Massacre To Encourage 'Fiscal Cliff' Compromise," *The Blaze*, Dec. 19, 2012: http://www.theblaze.com/stories/president-obama-cites-sandy-hook-massacre-to-encourage-fiscal-cliff-compromise/.
31. Matt Hadro, "CNN's Lemon Goes on Anti-Gun Tirade, Calls for Assault Weapons Ban," Newsbusters, Dec. 17, 2012: http://newsbusters.org/blogs/matt-hadro/2012/12/17/cnns-lemon-goes-anti-gun-tirade-calls-assault-weapons-ban.
32. The phrase "Bill of Needs" is borrowed from Mark Levin, conservative radio talk show host, who used the term when criticizing these Leftists who are asking "why do you need" such and such type of weapon. As heard on Dec. 17, 2012, on WRC 1260 AM radio.
33. Jeffrey Meyer, "In Wake of Conn. School Shooting, GMA Pushes for Greater Gun Control," *Newsbusters*, Dec. 17, 2012: http://newsbusters.org/blogs/jeffrey-meyer/2012/12/17/wake-conn-school-shooting-gma-pushes-greater-gun-control.
34. Matt Hadro, "Soledad O'Brien Bullies Gun Rights Activist; 'Your Position Completely Boggles Me'," *Newsbusters*, Dec. 17, 2012: http://newsbusters.org/blogs/matt-hadro/2012/12/17/soledad-obrien-bullies-gun-rights-activist-your-position-completely-bogg#ixzz2FOAgLXPN.
35. Madeleine Morganstern, "'You are a Dangerous Man...And You Shame Your Contry': CNN Anchor Lashes Out at Gun Lobby Director," *The Blaze*, Dec. 19, 2012: http://www.theblaze.com/stories/you-are-a-dangerous-man-and-you-shame-your-country-cnn-anchor-lashes-out-at-gun-lobby-director/.See also, John Nolte, "CNN's Piers Morgan Calls Pro-Gun Rights Guest 'Unbelievable Stupid Man'," *Breitbart*, Dec. 19, 2012:

http://www.breitbart.com/Big-Journalism/2012/12/19/Piers-Morgan-Flips-Out-Over-Gun-Control.

36. Jared Loughner Wikipedia page: http://en.wikipedia.org/wiki/Jared_Loughner.
37. http://www.wibw.com/home/headlines/Jared_Loughner_Had_5_Run-ins_with_College_Police_113254289.html.
38. David A. Fahrenthold, "Jared Loughner's college instructor: I was worried he might have a gun in class," *Washington Post*: http://voices.washingtonpost.com/44/2011/01/loughners-college-instructor-i.html.
39. David Brooks, "The politicized mind," *New York Times*: http://www.nytimes.com/2011/01/11/opinion/11brooks.html.
40. "Pima County Sheriff Clarence Dupnik Calls Out Vitriolic, Hateful Rhetoric," *YouTube*: http://www.youtube.com/watch?v=ccY9lNRiUWg.
41. Geoffrey Dickens, "Today Show Links Sarah Palin to Giffords Shooting," *Newsbusters*: http://newsbusters.org/blogs/geoffrey-dickens/2011/01/10/today-show-links-sarah-palin-giffords-shooting.
42. Geoffrey Dickens, "Matthews Links Palin&Bachmann to Giffords Shooting, Portrays U.S. as Gun Crazed Nation," *Newsbusters*: http://newsbusters.org/blogs/geoffrey-dickens/2011/01/10/matthews-links-palinbachmann-giffords-shooting-portrays-us-gun-cra.
43. Alex Fitzsimmons, "MSNBC's Mitchell Blames Palin, Again, for Tucson Shooting," *Newsbusters*: http://newsbusters.org/blogs/alex-fitzsimmons/2011/01/11/msnbcs-mitchell-blames-palin-again-tucson-shooting.
44. Geoffrey Dickens, "NBC's Lee Cowan Highlights Palin Map As Possible Rationale for Attack on Gabrielle Giffords," *Newsbusters*: http://newsbusters.org/blogs/geoffrey-dickens/2011/01/10/nbcs-lee-cowan-highlights-palin-map-possible-rationale-attack-gabr.
45. Ed Morrissey, "The Shame – and Hypocrisy – of CNN,"

Hotair: http://hotair.com/archives/2011/01/09/the-shame-and-hypocrisy-of-cnn/.

46. Matt Hadro, "Tom Brokaw Praises Sheriff Dupnik For Remarks Against Violent Rhetoric, Wishes More Would Speak Out," *Newsbusters*: http://newsbusters.org/blogs/matt-hadro/2011/01/10/tom-brokaw-praises-sheriff-dupnik-remarks-against-violent-rhetoric-wishe.
47. Tom Blumer, "AP Determined to Pin Giffords Shooting, Multiple Murders on Right, Ignores Lefist Rage at Her Failure to Back Pelosi," *Newsbusters*: http://newsbusters.org/blogs/tom-blumer/2011/01/08/ap-determined-pin-giffords-shooting-multiple-murders-right-ignores-lefis.
48. Brent Baker, "Network Journalists Advance Leftist Wish to Blame Palin (and Tea Party) for Shooting," *Newsbusters*: http://newsbusters.org/blogs/brent-baker/2011/01/09/network-journalists-advance-leftist-wish-blame-palin-and-tea-party-shoo#ixzz24wMuNF00.
49. Brad Wilmouth, "WaPo's Eugene Robinson Joins Olbermann in Linking Giffords Shooting to Political Rhetoric," *Newsbusters*: http://newsbusters.org/blogs/brad-wilmouth/2011/01/09/wapo-s-eugene-robinson-joins-olbermann-linking-giffords-shooting-poli.
50. Brent Baker, "Network Journalists Advance Leftist Wish to Blame Palin (and Tea Party) for Shooting," *Newsbusters*: http://newsbusters.org/blogs/brent-baker/2011/01/09/network-journalists-advance-leftist-wish-blame-palin-and-tea-party-shoo#ixzz24wMuNF00.
51. Brent Baker, "Network Journalists Advance Leftist Wish to Blame Palin (and Tea Party) for Shooting," *Newsbusters*: http://newsbusters.org/blogs/brent-baker/2011/01/09/network-journalists-advance-leftist-wish-blame-palin-and-tea-party-shoo#ixzz24wMuNF00.
52. Terry Trippany, "Chicago Sun Times Takes Low Road on Giffords Shooting," *Newsbusters*: http://newsbusters.org/blogs/

terry-trippany/2011/01/09/chicago-sun-times-takes-low-road-giffords-shooting.

53. Brent Baker, "Network Journalists Advance Leftist Wish to Blame Palin (and Tea Party) for Shooting," *Newsbusters*: http://newsbusters.org/blogs/brent-baker/2011/01/09/network-journalists-advance-leftist-wish-blame-palin-and-tea-party-shoo#ixzz24wMuNF00.
54. Noel Sheppard, "Debra Saunders Scolds Roger Simon for Tying Palin to Giffords Shooting," *Newsbusters*: http://newsbusters.org/blogs/noel-sheppard/2011/01/09/san-francisco-conservative-scolds-roger-simon-connecting-sarah-palin-.
55. Paul Krugman, "The Conscience of a Liberal," *New York Times*, January 8, 2011: http://krugman.blogs.nytimes.com/2011/01/08/assassination-attempt-in-arizona/. More: Meredith Jessup, "NY Times' Krugman Blames Shooting on GOP, 'Hate-Mongers' Beck & Limbaugh," *The Blaze*: http://www.theblaze.com/stories/ny-times-krugman-blames-shooting-on-gop-hate-mongers-beck-limbaugh/.
56. Brent Baker, "Network Journalists Advance Leftist Wish to Blame Palin (and Tea Party) for Shooting," *Newsbusters*: http://newsbusters.org/blogs/brent-baker/2011/01/09/network-journalists-advance-leftist-wish-blame-palin-and-tea-party-shoo#ixzz24wMuNF00.
57. Watch the video at "Keith Olbermann Compares Glenn to Shooter, Calls on Beck to Apologize for his Rhetoric," *The Blaze*: http://www.theblaze.com/stories/keith-olbermann-compares-glenn-to-shooter-calls-on-beck-to-apologize-for-his-rhetoric/.
58. Jonathon M. Seidl, "PA Rep. Brady Suggests Gunman Motivated by Sarah Palin's Website," *The Blaze*: http://www.theblaze.com/stories/pa-rep-brady-suggests-gunman-motivated-by-sarah-palins-website/.
59. Tim Graham, "Within Minutes of Shooting, CNN Finds Local Liberal to Blame State's 'Rabid Right' and Gun 'Fetish'," *Newsbusters*: http://newsbusters.org/blogs/tim-

graham/2011/01/09/within-minutes-shooting-cnn-finds-local-liberal-blame-states-rabid-right.

60. Ed Morrissey, "The Shame – and Hypocrisy – of CNN," *Hotair*: http://hotair.com/archives/2011/01/10/the-shame-and-hypocrisy-of-the-new-york-times/.
61. "'Politics in Arizona Have Become Fueled by Hate...Driven by Anger": Rep. Raúl Grijalva on Shooting of Giffords," Democracy Now!: http://www.democracynow.org/2011/1/10/politics_in_arizona_have_become_fueled.
62. Lachlan Markay, "Loughner Friend: 'He Did Not Watch TV' or 'Listen to Political Radio'," *Newsbusters*: http://newsbusters.org/blogs/lachlan-markay/2011/01/12/loughner-friend-he-did-not-watch-tv-or-listen-political-radio. More: Ed Morrissey, "Video: Shooter a nonpartisan nutcase, says friend," *Hotair*: http://hotair.com/archives/2011/01/12/video-shooter-a-nonpartisan-nutcase-says-friend/.
63. Paul Krugman, "The Conscience of a Liberal," *New York Times*: http://krugman.blogs.nytimes.com/2011/01/08/assassination-attempt-in-arizona/.
64. "CNN Poll: Blame game in Arizona shootings," *CNN*, Jan. 17, 2011: http://politicalticker.blogs.cnn.com/2011/01/17/cnn-poll-blame-game-in-arizona-shootings/. See, also: Allahpundit, "CNN poll: Majority of Dems, 35% overall think Palin's crosshairs map is at least partly to blame for Arizona shootings," *Hotair*: http://hotair.com/archives/2011/01/17/cnn-poll-majority-of-dems-35-overall-think-palins-crosshairs-map-is-at-least-partly-to-blame-for-arizona-shootings/.
65. Keach Hagey, "Pew: Political rhetoric focus of Tucson coverage," *Politico*: http://www.politico.com/blogs/onmedia/0111/Pew_Political_rhetoric_focus_of_Tucson_coverage.html.
66. Ed Morrissey, "Bummber: Pima County Attorny muzzles Supercop," *Hotair*: http://hotair.com/archives/2011/01/20/bummer-pima-county-attorney-muzzles-supercop/.
67. Victor Davis Hanson, "The Bloomberg Syndrome," *National*

Review Online, Jan. 20, 2011: http://www.nationalreview.com/articles/257560/bloomberg-syndrome-victor-davis-hanson.

68. Rick Moran, "Is Daily Kos to blame for Gifford Attack?" *American Thinker*: http://www.americanthinker.com/blog/2011/01/is_daily_kos_to_blame_for_giff.html.
69. "Democrat Harry Mitchell Places Opponent in Crosshairs," Youtube: http://www.youtube.com/watch?v=XqB4tyvxWKA.
70. Markos Moulitsas, "2012 will be primary season," *The Daily Kos*: http://www.dailykos.com/story/2008/6/25/1204/74882/511/541568.
71. Ben Smith, "Obama brings gun to a knife fight," *Poltiico*: http://www.politico.com/blogs/bensmith/0608/Obama_brings_a_gun_to_a_knife_fight.html.
72. Tim Graham, "WaPo Civility: 'Knock Every Racist and Homophobic Tooth Out of Their Cro-Magnon Heads'," *Newsbusters*: http://newsbusters.org/blogs/tim-graham/2010/03/24/wapo-civility-knock-every-racist-and-homophobic-tooth-out-their-cro-magn#ixzz23rDs2Loh.
73. Rusty Weiss, "Daily Kos Campaign Director Uses 'Target Lists' Frequently," *Newsbusters*: http://newsbusters.org/blogs/rusty-weiss/2011/01/10/daily-kos-campaign-director-uses-target-lists-frequently#ixzz23rEI6g7a.
74. Tom Blumer, "At NYT, Former Congressman Who Called for Rick Scott's Shooting Wants 'Atmosphere of Civility and Respect'," Newsbusters: http://newsbusters.org/blogs/tom-blumer/2011/01/11/nyt-former-congressman-who-called-rick-scotts-shooting-wants-atmosphere-#ixzz23rEXMwBp.
75. Jack Coleman, "Aghast From Past: Ed Schultz Producer Suggested Obama 'Put a Gun' to Heads of CEOs," *Newsbusters*: http://newsbusters.org/blogs/jack-coleman/2011/01/11/aghast-past-ed-schultz-producer-suggested-obama-put-gun-heads-ceos#ixzz23rEjC1Ds.
76. Noel Sheppard, "Chris Matthews' Violent Imagery: 'Sarah Palin is Going to be Erased as a Potential Candidate'," *Newsbusters*: http://newsbusters.org/blogs/noel-

sheppard/2011/01/11/chris-matthews-violent-imagery-sarah-palin-going-be-erased-potential-#ixzz23rEyKTjL.

77. Paul Krugman, "Pass the Bill," *New York Times* (Dec. 17, 2009): http://www.nytimes.com/2009/12/18/opinion/18krugman.html.
78. "Flashback: Barney Frank Jokes About Assassination Attempt on Cheney," *Breitbart*: http://www.breitbart.tv/flashback-barney-frank-jokes-about-assassination-attempt-on-cheney/.
79. Naked Emperor News, "#1 Lib Talker Hartmann: Beck is Like Bin Laden..." *The Blaze* (Jan. 14, 2011): http://www.theblaze.com/stories/1-lib-talker-thom-hartman-beck-is-like-bin-laden-palin-beck-right-are-activating-lone-wolf-terroists/.
80. Byron York, "Before banning 'crosshairs,' CNN used it to refer to Palin, Bachmann," *The Examiner* (Jan. 19, 2011): http://washingtonexaminer.com/blogs/beltway-confidential/2011/01/banning-crosshairs-cnn-used-it-refer-palin-bachmann#ixzz1BXt0ebnF.
81. Geoffrey Dickens, "Sheriff Civility AKA Chris Matthews Calls Michele Bachmann a 'Nut Case'," *Newsbusters*: http://newsbusters.org/blogs/geoffrey-dickens/2011/01/19/sheriff-civility-aka-chris-matthews-calls-michele-bachmann-nut-cas#ixzz23rGovuTg. See, also: http://redsounding.org/2012/03/05/maher-versus-limbaugh.aspx.
82. "New Tone: Dem Compares GOP to Nazis During Obamacare Repeal Speech," *Breitbart*: http://www.breitbart.tv/new-tone-dem-compares-gop-to-nazis-during-obamacare-repeal-speech/.
83. "Dem Congressman: Obamacare Repeal Will Kill People," *Breitbart*: http://www.breitbart.tv/dem-congressman-obamacare-repeal-will-kill-people/.
84. Jeff Poor, "Democratic congressman: Gabrielle Giffords shooting 'the start of the revolution'," *Daily Caller*: http://dailycaller.com/2011/01/13/democratic-congressman-gabrielle-giffords-shooting-the-start-of-the-revolution/.
85. See, for instance: http://www.zombietime.com/.

86. Seton Motley, "CNN Video from 2006: Bush With Hitler Mustache? No Outrage; Called A 'Look-Alike'," *Newsbusters*: http://newsbusters.org/blogs/seton-motley/2009/08/13/cnn-video-2006-bush-hitler-mustache-no-outrage-called-look-alike.
87. See Wikipedia: http://en.wikipedia.org/wiki/Death_of_a_President_(2006_film).
88. See, for instance: http://semiskimmed.net/bushhitler.html. Cite could not be accessed after August 2012.
89. "The Horror at Fort Hood," *New York Times*: http://www.nytimes.com/2009/11/07/opinion/07sat1.html.
90. "Bloodshed and Invective in Arizona," *New York Times*: http://www.nytimes.com/2011/01/10/opinion/10mon1.html.
91. Scott Whitlock, "Ex-Newsweek Editor Howard Fineman Counsels Obama on How to Spin Shooting for Political Gain," *Newsbusters*: http://newsbusters.org/blogs/scott-whitlock/2011/01/10/ex-newsweek-editor-howard-fineman-counsels-obama-how-spin-shooting-p#ixzz24ATb34sr.
92. Lachlan Markay, "Newsweek's Jonathan Alter Gives Obama Advice on Exploiting Tucson Tragedy for Political Gain," *Newsbusters*: http://newsbusters.org/blogs/lachlan-markay/2011/01/11/newsweeks-jonathan-alter-gives-obama-advice-exploiting-tucson-traged#ixzz24ATmoP6j.
93. Jonathon M. Seidl, "PA Rep. Brady Suggests Gunman Motivated by Sarah Palin's Website," *The Blaze*: http://www.theblaze.com/stories/pa-rep-brady-suggests-gunman-motivated-by-sarah-palins-website/.
94. Naked Emperor News, "Exploiting Tragedy," *The Blaze*: http://www.theblaze.com/stories/exploiting-tragedy-we-had-restraint-on-speech-back-then-rep-clyburn-calls-for-new-fairness-doctrine-gun-restrictions/.
95. Chris Moody, "Hinojosa voices support for bill that curbs 'threatening' speech against lawmakers," *The Daily Caller*: http://dailycaller.com/2011/01/10/hinojosa-voices-support-for-bill-that-curbs-threatening-speech-against-lawmakers.

96. Rusty Weiss, "Congresswoman Wants to Kill the Phrase 'Job Killing'," *Newsbusters*: http://newsbusters.org/blogs/rusty-weiss/2011/01/11/congresswoman-wants-kill-phrase-job-killing#ixzz24AVEvYyT.
97. Noel Sheppard, "Bill Maher Heckled by 'Tonight Show' Crowd for Saying Conservatives Want to Kill People They Disagree With," *Newsbusters*: http://newsbusters.org/blogs/noel-sheppard/2011/01/12/bill-maher-heckled-tonight-show-crowd-saying-conservatives-want-kill-#ixzz24AXHzk3t.
98. All of these statements are cited on my blog: http://redsounding.org/2011/01/21/the-anatomy-of-a-smear-campaign.aspx.
99. Madeleine Morgenstern, "Scathing New Video Slams Obama's 'Double Standard' on Maher and Limbaugh," *The Blaze*: http://www.theblaze.com/stories/scathing-new-video-slams-obamas-double-standard-on-maher-and-limbaugh/.
100. Stephen Gutowski, "Michael Moore: People Own Guns Because They're Racists," *Media Research Center*: http://www.mrctv.org/2011/01/michael-moore-people-own-guns-because-they%E2%80%99re-racists/.
101. David Wright, "Gabrielle Giffords Tucson Shooting Puts Arizona's Gun Culture in Spotlight," *ABC News*: http://abcnews.go.com/US/tucson-shooting-puts-arizonas-gun-culture-spotlight/story?id=12578817.
102. Kyle Drennen, "NBC: 'Colorado Has Some of the Weakest Gun Laws in the Country'," *Newsbusters*: http://newsbusters.org/blogs/kyle-drennen/2012/07/23/nbc-colorado-has-some-weakest-gun-laws-country#ixzz21U5n4WWa.
103. David Kopel, "Colorado Consensus on Gun Laws," *Cato Institute*: http://www.cato.org/publications/commentary/colorado-consensus-gun-laws.
104. See, for instance, David B. Kopel, "Pretend 'Gun-Free' School Zones: A Deadly Fiction," *Connecticut Law Review*, Vol. 42, No. 2, pp. 515-584, December 2009; available online at: http://papers.ssrn.com/sol3/papers.cfm?abstract_id=1369783.
105. Matt Hadro, "Soledad O'Brien Bullies Gun Rights Activist; 'Your Position Completely Boggles Me'," *Newsbusters*, Dec. 17, 2012: http://newsbusters.org/blogs/matt-hadro/2012/12/17/

soledad-obrien-bullies-gun-rights-activist-your-position-completely-bogg#ixzz2FOCnwEsn.

106. David Kopel, Colorado Consensus on Gun Laws," *Cato Institute*: http://www.cato.org/publications/commentary/colorado-consensus-gun-laws. Emphasis his.
107. Erica Ritz, "Michael Moore: Guns today 'not really' what Founding Fathers meant when they said 'right to bear arms'," *The Blaze*: http://www.theblaze.com/stories/michael-moore-guns-today-not-really-what-founding-fathers-had-in-mind-when-they-said-right-to-bear-arms/.
108. Erika Harrell, Ph.D. "Black Victims of Violent Crime," August 2007, NCJ 214258: http://bjs.ojp.usdoj.gov/content/pub/pdf/bvvc.pdf.
109. http://pjmedia.com/instapundit/146061/
110. See, for instance, Max Fisher, "Chart: The U.S. has far more gun-related killings than any other developed country," *Washington Post*, Dec. 14, 2012: http://www.washingtonpost.com/blogs/worldviews/wp/2012/12/14/chart-the-u-s-has-far-more-gun-related-killings-than-any-other-developed-country/.
111. James Alan Fox and Marianne W. Zawitz, "Homicide Trends in the U.S.," *Bureau of Justice Statistics*, no date: http://bjs.ojp.usdoj.gov/content/homicide/homtrnd.cfm.
112. *District of Columbia* v. *Heller*, 554 U.S. 570 (2008).
113. *McDonald* v. *Chicago*, 561 U.S. 3025 (2010).
114. See John R. Lott, More Guns Less Crime: http://www.amazon.com/More-Guns-Less-Crime-Understanding/dp/0226493644/.
115. Prof. Carl T. Bogus, "The Hidden History of the Second Amendment," Violence Policy Center, 1998: http://www.vpc.org/fact_sht/hidhist.htm.
116. Stephanie Mencimer, "Whitewashing the Second Amendment," Mother Jones (Mar. 20, 2008): http://www.motherjones.com/politics/2008/03/whitewashing-second-amendment.
117. Justice Clarence Thomas, Concurrence (Cornell Univ. Law School, 2012): http://www.law.cornell.edu/supct/html/08-1521.ZC1.html.

118. Courtland Milloy, "In Clarence Thomas's gun rights opinion, race plays a major role," *Washington Post* (Jun. 30, 2010): http://www.washingtonpost.com/wp-dyn/content/article/2010/06/29/AR2010062905329.html
119. Kyle Drennen, "MSNBC: ObamaCare Protesters 'Racist,' Including Black Gun-Owner," *Newsbusters*: http://newsbusters.org/blogs/kyle-drennen/2009/08/18/msnbc-no-mention-black-gun-owner-among-racist-protesters.
120. Lizette Alverez, "City Criticizes Police Chief After Shooting," *New York Times*: http://www.nytimes.com/2012/03/22/us/police-chief-draws-fire-in-trayvon-martin-shooting.html: "Mr. Zimmerman, 28, a white Hispanic, told the police that he shot Trayvon in self-defense after an altercation." See also, Yamiche Alcindor, "Zimmerman's bail set at $1M in Trayvon Martin case," *USA Today*: http://www.wcsh6.com/news/national/article/206265/44/Zimmermans-bail-set-at-1M-in-Trayvon-Martin-case: "Zimmerman, a white Hispanic, is charged with second-degree murder in the shooting of Martin on Feb. 26."
121. Erik Wemple, "Why did New York Times call Zimmerman 'white Hispanic'?" *Washington Post*: http://www.washingtonpost.com/blogs/erik-wemple/post/why-did-new-york-times-call-george-zimmerman-white-hispanic/2012/03/28/gIQAW6fngS_blog.html.
122. Robert Gooding-Williams, "Fugitive Slave Mentality," *New York Times*: http://opinionator.blogs.nytimes.com/2012/03/27/fugitive-slave-mentality/.
123. Randy Hall, "In Haste to Cast Zimmerman as Racist, CNN Went Against Internal Recommendations," *Newsbusters*: http://newsbusters.org/blogs/randy-hall/2012/04/12/haste-cast-zimmerman-racist-cnn-went-against-internal-recommendations#ixzz202srTqLg.
124. "Did Trayvon Martin's shooter use slur in 911 tapes?" CNN: http://ac360.blogs.cnn.com/2012/03/22/did-trayvon-martins-shooter-use-slur-in-911-tapes/.
125. Bret LoGiurato, "CNN Backtracks, Now Thinks George Zimmerman Didn't Call Trayvon Martin a 'Coon'," *Business Insider*: http://articles.businessinsider.com/2012-04-06/

politics/31298195_1_racial-slur-audio-expert-anderson-cooper.

126. Paul Bond, "CNN Report of Racial Slur in Trayvon Martin Case Under Scrutiny (Video)," *The Hollywood Reporter*: http://www.hollywoodreporter.com/news/trayvon-martin-cnn-report-racial-slur-wolf-blitzer-308849.
127. Tommy Christopher, "CNN Isolates Audio on Alleged 'F**king C**ns' Trayvon Martin 911 Call," Mediaite.com: http://www.mediaite.com/tv/cnn-isolates-audio-on-alleged-%E2%80%98fcking-cns%E2%80%99-trayvon-martin-911-call/.
128. Charles Blow, "The Curious Case of Trayvon Martin," *New York Times*: http://www.nytimes.com/2012/03/17/opinion/blow-the-curious-case-of-trayvon-martin.html.
129. Charles Blow, "A Mother's Grace and Grieving," *New York Times*: http://www.nytimes.com/2012/03/26/opinion/blow-a-mothers-grace-and-grieving.html. Charles Blow, "From O.J. to Trayvon," *New York Times*: http://www.nytimes.com/2012/04/07/opinion/blow-from-oj-to-trayvon.html.
130. "Spike Lee apologizes for retweeting wrong Zimmerman address," CNN: http://articles.cnn.com/2012-03-28/justice/justice_florida-teen-spike-lee_1_apology-skittles-director-spike-lee?_s=PM:JUSTICE.
131. Benny Johnson, "New Black Panther Goes on Racist Rant After Release From Jail," *The Blaze*: http://www.theblaze.com/stories/racist-bastard-monkey-a-new-black-panther-spiritual-leader-gets-out-of-jail-goes-on-shouting-shock-rant-vowing-zimmerman-gotta-pay/.
132. Dan Riehl, "MSNBC's Convenient ellipses make Zimmerman look racist," Breitbart.com: http://www.breitbart.com/Big-Journalism/2012/03/28/MSNBC-ZImmerman-Ellipses.
133. Tim Graham, "A Win for NewsBusters: NBC Apologizes for Shoddy Editing of Zimmerman Call": http://newsbusters.org/blogs/tim-graham/2012/04/03/win-newsbusters-nbc-apologizes-shoddy-editing-zimmerman-call#ixzz2030kFIjT. Also, see Michael Brendan Dougherty, "NBC Edited the 911 Tape Audio And Made George Zimmerman Sound Racist," *Business Insider*: http://www.businessinsider.com/nbc-

is-investigating-how-its-news-edited-the-audio-to-make-george-zimmerman-look-really-racist-2012-4.

134. Matthew Sheffield, "NBC News President Insists Zimmerman Edit 'Not a Deliberate Act to Misrepresent," Newsbusters.org: http://newsbusters.org/blogs/matthew-sheffield/2012/04/08/nbc-insists-zimmerman-audio-edit-not-deliberate-act-misrepresent#ixzz202xiZsb7.
135. "George Zimmerman's head wounds after Trayvon Martin shooting likely bolster self-defense claims," CBS News: http://www.cbsnews.com/8301-505263_162-57435247/george-zimmermans-head-wounds-after-trayvon-martin-shooting-likely-bolster-self-defense-claims/.
136. Jelani Cobb, "What Got George Zimmerman Charged With Second-Degree Murder," *The Daily Beast*: http://www.thedailybeast.com/articles/2012/04/12/what-got-george-zimmerman-charged-with-second-degree-murder.html.
137. Frances Robles, "Detective in Zimmerman case said he was pressured to file charges," *The Miami Herald*: http://www.miamiherald.com/2012/07/12/2892510/more-evidence-released-in-zimmerman.html.
138. Frances Robles, "FBI records: Sanford police investigator felt pressured to arrest George Zimmerman in Trayvon Martin shooting," *Tampa Bay Times*: http://www.tampabay.com/news/publicsafety/crime/fbi-records-agents-found-no-evidence-that-george-zimmerman-was-racist/1239956.
139. Elizabeth Rosenthal, "More Guns = More Killing," *New York Times*, Jan. 5, 2012: http://www.nytimes.com/2013/01/06/sunday-review/more-guns-more-killing.html. The author buried, way down in paragraph fourteen, the fact that violent crime rates in the U.S. have been declining overall, but are still sky high in Chicago.
140. Neil Steinberg, "Gun violence reverberates through nation in a year of mass killings," *Chicago Sun-Times*, Dec. 28, 2012: http://www.suntimes.com/news/17268637-418/2012-in-with-a-bang.html.
141. Julie Pace, "White House ramping up gun violence discussions," *Yahoo News* (Associated Press), Jan. 8, 2013:

http://news.yahoo.com/white-house-ramping-gun-violence-discussions-110136366--politics.html.
142. "Crime in the United States: 2011," Federal Bureau of Investigation (FBI): http://www.fbi.gov/about-us/cjis/ucr/crime-in-the-u.s/2011/crime-in-the-u.s.-2011/tables/table-1. See also, "Choose Your Own Crime Stats," Youtube: http://youtu.be/Ooa98FHuaU0.
143. "Crime in the United States: 2011," Federal Bureau of Investigation (FBI): http://www.fbi.gov/about-us/cjis/ucr/crime-in-the-u.s/2011/crime-in-the-u.s.-2011/tables/expanded-homicide-data-table-8.
144. "Crime in the United States: 2011," Federal Bureau of Investigation (FBI): http://www.fbi.gov/about-us/cjis/ucr/crime-in-the-u.s/2011/crime-in-the-u.s.-2011/tables/expanded-homicide-data-table-3.
145. "Crime in the United States: 2011," Federal Bureau of Investigation (FBI): http://www.fbi.gov/about-us/cjis/ucr/crime-in-the-u.s/2011/crime-in-the-u.s.-2011/tables/expanded-homicide-data-table-3.
146. Warren Farrell, "Column: Guns don't kill people – our sons do," *USA Today*, Jan. 6, 2013: http://www.usatoday.com/story/opinion/2013/01/06/guns-newtown-sandy-hook-adam-lanza-boys/1566084/.
147. Robert Rector, "Marriage: America's Greatest Weapon Against Child Poverty," *The Heritage Foundation*, Sep. 5, 2012: http://www.heritage.org/research/reports/2012/09/marriage-americas-greatest-weapon-against-child-poverty.
148. William Raspberry, "Why Our Black Families Are Failing," *The Washington Post*, Jul. 25, 2005: http://www.washingtonpost.com/wp-dyn/content/article/2005/07/24/AR2005072401115.html.
149. Kay S. Hymowitz, "The Black Family: 40 Years of Lies," *City Journal*, Aug. 25, 2005: http://archive.frontpagemag.com/readArticle.aspx?ARTID=7590.
150. George A. Akerlof and Janet L. Yellen, "An Analysis of Out-Of-Wedlock Births in the United States," *Brookings Institution*, Policy Brief Series #4, Aug. 1996: http://www.brookings.edu/research/papers/1996/08/childrenfamilies-akerlof.

151. "Total Welfare Spending Is Rising Despite Attempts at Reform," Heritage Foundation: http://www.heritage.org/federalbudget/welfare-spending.
152. "Number in Poverty and Poverty Rate: 1959 to 2009," U.S. Census Bureau: http://www.census.gov/hhes/www/poverty/data/incpovhlth/2009/pov09fig04.pdf.
153. Deputy shoots gunman at San Antonio movie theater," WOAI News, Dec. 16, 2012: http://www.woai.com/news/local/story/Deputy-shoots-gunman-at-San-Antonio-movie-theater/2wFsix5ntU2CDrsHjXx2kQ.cspx; see also, Stacia Willson, "Deputy awarded Medal of Valor for shooting movie theater gunman," KENS 5, Dec. 19, 2012: http://www.kens5.com/home/Deputy-awarded-medal-of-valor-for-shooting-movie-theater-gunman-184193611.html.
154. Ann Coulter, "Coulter Column: We Know How to Stop School Shootings," *Newsbusters*, Dec. 19, 2012: http://newsbusters.org/blogs/ann-coulter/2012/12/19/coulter-column-we-know-how-stop-school-shootings#ixzz2I0pPgQH6. See also, "Latest Ed Schultz Whopper: 'We've Never Had a Civilian Stop a Shooting'," *Newsbusters*, Jan. 11, 2013: http://newsbusters.org/blogs/jack-coleman/2013/01/11/latest-ed-schultz-whopper-weve-never-had-civilian-stop-shooting#ixzz2I0t9azuX.
155. "Shots fired, patrons panic at San Antonio theater," *CBS News online*, Dec. 17, 2012: http://www.cbsnews.com/8301-201_162-57559506/shots-fired-patrons-panic-at-san-antonio-theater/.
156. National Rifle Association (NRA), "Armed Citizen," http://www.nraila.org/gun-laws/armed-citizen.aspx.

CHAPTER THREE

1. "Senate approves Iraq war resolution," *CNN*, October 11, 2002: http://archives.cnn.com/2002/ALLPOLITICS/10/11/iraq.us/.
2. Wikipedia: Iraq Resolution: http://en.wikipedia.org/wiki/Iraq_Resolution.
3. President Barack Obama, "Remarks by the President in Address to the Nation on Libya," White House Press Briefing Room, Mar. 21, 2011: http://www.whitehouse.gov/the-press-office/2011/03/28/remarks-president-address-nation-libya.

4. Tom Blumer, "Reuters 'Analysis': Obama Not 'Going It Alone' Like Bush Did; Oil Now a 'Concrete Interest'," *Newsbusters*: http://newsbusters.org/blogs/tom-blumer/2011/03/25/reuters-analysis-obama-not-going-it-alone-bush-did-oil-now-concrete-inte#ixzz25irhYXNj.
5. Mark Finkelstein, "Alter: Obama 'A Reluctant Warrior,' Not Cowboy Like Bush," *Newsbusters*: http://newsbusters.org/blogs/mark-finkelstein/2011/03/21/alter-obama-reluctant-warrior-not-cowboy-bush#ixzz25isqzJHO.
6. Noel Sheppard, "Monica Crowley Laughs at Eleanor Clift's Foolish Comment About Obama, Reagan and Libya," *Newsbusters*: http://newsbusters.org/blogs/noel-sheppard/2011/03/27/monica-crowley-laughs-eleanor-clifts-foolish-comment-about-obama-reag#ixzz25itDo3Fv.
7. Clay Waters, "No! George Bush Didn't 'Go It Alone' in Iraq," *Newsbusters*: http://newsbusters.org/blogs/clay-waters/2011/12/22/no-george-bush-didnt-go-it-alone-iraq#ixzz25iLjnPvW.
8. Rep. Anthony Weiner; watch the video at *Real Clear Politics*: http://www.realclearpolitics.com/video/2011/03/29/weiner_whats_the_point_of_being_powerful_without_stepping_in_and_helping.html.
9. "Libya intervention: Praising President Obama," *The Los Angeles Times*, Mar. 25, 2011: http://opinion.latimes.com/opinionla/2011/03/libya-intervention-praising-president-obama.html.
10. "Libya intervention: Praising President Obama," *The Los Angeles Times*, Mar. 25, 2011: http://opinion.latimes.com/opinionla/2011/03/libya-intervention-praising-president-obama.html.
11. "Pentagon poised as pressure mounts on Qaddafi," *CBS News*, Mar. 1, 2011: http://www.cbsnews.com/stories/2011/03/01/earlyshow/main20037638.shtml.
12. Geoffrey Dickens, "Flashback: Media Amazed by Obama's 'Deft' Libya Policy," *Newsbusters*: http://newsbusters.org/

blogs/geoffrey-dickens/2012/09/12/flashback-media-amazed-obamas-deft-libya-policy#ixzz26He1lBnm.

13. Nile Gardiner, "The Myth of U.S. Isolation: Why America Is Not Alone in the War on Terror," *The Heritage Foundation*, Sep. 7, 2004: http://www.heritage.org/research/reports/2004/09/the-myth-of-us-isolation-why-america-is-not-alone-in-the-war-on-terror.
14. Stephen Dinan, "Bipartisan Congress rebuffs Obama on Libya mission," *Washington Times*, Jun. 3, 2011: http://www.washingtontimes.com/news/2011/jun/3/bipartisan-congress-rebuffs-obama-libya-mission/.
15. Wikipedia: Iraq Liberation Act: http://en.wikipedia.org/wiki/Iraq_Liberation_Act.
16. "Sean Penn urges peace with Iraq," *BBC News*, Dec. 16, 2002: http://news.bbc.co.uk/2/hi/middle_east/2577981.stm.
17. Kenneth R. Timmerman, *Shadow Warriors: The Untold Story of Traitors, Saboteurs, and the Party of* Surrender (New York: Random House, Inc., 2007), p. 100.
18. There remains some controversy about whether the documents were forgeries planted in Niger by Italian or perhaps French agents in an attempt to embarrass the United States. There's also some evidence that some agents at the CIA were complicit in the attempt to make the U.S. look bad, motivated by their abject hatred of George W. Bush. See, for instance, Timmerman, pp. 53-68.
19. Timmerman, pp. 102-103.
20. See, http://www.davidstuff.com/political/wmdquotes.htm. See, also: Philip J. Eveland, "Bush Didn't Lie," *Redsounding*: http://redsounding.org/2008/06/10/bush-didnt-lie.aspx. See, also: http://www.snopes.com/politics/war/wmdquotes.asp.
21. Kyle Drennen, "CBS Marks Iraq War Anniversary by Hitting Bush Administration on WMD Intel," *Newsbusters*: http://newsbusters.org/blogs/kyle-drennen/2011/03/14/cbs-marks-iraq-war-anniversary-hitting-bush-administration-wmd-intel#ixzz2602x136s.

22. Mark Finkelstein, "Morning Joe Skirmish As PBS Host Smiley Recycles 'Bush Lied'," *Newsbusters*: http://newsbusters.org/blogs/mark-finkelstein/2011/09/12/morning-joe-skirmish-smiley-recycles-bush-lied#ixzz2607iQfJf.
23. Noel Sheppard, "Condoleezza Rice Schools Katie Couric on Why U.S. Invaded Iraq," Newsbusters: http://newsbusters.org/blogs/noel-sheppard/2010/12/12/condoleezza-rice-schools-katie-couric-iraq-and-wmd#ixzz2608z273v.
24. Kyle Drennen, "NBC's Ann Curry to Joe Biden: With No WMD, Can U.S. 'Claim Victory' in Iraq?," *Newsbusters*: http://newsbusters.org/blogs/kyle-drennen/2011/12/01/nbcs-ann-curry-joe-biden-no-wmd-can-us-claim-victory-iraq#ixzz260C1pKBx.
25. Jack Coleman, "Rachel Maddow Clings to Baathist Party Line That 'Saddam Wasn't Pursuing' WMD," Newsbusters: http://newsbusters.org/blogs/jack-coleman/2010/11/11/rachel-maddow-clings-baathist-party-line-saddam-wasnt-pursuing-wmd#ixzz2609cmr9i.
26. Dave Pierre, "Al Franken: Duelfer Report Said Iraq's WMD 'Were Destroyed by President Clinton',"Newsbusters: http://newsbusters.org/blogs/dave-pierre/2005/12/09/al-franken-duelfer-report-said-iraqs-wmd-were-destroyed-president-clint#ixzz260ADAgc9.
27. Timmerman, pp. 277-278.
28. See Timmerman, pp. 277-278 and 285-288.
29. "U.S. removed nuclear material from Iraq," *CNN*, July 14, 2004: http://articles.cnn.com/2004-07-07/world/iraq.nuclear_1_nuclear-materials-tuwaitha-nuclear-research-center-nuclear-weapons?_s=PM:WORLD. See, also, "U.S. transferred uranium from Iraq without U.N. authorization," USA Today, July 7, 2004: http://www.usatoday.com/news/world/iraq/2004-07-07-iraq-uranium_x.htm.
30. Ellen Knickmeyer, "Iraqi Chemical Stash Uncovered," *The Washington Post*, August 14, 2005, p. A18.
31. Noah Shachtman, "WikiLeaks Show WMD Hunt Continued

in Iraq – With Surprising Results," Wired, October 23, 2010: http://www.wired.com/dangerroom/2010/10/wikileaks-show-wmd-hunt-continued-in-iraq-with-surprising-results/.

32. Timmerman, pp. 268-269. Also, watch Jon Stewart's interview with Gen. Sada: http://www.thedailyshow.com/watch/tue-march-21-2006/general-georges-sada.
33. Timmerman, pp. 191-194.
34. Timmerman, pp. 124-129, and 191-194.
35. Timmerman, pp. 129, and 269-270.
36. Warren P. Strobel, "Exhaustive review finds no link between Saddam and al Qaida," *McClatchy Newspapers*: http://www.mcclatchydc.com/2008/03/10/29959/exhaustive-review-finds-no-link.html#storylink=cpy.
37. See, Discover The Networks: http://www.discoverthenetworks.org/viewSubCategory.asp?id=24.
38. Ryan Mauro, "New Evidence of Saddam-Terrorist Links," PJ Media: http://pjmedia.com/blog/new-evidence-of-saddam-terrorism-links/.
39. For instance: In the Valley of Elah, Lions for Lambs, Redacted, Grace is Gone, and the remake of The Manchurian Candidate.
40. President Barack Obama, The White House, Apr. 16, 2009: http://www.whitehouse.gov/the_press_office/Statement-of-President-Barack-Obama-on-Release-of-OLC-Memos/.
41. Suzanne Ito, America Civil Liberties Union (ACLU), Nov. 19, 2008: http://www.aclu.org/blog/national-security/cheers-obamas-committment-close-guantanamo.
42. See Youtube video: http://youtu.be/wrW4fOGIMVY.
43. President Barack Obama, May 21, 2009: http://www.whitehouse.gov/the-press-office/remarks-president-national-security-5-21-09.
44. Matt Negrin, *ABC News*, July 3, 2102: http://abcnews.go.com/Politics/OTUS/guantanamo-bay-open-promises/story?id=16698768.
45. Barack Obama, "Renewing American Leadership," *Foreign*

Policy, July/August 2007: http://www.foreignaffairs.com/articles/62636/barack-obama/renewing-american-leadership. See also, Larry O'Connor, "Press Mum as Renditions Continue Under Obama," *Breitbart*, Jan. 2, 2013: http://www.breitbart.com/Big-Journalism/2013/01/02/Obama-Rendition-Press-Mum.

46. Executive Order 13491, "Ensuring Lawful Interrogations," Whitehouse.gov, accessed Jan. 3, 2013: http://www.whitehouse.gov/the_press_office/EnsuringLawfulInterrogations.
47. Amshula Jayaram, "Shedding Light on the Dark Side – A Call to Congress to Release the SSCI Report," American Civil Liberties website, Dec. 18, 2012: http://www.aclu.org/blog/human-rights-national-security-immigrants-rights/shedding-light-dark-side-call-congress-release.
48. Jason Ditz, "Obama's Renditions: Short on Evidence, Long on Secrecy," Antiwar.com, Jan. 1, 2013: http://news.antiwar.com/2013/01/01/obamas-renditions-short-on-evidence-long-on-secrecy/.
49. Craig Whitlock, "Renditions continue under Obama, despite due-process concerns," *Washington Post*, Jan. 1, 2013: http://www.washingtonpost.com/world/national-security/renditions-continue-under-obama-despite-due-process-concerns/2013/01/01/4e593aa0-5102-11e2-984e-f1de82a7c98a_story.html.
50. Greg Miller, "Under Obama, an emerging global apparatus for drone killing," *Washington Post*, Dec. 27, 2011: http://www.washingtonpost.com/national/national-security/under-obama-an-emerging-global-apparatus-for-drone-killing/2011/12/13/gIQANPdILP_story.html.
51. Peter Bergen, "Drone is Obama's Weapon of Choice," *CNN*, Sep. 5, 2012: http://articles.cnn.com/2012-09-05/opinion/opinion_bergen-obama-drone_1_drone-strikes-drone-attacks-drone-program.
52. Jo Becker and Scott Shane, "Secret 'Kill List' Proves a Test of Obama's Principles and Will," *New York Times*, May 29,

2012: http://www.nytimes.com/2012/05/29/world/obamas-leadership-in-war-on-al-qaeda.html.

53. Peter Bergen, "Warrrior in Chief," *New York Times*, Apr. 29, 2012: http://www.nytimes.com/2012/04/29/opinion/sunday/president-obama-warrior-in-chief.html.
54. Of note, a federal judge, a Bill Clinton appointee, ruled that the Obama administration "has no legal duty to disclose legal opinions justifying the use of drones to kill suspected terrorist operatives abroad." See Josh Gerstein, "Court: Feds can keep drone legal opinions secret," *Politico*, Jan. 2, 2013: http://www.politico.com/blogs/under-the-radar/2013/01/court-feds-can-keep-drone-legal-opinions-secret-153169.html.
55. Watch: http://youtu.be/P_igpyewuzQ.
56. Wikipedia: http://en.wikipedia.org/wiki/MoveOn.org_ad_controversy.
57. See: http://www.icasualties.org/.
58. See, for instance, Thomas E. Ricks, *The Gamble: General Patraeus and the American Military Adventure in Iraq* (New York: Penguin Books, 2009), pp. 237-243.
59. Andrew Malcolm, "Joe Biden update: Iraq one of Obama's 'great' achievements," *LA Times*: http://latimesblogs.latimes.com/washington/2010/02/joe-biden-update-larry-king-iraq-obama-sarah-palin.html.
60. President Obama: http://www.whitehouse.gov/the-press-office/2011/12/12/remarks-president-obama-and-prime-minister-al-maliki-iraq-joint-press-co.
61. Matt Loffman, "Vice President Biden: Iraq 'Could Be One of the Great Achievements of This Administration," *ABC News blog*: http://abcnews.go.com/blogs/politics/2010/02/vice-president-biden-iraq-could-be-one-of-the-great-achievements-of-this-administration/.
62. Tim Graham, "Editing Reverend Wright's Wrongs: How the Networks Censored and Manipulated Jeremiah Wright Soundbites and Glorified Barack Obama's Race Speech,"

Media Research Center: http://www.mrc.org/special-reports/editing-reverend-wrights-wrongs.

63. Tucker Carlson and Vince Coglianese, "Exclusive: In heated '07 speech, Obama lavishes praise on Wright, says feds 'don't care' about New Orleans," *Daily Caller*: http://dailycaller.com/2012/10/02/obama-speech-jeremiah-wright-new-orleans/.
64. Tim Graham, "Editing Reverend Wright's Wrongs," *MRC*: http://www.mrc.org/special-reports/editing-reverend-wrights-wrongs.
65. "New Details on the Attack on the American Mission in Benghazi, Libya," *New York Times*: http://www.nytimes.com/interactive/2012/09/20/world/africa/the-attack-on-the-american-mission-in-benghazi-libya.html.
66. Jamie Weinstein, "Evidence mounts that al-Qaeda group killed U.S. ambassador in Libya," *Daily Caller*: http://dailycaller.com/2012/09/21/evidence-mounts-that-al-qaida-group-killed-us-ambassador-to-libya/. See, also, Jamie Dettmer, Christopher Dickey, and Eli Lake, "The Truth Behind the Benghazi Attack," *Newsweek* (The Daily Beast): http://www.thedailybeast.com/newsweek/2012/10/21/truth-behind-the-benghazi-attack.html.
67. Matthew Boyle, "FLASHBACK: JouroList plotted to kill Jeremiah Wright story in 2008," *Daily Caller*: http://dailycaller.com/2012/10/02/flashback-journolist-plotted-to-kill-jeremiah-wright-story-in-2008/. See also: Wikipedia: http://en.wikipedia.org/wiki/JournoList.
68. Tim Graham, "Video: CBS and NPR Reporter Plot to Insure Romney's Asked If He Regrets Obama Critique," *Newsbusters*: http://newsbusters.org/blogs/tim-graham/2012/09/12/video-cbs-and-npr-reporter-plot-insure-romneys-asked-if-he-regrets-obama#ixzz26MroFD9n. See, also, Noel Sheppard, "Michelle Malkin: Reporters Plotting Questions for Romney Are Obama's 'Tools' and 'Stenographers'," *Newsbusters*: http://newsbusters.org/blogs/noel-sheppard/2012/09/13/michelle-

malkin-reporters-plotting-questions-romney-are-obamas-tools#ixzz26MnaxB00.

69. Scott Whitlock, "Journalists Freak Out as Romney Condemns Obama's Handling of Libya," *Newsbusters*: http://newsbusters.org/blogs/scott-whitlock/2012/09/12/journalists-freak-out-romney-condemns-obamas-handling-libya#ixzz26MlnBPXij.
70. President Barack Obama, "Remarks by the President on the Deaths of U.S. Embassy Staff in Libya," Sep. 12, 2012: http://www.whitehouse.gov/the-press-office/2012/09/12/remarks-president-deaths-us-embassy-staff-libya.
71. Stephen F. Hayes, "Permanent Spin," *Weekly Standard*: http://www.weeklystandard.com/articles/permanent-spin_652887.html. Watch: http://mrctv.org/videos/white-house-says-linking-libya-attack-911-anniversary-%E2%80%98conveniently-conflating%E2%80%99.
72. John Nolte, "Cover Up: Report Says U.S. Knew Al-Qaeda Behind Libya Attack Within 24 Hours," *Breitbart*: http://www.breitbart.com/Big-Peace/2012/09/26/Report-Says-US-Knew-Al-Qaeda-Behind-Libya-Attack-Within-24-Hours.
73. President Barack Obama, "Remarks by the President in a News Conference," The White House Briefing Room, November 14, 2012: http://www.whitehouse.gov/the-press-office/2012/11/14/remarks-president-news-conference.
74. Caroline Kennedy, "Speech to the Democratic National Convention," *Fox News*, September 6, 2012: http://foxnewsinsider.com/2012/09/06/transcript-caroline-kennedys-speech-to-the-democratic-national-convention/.
75. Nancy Keenan, "Speech to the Democratic National Convention," *Daily Kos*, September 4, 2012: http://www.dailykos.com/story/2012/09/04/1127754/-Transcript-of-NARAL-s-Nancy-Keenan-remarks-Democratic-National-Convention.
76. Lilly Ledbetter, "Speech to the Democratic National Convention," Daily Kos, September 4, 2012: http://www.

dailykos.com/story/2012/09/04/1127787/-Transcript-of-Lilly-Ledbetter-remarks-Democratic-National-Convention.

77. House Women, "Speech to the Democratic National Convention," *Daily Kos*, September 4, 2012: http://www.dailykos.com/story/2012/09/04/1127752/-Transcript-of-House-Women-remarks-as-prepared-for-delivery-Democratic-National-Convention.
78. Noel Sheppard, "MSNBC's Finney: Romney-Ryan Plan Would Kill Women By Their Mid-30s," *Newsbusters*: http://newsbusters.org/blogs/noel-sheppard/2012/05/04/msnbcs-finney-romney-ryan-plan-will-kill-women-their-mid-30s#ixzz2FF9zbsKt.
79. Clay Waters, "Panic at New York Times? Two Lead Editorials Tar Romney as Sexist and Radical," *Newsbusters*: http://newsbusters.org/blogs/clay-waters/2012/10/18/panic-new-york-times-two-lead-editorials-tar-romney-sexist-and-radical#ixzz2FFAV9M79.
80. Brad Wilmouth, "CBS's Nancy Giles Insists There is a GOP 'War on Women'," *Newsbusters*: http://newsbusters.org/blogs/brad-wilmouth/2012/07/23/cbss-nancy-giles-insists-there-gop-war-women#ixzz2FFAwcEjz.
81. Kyle Drennen, "NBC Keeps Up Drumbeat of GOP 'War Against Women's Health'," *Newsbusters*: http://newsbusters.org/blogs/kyle-drennen/2012/03/21/nbc-keeps-drumbeat-gop-war-against-womens-health#ixzz2FFBzrXFi.
82. Kyle Drennen, "NBC's Todd: Romney Response to Embassy Attacks 'Looks Crass and Tone Deaf'," *Newsbusters*: http://newsbusters.org/blogs/kyle-drennen/2012/09/12/nbcs-todd-romney-response-embassy-attacks-looks-crass-and-tone-deaf#ixzz26MmLRBcX.
83. Tim Graham, "Newsweek Trashes Romney for Exploiting Tragedy, Touts Obama's 'Diplomatic Fury'," *Newsbusters*: http://newsbusters.org/blogs/tim-graham/2012/09/12/newsweek-trashes-romney-exploiting-tragedy-touts-obamas-diplomatic-fury#ixzz26MpKZ0kr.

84. Howard Kurtz, "Mitt Romney's Ill-Timed Assault on President Obama as Americans Are Killed Abroad," *The Daily Beast*: http://www.thedailybeast.com/articles/2012/09/12/mitt-romney-s-ill-timed-assault-on-president-obama-as-americans-are-killed-abroad.html.
85. Ken Shepherd, "Time's Foroohar Compares Glenn Beck to Islamist 'Industry of Outrage' in Arab World That Whips Up Violent Mobs," *Newsbusters*: http://newsbusters.org/blogs/ken-shepherd/2012/09/12/times-foroohar-compares-glenn-beck-islamist-industry-outrage-arab-worl#ixzz26Mr41TZo.
86. Clay Waters, "NYT's Ashley Parker's Opening Line on Romney Speech: 'Facing Criticism...'," *Newsbusters*: http://newsbusters.org/blogs/clay-waters/2012/09/12/nyts-ashley-parkers-opening-line-romney-speech-facing-criticism#ixzz26MrJxjDM.
87. Matt Hadro, "Romney Adviser Hammers CNN Anchor Over 'Silly Question'," *Newsbusters*: http://newsbusters.org/blogs/matt-hadro/2012/09/12/romney-adviser-hammers-cnn-anchor-over-silly-question#ixzz26MsioH7J.
88. Kyle Drennen, "NBC's Mitchell: Is Romney 'Injecting Politics Into a National Tragedy?'," *Newsbusters*: http://newsbusters.org/blogs/kyle-drennen/2012/09/12/nbcs-mitchell-romney-injecting-politics-national-tragedy#ixzz26Mt0o9oi.
89. Scott Whitlock, "ABC's Diane Sawyer Hypes 'Secret' Mitt Romney Tapes: A 'Seismic' 'Political Earthquake'," *Newsbusters*: http://newsbusters.org/blogs/scott-whitlock/2012/09/19/abcs-diane-sawyer-hypes-secret-mitt-romney-tapes-seismic-political-e#ixzz28BBDi9SY.
90. Kyle Drenned, "NBC Brings on Pelosi to Bash Romney Over Video, A 'Gift From Above' for Democrats" *Newsbusters*: http://newsbusters.org/blogs/kyle-drennen/2012/09/19/nbc-brings-pelosi-bash-romney-over-video-gift-above-democrats#ixzz28BBn2flx.
91. Matthew Balan, "CBS's Norah O'Donnell: Did Romney 'Insult' GOP Voters In Secret Video?" *Newsbusters*: http://newsbusters.

org/blogs/matthew-balan/2012/09/18/cbss-norah-odonnell-did-romney-insult-gop-voters-secret-video#ixzz28BCbbpg9.

92. Tom Blumer, "Desperately Spinning Romney: Reuters Says 'Gaffe-Plagued' Romney Campaign (Gaining and Ahead in Non-cooked Polls) Is 'Reeling'," *Newsbusters*: http://newsbusters.org/blogs/tom-blumer/2012/09/18/desperately-spinning-romney-reuters-says-gaffe-plagued-romney-campaign-g#ixzz28BDPziWq.
93. Matt Hadro, "CNN Hypes 'Tsunami' of Romney Campaign Problems," *Newsbusters*: http://newsbusters.org/blogs/matt-hadro/2012/09/18/cnn-hypes-tsunami-romney-campaign-problems.
94. Kyle Drennen, "NBC: Ohio 'Slipping Away' From Romney After 'Damage From That 47% Comment'," *Newsbusters*: http://newsbusters.org/blogs/kyle-drennen/2012/09/27/nbc-ohio-slipping-away-romney-after-damage-47-comment#ixzz28BF8pn2l.
95. Tim Graham, "NPR Asks: 'Did the Wheels Just Fall Off the GOP Campaign?' David Brooks Says Yes, Mitt's Worse Than Gore, McCain," *Newsbusters*: http://newsbusters.org/blogs/tim-graham/2012/09/22/npr-asks-did-wheels-just-fall-gop-campaign-david-brooks-says-yes-mitts-w#ixzz28BFpqQps.
96. Geoffrey Dickens, "ABC, CBS, NBC Devote More Time (20 to 1) to Romney Flap Than Obama Mideast Mistakes," *Newsbusters*: http://newsbusters.org/blogs/geoffrey-dickens/2012/09/13/abc-cbs-nbc-devote-more-time-20-1-romney-flap-obama-mideast-mistak#ixzz26Ul5oq7V.
97. Matthew Balan, "CBS Gets in Senator Portman's Face on Embassy Apology Dispute, Breaks Out Kid Gloves For Obama," *Newsbusters*: http://newsbusters.org/blogs/matthew-balan/2012/09/13/cbs-gets-senator-portmans-face-embassy-apology-dispute-breaks-out-kid#ixzz26UpQplDs.
98. Allahpundit, "Kirsten Powers: Yes, the media's reaction to Romney's Egypt statement yesterday was utterly insane," *Hot Air*: http://hotair.com/archives/2012/09/13/kirsten-powers-

yes-the-medias-reaction-to-romneys-egypt-statement-yesterday-was-utterly-insane/.

99. Noel Sheppard, "NYT's Helene Cooper: 'Death of Four Americans Is Peripheral To What's Going on Right Now'," *Newsbusters*: http://newsbusters.org/blogs/noel-sheppard/2012/10/21/nyts-helene-cooper-death-four-americans-libya-peripheral-whats-going#ixzz2A2fMySrd.
100. Noel Sheppard, "Joe Klein: Benghazi Consulate Controversy 'The October Mirage - It Really Isn't An Issue'," *Newsbusters*: http://newsbusters.org/blogs/noel-sheppard/2012/10/21/joe-klein-benghazi-consulate-attack-controversy-october-mirage-it-rea#ixzz2A2fugzEm.
101. Brent Baker, "Friedman Contends Benghazi Controversy 'Utterly Contrived,' Stephanopoulos Hails White House 'Transparency'," *Newsbusters*: http://newsbusters.org/blogs/brent-baker/2012/10/21/friedman-contends-benghazi-controversy-utterly-contrived-stephanopoulos#ixzz2A2gQJ3sz.
102. Noel Sheppard, "NPR's Nina Totenberg: 'There'd Be No Reason to Send Susan Rice Out to Lie'," *Newsbusters*: http://newsbusters.org/blogs/noel-sheppard/2012/10/20/nina-totenberg-thered-be-no-reason-send-susan-rice-out-lie#ixzz2A2hIKBiV.
103. Ed Morrissey, "Flashback: Major-party nominee uses war deaths to score political points," *Hotair*: http://hotair.com/archives/2012/09/13/flashback-major-party-nominee-uses-war-deaths-to-score-political-points/.
104. Josh Rogin, "White House clarifies Obama's statement that Egypt is not an 'ally'," *Foreign Policy*: http://thecable.foreignpolicy.com/posts/2012/09/13/white_house_clarifies_obama_s_statement_that_egypt_is_not_an_ally.
105. Byron Tau, "State Dept.: Egypt's still an ally," *Politico*: http://www.politico.com/politico44/2012/09/state-dept-egypts-still-an-ally-135479.html.
106. Ed Morrissey, "Obama: Sacked consulate and dead ambassador 'bumps in the road'," *Hotair*: http://hotair.com/archives/2012/09/24/obama-sacked-consulate-and-dead-ambassador-bumps-in-the-road/.

107. Allahpundit, "Obama on Benghazi: 'If four Americans get killed, it is not optimal'," *Hotair*: http://hotair.com/archives/2012/10/18/obama-on-benghazi-if-four-americans-get-killed-it-is-not-optimal/.
108. Eric Erickson, "The American Media Beclowned Themselves Yesterday," *Red State*: http://www.redstate.com/2012/09/13/the-american-media-beclowned-themselves-yesterday/.
109. Wynton Hall, "Exclusive: No Record of Intel Briefings For Obama During Week Before Embassy Attacks," *Breitbart*: http://www.breitbart.com/Big-Peace/2012/09/12/Exclusive-Obama-Skipped-Intel-Briefings-Week-Before-Embassy-Attacks.
110. George Stephanopolous, "Romney tends to 'shoot first, aim later,' Obama retorts after Romney's Mideast criticism," *Washington Post*: http://www.washingtonpost.com/national/obama-romney-return-to-campaigning-after-sept-11-anniversary-new-jockeying-in-wisconsin/2012/09/12/a864c8a2-fca7-11e1-98c6-ec0a0a93f8eb_story.html.
111. Noel Sheppard, "CNNer and FNCer Agree: Obama Wrong to Say 'Cambridge Police Acted Stupidly'," *Newsbusters*: http://newsbusters.org/blogs/noel-sheppard/2009/07/24/cnner-fncer-agree-obama-wrong-say-cambridge-police-acted-stupidly#ixzz26UtN4O8a. See, also: http://newsbusters.org/blogs/noel-sheppard/2009/07/24/jon-stewart-obama-handled-gates-racism-question-stupidly.
112. Ed Morrissey, "Sacking of Benghazi consulate 'a catastrophic intelligence loss'," *Hot Air*: http://hotair.com/archives/2012/09/24/sacking-of-benghazi-consulate-a-catastrophic-intelligence-loss/. See also, Ed Morrissey, "Obama: Sacked consulate and dead ambassador 'bumps in the road'," *Hot Air*: http://hotair.com/archives/2012/09/24/obama-sacked-consulate-and-dead-ambassador-bumps-in-the-road/.
113. Ed Morrissey, "Rasmussen: Only 23% believe embassy sieges related to YouTube video," *Hot Air*: http://hotair.com/archives/2012/09/24/rasmussen-only-23-believe-embassy-sieges-related-to-youtube-video/.

114. Matthew Balen, "ABC's GMA, NBC's Today Fail to Report Susan Rice's Now-Disputed Claims About Libya Consulate Attack," *Newsbusters*: http://newsbusters.org/blogs/matthew-balan/2012/09/27/abcs-gma-nbcs-today-fail-report-susan-rices-now-disputed-claims-about#ixzz27iSqv9iB.
115. Plutarch, "New York Times Streak of Page One Stories on Abu Ghraib ends at 32 Days!" *Free Republic*, Jun. 2, 2004: http://www.freerepublic.com/focus/f-news/1145998/posts.
116. Jack Rosenthal, "THE PUBLIC EDITOR; What Belongs on the Front Page of The New York Times," *New York Times*, Aug. 22, 2004: http://www.nytimes.com/2004/08/22/weekinreview/the-public-editor-what-belongs-on-the-front-page-of-the-new-york-times.html.
117. John Hideraker, Al Qaqaa and Benghazi: That Was Then, This Is Now," *Powerline*: http://www.powerlineblog.com/archives/2012/10/al-qaqaa-and-benghazi-that-was-then-and-this-is-now.php.
118. AWR Hawkins, "'Stand Down': U.S. Had Two Drones, AC-130 Gunship, and Targets Painted in Benghazi," *Breitbart*: http://www.breitbart.com/Big-Peace/2012/10/27/U-S-Had-Two-Drones-AC-130-Gunship-and-Targets-Painted-In-Benghazi-But-Obama-Didn-t-Pull-The-Trigger. See also, Joel B. Pollak, Petraeus, on Benghazi: It Wasn't Me," *Breitbart*: http://www.breitbart.com/Big-Peace/2012/10/26/Petraeus-on-Benghazi-It-Wasnt-Me.
119. Tony Lee, "Obama Refuses to Answer Whether WH Denied Benghazi Requests for Help," *Breitbart*: http://www.breitbart.com/Big-Government/2012/10/26/Obama-Refuses-To-Answer-Twice-Whether-His-Admin-Denied-Requests-for-Help-by-Americans-Under-Attack-In-Libya.
120. Joel B. Pollak, "Media Blackout: Aside From Fox, Sunday News Hosts Fail to Raise Benghazi," *Breitbart*: http://www.breitbart.com/Big-Journalism/2012/10/28/Media-Cover-Up-Aside-from-FOX-Sunday-Shows-Fail-to-Raise-Benghazi; see also, Clay Waters, "New York Times Relegates Libya Email Bombshell to Page A5 Under Dull Headline," *Newsbusters*: http://newsbusters.org/blogs/clay-waters/2012/10/25/new-york-times-relegates-libya-email-bombshell-page-a5-

under-dull-headl#ixzz2ALpNiwQE; See also, Ken Sheppard, "WashPost Buries Benghazi Emails Story on A9, Plastered Front Page with Puffy Piece on Obama Counterrorism Advisor," *Newsbusters*: http://newsbusters.org/blogs/ken-shepherd/2012/10/25/washpost-buries-benghazi-emails-story-a8-plastered-front-page-puffy-pi#ixzz2ALpavVhA;also, Scott Whitlock, "Instead of Exposing Libya Bombshell, ABC Hypes 'Mystery Monkey' and Yawning Dogs," Newsbusters: http://newsbusters.org/blogs/scott-whitlock/2012/10/26/instead-exposing-libya-bombshell-abc-hypes-mystery-monkey-and-yawnin#ixzz2AS8DaCMn.

CHAPTER FOUR

1. "Cleveland's Veto of the Texas Seed Bill," *Wikisource*: http://en.wikisource.org/wiki/Cleveland%27s_Veto_of_the_Texas_Seed_Bill.
2. Michael Medved, *The Ten Big Lies About America: Combating the Destructive Distortions About Our Nation* (New York: Random House, Inc., 2008), p. 152.
3. Steven Hayward and Erik Peterson, "The Medicare Monster," Reason Magazine (Jan. 1993): http://reason.com/archives/1993/01/01/the-medicare-monster. See, also, Office of Management and Budget "Historical Tables": http://www.whitehouse.gov/omb/budget/Historicals/.
4. Burton Folsom, *New Deal or Raw Deal? How FDR's Economic Legacy Has Damaged America* (New York: Simon & Schuster, Inc., 2008), p. 78.
5. Folsom, pp. 80-81.
6. Tim Dickinson, "How the GOP Became the Party of the Rich," *Rolling Stone*, Nov. 9, 2011: http://www.rollingstone.com/politics/news/how-the-gop-became-the-party-of-the-rich-20111109.
7. "A dangerous game," *The Economist*, Nov. 5, 2011: http://www.economist.com/node/21536603.
8. Brent Budowsky, "Mitt Romney, Paul Ryan, and the party of Ayn Rand," *The Hill*, Jul. 12, 2012: http://thehill.com/blogs/

pundits-blog/presidential-campaign/243267-mitt-romney-paul-ryan-and-the-party-of-ayn-rand.

9. Full Text of President Obama Speech in Osawatomie, Kansas, Dec. 6, 2011, *The Guardian*: http://www.guardian.co.uk/world/2011/dec/07/full-text-barack-obama-speech.
10. Janet Hook and Dan Morain, "Democrats are darlings of Wall St.," *Los Angeles Times*, Mar. 21, 2008: http://articles.latimes.com/2008/mar/21/nation/na-wallstdems21.
11. Emily Kaiser, "Wall Street puts its money behind Obama," *Reuters*, Jun. 5, 2008: http://uk.reuters.com/article/2008/06/05/analysis-shares-obama-idUKNOA53525520080605.
12. Julia La Roche, " These 22 Wall Street Titans Have Visited President Obama's White House," *Business Insider*: http://www.businessinsider.com/wall-street-titans-visited-president-barack-obamas-white-house-2012-1?op=1#ixzz25QoqgeQZ.
13. "Obama White House 'Full of Wall Street Executives'?" Factcheck.org, Feb. 29, 2012, corrected on Mar. 1, 2012: http://www.factcheck.org/2012/02/obama-white-house-full-of-wall-street-executives/.
14. Annie Lowry, "It's Mostly Wonks," *Slate*: http://www.slate.com/articles/business/moneybox/2011/01/its_mostly_wonks.html.
15. Lauren Ezell, "From Bear to Lehman: Documents Reveal an Alternate History," *PBS Frontline*, May 1, 2012: http://www.pbs.org/wgbh/pages/frontline/business-economy-financial-crisis/money-power-wall-street/from-bear-to-lehman-documents-reveal-an-alternate-history/.
16. "Most say Romney policies favor the rich," *CBS News*, Jul. 18, 2012: http://www.cbsnews.com/8301-503544_162-57475189-503544/most-say-romney-policies-favor-the-rich/.
17. "Q: Who do you think would do more to advance the economic interests of wealthy Americans," *Washington Post*, Jul. 9, 2012: http://www.washingtonpost.com/politics/polling/americans-romney-obama-interests/2012/05/25/gJQAOyjjoU_page.html.

18. David E. Rosenbaum, "Doing the math on Bush's tax cuts," *New York Times*, March 4, 2001, as quoted in Groseclose, p. 181.
19. Anne Sorock, "The Congressional Wealth Gap," *Legal Insurrection* (Aug. 2, 2012): http://legalinsurrection.com/2012/08/the-congressional-wealth-gap/.
20. Mike Bates, "CNN's Banfield Fixates on Romney's Tax Returns, 'If There Is Something With Regard to Amnesty'," *Newsbusters*:http://newsbusters.org/blogs/mike-bates/2012/08/18/cnns-banfield-fixates-romneys-tax-returns-if-there-something-regard-amne#ixzz23wfL0A00.
21. B. Daniel Blatt, "Tax returns show Mitt Romney's empathy," *Gay Patriot*: tax-returns-show-mitt-romneys-empathy. See also, Becket Adams, "Here is Romney's Official 2011 Tax Returns," *The Blaze*: http://www.theblaze.com/stories/here-are-romneys-official-2011-tax-return-numbers/.
22. Matt Kelley, "Biden gave average of $369 to charity a year," *USA Today*: http://www.usatoday.com/news/politics/election2008/2008-09-12-biden-financial_N.htm.
23. Glenn Kessler, "Obama's gifts to charity: Just 1 percent?" *Washington Post*: http://www.washingtonpost.com/blogs/fact-checker/post/obamas-gifts-to-charity-just-1-percent/2012/02/14/gIQAXuMDER_blog.html. See, also: Howard Portnoy, "Romney charitable giving has outpaced Obama's," *Hotair*: http://hotair.com/archives/2012/08/26/romney-charitable-giving-has-outpaced-obamas/.
24. Robert Frank, "'Tax Me More,' Says Wealthy Entrepreneur," *Wall Street Journal*: http://blogs.wsj.com/wealth/2010/09/20/tax-me-more-says-wealthy-entrepreneur/. Also, watch Gruener discuss his patriotism and beneficence on PBS's New Hour: http://youtu.be/7b682jzn_B0 (official News Hour site: http://www.pbs.org/newshour/bb/politics/july-dec11/millionaires_11-16.html).
25. See, for example, "Garrett Gruener Political Campaign Contributions 2012 Election Cycle," at http://www.

campaignmoney.com/political/contributions/garrett-gruener.asp?cycle=12.

26. Leftists will, of course, make the case that I'm giving Mitt Romney a pass because his hands are just as soft and pink and chubby as those of the "Patriotic Millionaires." But, the difference is that presidential candidate Mitt Romney was not asking for the federal government to raise my taxes; in fact, he was proposing the opposite, and with the selection of Rep. Paul Ryan, both devoted tax-reducers, the likelihood that taxes would have increased under a Romney-Ryan administration was far smaller than under another Obama-Biden administration.
27. "Mr. Obama's stand on taxes," *Washington Post*, Jul. 22, 2012: http://www.washingtonpost.com/opinions/the-presidents-stand/2012/07/22/gJQAeAKy2W_story.html. See, also, Noel Sheppard, "WaPo: 'It's Impossible to Tackle the Federal Debt by Taxing Only the Wealthy'," *Newsbusters*: http://newsbusters.org/blogs/noel-sheppard/2012/07/23/wapo-admits-it-s-impossible-tackle-federal-debt-taxing-only-wealthy#ixzz23waJl1gM.
28. Michelle Fields, "'Patriotic millionaires' demand higher taxes, but unwilling to pay up," *Daily Caller*: http://dailycaller.com/2011/11/17/patriotic-millionaires-demand-higher-taxes-but-unwilling-to-pay-up-video/. See, also: http://redsounding.org/2011/11/18/rich-want-higher-taxes.aspx.
29. Sen. Claire McCaskill press conference, Dec. 3, 2010: http://youtu.be/HdcDjQz01z4.
30. Robert Gibbs, White House press conference, Mar. 16, 2009: http://www.whitehouse.gov/the_press_office/Briefing-by-WH-Press-Secretary-Gibbs-3-16-09/. See, also, http://redsounding.org/2009/03/18/press-secretary-gibbs-and-government-rewards.aspx.
31. CNN's Late Edition, Oct. 5, 2008: http://transcripts.cnn.com/TRANSCRIPTS/0810/05/le.01.html. See, also, http://

redsounding.org/2009/03/18/press-secretary-gibbs-and-government-rewards.aspx.

32. See, for instance, the Wikipedia page "Theological virtues": http://en.wikipedia.org/wiki/Three_theological_virtues.
33. Ken Shepherd, "MSNBC's O'Donnell Slams Limbaugh As Biblically Ignorant; Contorts Scripture to Paint Jesus As Socialist," *Newsbusters*: http://newsbusters.org/blogs/ken-shepherd/2011/04/26/msnbcs-odonnell-slams-limbaugh-biblically-ignorant-goes-contort-script#ixzz25E0IQMLd.
34. See, for instance, Exodus 20:17; Deuteronomy 5:21; Deuteronomy 7:25; Joshua 7:21; Micah 2:2; Acts 20:33; Romans 7:7-8; Romans 13:9.
35. See: http://dictionary.reference.com.
36. Gregory Paul, "From Jesus' socialism to capitalistic Christianity," *Washington Post*: http://www.washingtonpost.com/blogs/guest-voices/post/from-jesus-socialism-to-capitalistic-christianity/2011/08/12/gIQAziaQBJ_blog.html.
37. Richard Bauckham, *The Book of Acts in Its Palestinian Setting* (Grand Rapids, MI: Wm. B. Eerdmans Publishing, 1995), p. 337.
38. Bauckham, p. 340.
39. See The Chronicle of Philanthropy website for the results of the study: http://philanthropy.com/section/How-America-Gives/621/. See also: "Study: Religious Regions Give More Money to Charity, Red States More Generous Than Blue," *The Blaze*: http://www.theblaze.com/stories/study-religious-regions-give-more-to-charity-red-states-more-generous-than-blue/.
40. "The Politics of Giving," *Chronicle of Philanthropy*: http://philanthropy.com/article/The-Politics-of-Giving/133609/.
41. "Biden calls paying higher taxes a patriotic act," *MSNBC*: http://www.msnbc.msn.com/id/26771716/.
42. Ed Morrissey, "Biden: Taxes not just a patriotic duty — but also a religious experience," *Hotair*: http://hotair.com/

archives/2008/09/18/biden-taxes-not-just-a-patriotic-duty-but-also-a-religious-experience/.

43. Ed Morrissey, "Santorum's tax returns: a lack of charity?" *Hotair*: http://hotair.com/archives/2012/02/16/santorums-tax-returns-a-lack-of-charity/.
44. Clay Waters, "Really? Obama's 'You Didn't Built That' Remark in 'Context' Shows 'He Celebrates Individual Achievement': NYTimes," *Newsbusters*: http://newsbusters.org/blogs/clay-waters/2012/07/19/really-obamas-you-didnt-built-remark-context-shows-he-celebrates-indivi#ixzz216LlDshb.
45. Rich Lowry, "Obama's Statism vs. the Self-Made Man," *Real Clear Politics*: http://www.realclearpolitics.com/articles/2012/07/18/obama_you_didnt_build_that_114830.html.
46. Tom Blumer, "AP's Peoples Tells Readers What Obama 'Intended' in 'You Didn't Build That, Somebody Else Made That Happen' Remark," *Newsbusters*: http://newsbusters.org/blogs/tom-blumer/2012/07/19/aps-peoples-tells-readers-what-obama-intended-you-didnt-build-somebody-e#ixzz216MY7dpY.
47. Brent Baker, "Moderating a Debate About Size of Government, Amanpour Takes the Liberal Side," *Newsbusters*: http://newsbusters.org/blogs/brent-baker/2011/12/19/moderating-debate-about-size-government-amanpour-takes-liberal-side#ixzz260GxnDSn.
48. Lachlan Markley, "Obama's Green Energy Corporatism," *Breitbart*: http://www.breitbart.com/Big-Government/2012/07/19/Markay-On-Venture-Coporatism.
49. "Democrats: Let's Ban Profits!" *Youtube*: http://youtu.be/07fTsF5BiSM.
50. DNC Video: http://www.breitbart.com/Breitbart-TV/2012/09/04/DNC-Video-Government-Only-Thing-We-All-Belong-To.
51. Michael E. Newton, *The Path to Tyranny: A History of Free*

Society's Descent into Tyranny (Eleftheria Publishing, Kindle Edition, 2010), Kindle Locations 4571-4574.

52. For instance, see the story about Hollywood stars jetting around the globe on New Year's Eve to party in Australia and Las Vegas: Breitbart News, "Green Advocate Leonardo DiCaprio Flies to Sydney and Las Vegas to Ring in 2013," *Breitbart*, Jan. 2, 2013: http://www.breitbart.com/Big-Hollywood/2013/01/02/dicaprio-eco-hypocrite-flying.
53. George Alfred Townsend, *The Life, Crime and Capture of John Wilkes Booth* (New York: Dick and Fitzgerald, 1865 [1977 edition]), p. 22. Available online: http://openlibrary.org/books/OL13490302M/The_life_crime_and_capture_of_John_Wilkes_Booth.
54. Jeffrey W. Seibert, *I Done My Duty: The Complete Story of the Assassination of President McKinley* (Bowie, MD: Heritage Books, 2002), n.p. Quoted in Wikipedia: http://en.wikipedia.org/wiki/Leon_Czolgosz.
55. Humberto Fontova, *Fidel: Hollywood's Favorite Tyrant* (Washington, D.C.: Regnery Publishing, Inc., 2005), pp. 1-6.
56. Dennis Prager, "Understanding the Politics of the Left," *Real Clear Politics*, Jul. 22, 2009: http://www.realclearpolitics.com/articles/2009/07/22/understanding_the_politics_of_the_left.html.
57. Becket Adams, "Dem. Rep. Accuses GOP of 'Literally' Trying to 'Take Food Out of the Mouths of Hungry Babies'," *The Blaze*, Dec. 29, 2012: http://www.theblaze.com/stories/dem-rep-accuses-gop-of-literally-trying-to-take-food-out-of-the-mouths-of-hungry-babies/.
58. Becket Adams, "Dem. Rep. Compares GOP Leaders to Psychopaths: It's Like 'I'm Going to Shoot My Child' If I Get What I Want," *The Blaze*, Dec. 28, 2012: http://www.theblaze.com/stories/dem-rep-compares-gop-leaders-to-psychopaths-its-like-im-going-to-shoot-my-child-if-i-dont-get-what-i-want/.
59. Laura Vozzella, "Va. state senator blames racism for

Romney gains," *Washington Post*, July 24, 2012: http://www.washingtonpost.com/blogs/virginia-politics/post/va-state-senator-blames-racism-for-romney-gains/2012/07/24/gJQAArsQ7W_blog.html.

60. Billy Halllowell, "Rep. Clyburn Questions Republicans' Faith: They Think 'There's Something Wrong With Feeding People When They're Hungry," *The Blaze*, Sep. 6, 2012 http://www.theblaze.com/stories/rep-clyburn-questions-republicans-christian-faith-they-think-theres-something-wrong-with-feeding-people-when-theyre-hungry/.
61. See the videos at MSNBC's website: http://video.msnbc.msn.com/martin-bashir/48848738#48848738.
62. PJ Tatler, "Behold the Self-Hating White Person," *PJ Media*: http://pjmedia.com/tatler/2012/08/31/behold-the-self-hating-white-person/.
63. Jack Coleman, "Chris Matthews Claims to Live in 'Black Majority' DC, Resides in MD Village Less Than 1% Black," *Newsbusters*: http://newsbusters.org/blogs/jack-coleman/2012/08/30/chris-matthews-claims-live-black-majority-dc-resides-md-village-less-1#ixzz254omHTRg.
64. Allahpundit, "Newest racist dog whistle: 'Chicago'," *Hotair*: http://hotair.com/archives/2012/08/30/newest-racist-dog-whistle-chicago/.
65. Matthew Balan, "CNN's Spitzer: 'Every One of Us is Being Held Hostage' By Senate GOP," *Newsbusters*, Dec. 2, 2012: http://newsbusters.org/blogs/matthew-balan/2010/12/02/cnns-spitzer-every-one-us-being-held-hostage-senate-gop#ixzz2GmGFsitB.
66. Tom Blumer, "Politico's Tau Ignores 'Hostage' Language in Obama Admin Econ Advisers' Report," *Newsbusters*, Nov. 26, 2012: http://newsbusters.org/blogs/tom-blumer/2012/11/26/politicos-tau-ignores-hostage-language-obama-admin-econ-advisers-report#ixzz2GmChMoPY.
67. Jack Coleman, "Sheila Jackson Lee Actually Compares Bush Tax Cuts to Iranian Hostage Crisis," *Newsbusters*, Dec. 8, 2012:

http://newsbusters.org/blogs/jack-coleman/2011/12/08/sheila-jackson-lee-actually-compares-bush-tax-cuts-americans-taken-hos#ixzz2GmDWFYwc.

68. Tim Graham, "NPR Host Tweets That al-Qaeda Can't Compete with How (GOP) Congress 'Terrorizes Americans'," *Newsbusters*, Dec. 29, 2012: http://newsbusters.org/blogs/tim-graham/2012/12/29/npr-host-tweets-al-qaeda-cant-compete-how-gop-congress-terrorizes-americ#ixzz2GmHWLFU4.
69. Julia A. Seymour, "Media Follow Lead of Left-Wing Groups in Grover Norquist Attack," *Newsbusters*, Dec. 5, 2012: http://newsbusters.org/blogs/julia-seymour/2012/12/05/media-follow-lead-left-wing-groups-grover-norquist-attack#ixzz2GmIFzjbE.
70. Louis Michael Seidman, "Let's Give Up on the Constitution," *New York Times*, Dec. 30, 2012: http://www.nytimes.com/2012/12/31/opinion/lets-give-up-on-the-constitution.html.
71. An excellent critique of Seidman's article was written by W. James Antle III, "We already gave up on the Constitution," *Daily Caller*, Jan. 1, 2013: http://dailycaller.com/2013/01/01/we-already-gave-up-on-the-constitution/.

CONCLUSION

1. What was edited from the exchange was Romney stating: "It is a low rate. And one of the reasons why the capital gains tax rate is lower is because capital has already been taxed once at the corporate level, as high as thirty-five percent." See Noel Sheppard, "Does CBS News Approve Obama Using and Deceptively Editing 60 Minutes Piece for Anti-Romney Ad?" *Newsbusters*: http://newsbusters.org/blogs/noel-sheppard/2012/10/18/does-cbs-news-sanction-obama-using-and-deceptively-editing-60-minutes#ixzz29s7XCt2Z.
2. Lydia Saad, "Generational Differences on Abortion Narrow," *Gallup*, Mar. 12, 2010: http://www.gallup.com/poll/126581/Generational-Differences-Abortion-Narrow.aspx.

3. Groseclose, pp. 201-240.
4. Groseclose, pp. 211-212.
5. For numerous admissions, see the *Media Research Center*: http://archive.mrc.org/biasbasics/biasbasics2.asp See also: http://youtu.be/d2Rz5hDvJeo.
6. Campbell Brown, "Confessions of a Romney Wife," *Slate*: http://www.slate.com/articles/news_and_politics/politics/2012/08/campbell_brown_on_being_a_romney_wife_you_can_still_have_your_own_opinions_when_your_husband_works_for_a_presidential_candidate_.html.
7. See, for instance, Groseclose, pp. 241-256.
8. "U.S. Distrust in Media Hits New High," *Gallup*: http://www.gallup.com/poll/157589/distrust-media-hits-new-high.aspx.
9. See Wikipedia: http://en.wikipedia.org/wiki/Journalistic_scandal.
10. David Knowles, "Poll: Jon Stewart is America's Most Trusted Newsman," *Huffington Post*: http://www.politicsdaily.com/2009/07/23/poll-jon-stewart-is-americas-most-trusted-newsman/.